CRITICAL
INSIGHTS

Louise Erdrich

CRITICAL INSIGHTS

Louise Erdrich

Editor
P. Jane Hafen
University of Nevada, Las Vegas

SALEM PRESS
A Division of EBSCO Publishing
Ipswich, Massachusetts

Editor's text © 2013 by P. Jane Hafen

Library of Congress Cataloging-in-Publication Data
Louise Erdrich / editor P. Jane Hafen.
   p. cm. -- (Critical insights)
Includes bibliographical references and index.
   ISBN 978-1-4298-3723-1 (hardcover) -- ISBN 978-1-4298-3771-2 (ebook) 1.
Erdrich, Louise--Criticism and interpretation. I. Hafen, P. Jane, 1955-
PS3555.R42Z76 2012
813'.54--dc23
                              2012019009

Contents_____

About This Volume, P. Jane Hafen   vii

Career, Life, and Influence

On Louise Erdrich, P. Jane Hafen   3
Biography of Louise Erdrich, A. LaVonne Brown Ruoff   18

Critical Contexts

Re/creating the Past: Anishinaabe History in the Novels of
    Louise Erdrich, Margaret Huettl   29
The Work of Louise Erdrich: A Survey of Critical Responses,
    Gregory A. Wright   47
Louise Erdrich in Company: The American Writer and
    Her Communities, Thomas Austenfeld   68
Zwischenraum: "The Space Between" Ecologies in Louise Erdrich's
    The Painted Drum, William Huggins   86

Critical Readings

Louise Erdrich Anishinaabezhibiiaan, Margaret Noori / Giiwedinoodin   105
The Relentless Throat Call: Louise Erdrich and Poetic Voice,
    Dean Rader   120
Relative Identities: Connecting Chance and Continuance in
    Love Medicine, Jill Doerfler   137
"What I wished for and what I expected were two different futures":
    A Narratological Interpretation of Gender/Kinship Systems in
    The Beet Queen, Sandra Cox   154
Walking Between Worlds in Louise Erdrich's Novels, Amy T. Hamilton   172
"Life will break you. . . . You have to love": Historical/
    Intergenerational Trauma and Healing in Louise Erdrich's
    The Painted Drum, Patrice Hollrah   191
From Wallace to Wishkob: Queer Relationships and Two-Spirit
    Characters in *The Beet Queen*, *Tales of Burning Love*, and
    The Last Report on the Miracles at Little No Horse, Lisa Tatonetti   207
There are No Burning Wagons, Beads, or Feathers in
    Louise Erdrich's *The Plague of Doves*, Debra K. S. Barker   229

Sister Lost, Sister Found: Redemption in *The Painted Drum* and
  Shadow Tag, Gwen N. Westerman   245
Picturing a Thousand Words: Story and Image in Louise Erdrich's
  "Fiction," Joanne DiNova   256

Resources

Chronology of Louise Erdrich's Life   275
Works by Louise Erdrich   278
Bibliography   280

About the Editor   285
Contributors   287
Index   291

About This Volume

P. Jane Hafen

What makes this volume unique is how the essay topics span Louise Erdrich's career. From her early writing of *Jacklight* (1984) and *Love Medicine* (1984) through her recent novel, *Shadow Tag* (2010), this group of authors finds similar themes yet utilizes varied critical approaches and interpretations. These authors include seasoned academics who played important roles in establishing American Indian literatures as a valid area of study, as well as younger scholars who have benefited from this university discipline. Consequently, some of the thematic approaches include decolonization, trauma theory, comparative analysis, resistance writing, cultural studies, linguistics, and gender analysis.

Additionally, a number of contributors have established voices in the varied landscape of indigenous criticism, including tribalography. While other collections of Erdrich criticism have an occasional Native critic, this book draws from the expertise of international Ojibwe critics as well as Dakota and Lakota scholars. Having an indigenous perspective is neither essentialist nor an end in and of itself. However, these Native critics understand the compelling survivance, survival and continuance, of Erdrich's writing and the critical voice. The non-Native critics are also very strong in their presentations of both indigenist readings and general academic literary analysis. The combination of these critical techniques reflects Erdrich's own writing and the multivalanced world she presents and lives in. While many of the essays address Erdrich's Ojibwe heritage, culture, and language, they also discuss the complicated ways Ojibwe characters interact with non-Indians. Several critics consider how the novels show the interracial relationships in border towns and assess these challenging dynamics.

Louise Erdrich is an enrolled member of the Turtle Mountain Chippewas, or Ojibwes. The traditional tribal name is Anishinaabe, meaning "Original People." Some critics will use "Anishinaabe" in a larger cultural and historical sense, and others will use "Ojibwe" or "Chippewa." Erdrich herself has used all three nomenclatures over the course of her career. The authors of this volume use various versions in naming Erdrich's tribal heritage. Some of the authors recognize that while Erdrich belongs to a specific sovereign tribe, circumstances and experiences in her writing can be pan-Indian.

A. LaVonne Brown Ruoff, one of the pioneers in establishing American Indian literature in the academy, writes Erdrich's biography. Based on her personal association with Erdrich and her scholarly expertise, Ruoff offers a unique insight to the events of Erdrich's life while placing them in a scholarly and literary context.

Margaret Huettl (Ojibwe) establishes a historical and cultural context for Erdrich's writing. After giving context for the large Anishinaabe culture groups, she discusses particulars of Erdrich's own Turtle Mountain Reservation. Huettl outlines the impacts of the reservation system and the general allotment acts as represented in the novels. She identifies the historical influences of Louis Riel, a Métis leader, and the Ojibwe founding members of the American Indian Movement (AIM). Huettl also wisely observes that cultural revival resurfaces in Erdrich's characters and plots.

Gregory A. Wright analyzes a representative survey of Erdrich criticism. After summarizing general reviews and awards, he discusses major representative works and locates them within larger trends of general literary criticism and, more specifically, of American Indian criticism such as hybridity and nationalism.

Thomas Austenfeld, a professor of American literature and a German native, has previously written on Erdrich's German background in an analysis of *The Master Butchers Singing Club*. Here, he situates Erdrich primarily as an American writer without relegating her to minority literatures. With comparisons to Toni Morrison, Flannery O'Connor, and others, he demonstrates that Erdrich's skills transcend ethnicity.

William Huggins relies on his experience and involvement with environmental activism and literature to evaluate ecocritical theories of indigenous literatures. Rather than defaulting to common stereotypes of American Indians having supernatural ties to nature, Huggins presents a critical context for considering environmental issues and closely reads the roles of landscape and animals in complex relationships.

Margaret Noori / Giiwedinoodin, an Anishinaabe linguist, writer, and educator, outlines critical themes and issues evident in Erdrich's use of Anishinaabemowin. Through a complex linguistic analysis, Noori illustrates that language is a means of indigenous survival and shows its role in identity and community. Native language reveals ideas and concepts to readers, building bridges while asserting sovereignty and continuance.

Award-winning poet Dean Rader discusses Erdrich's poetry both in the context of its original publication and in reprinting with new poems in *Original Fire*. In offering a detailed analysis of the poems, Rader identifies and explicates the lyricism of Erdrich's voice within the genre.

Jill Doerfler (White Earth Ojibwe) reassesses *Love Medicine* and its various incarnations. Adding to a large body of previous critical work, Doerfler gives a fresh interpretation and demonstrates its applicability to contemporary Anishinaabe identity. Her main themes of chance and continuance reflect the indeterminacy of life on the reservation during the timeframe of the novel. By fleshing out the characterizations, Doerfler shows how Erdrich individualizes the various members of the tribal community and how random events encourage survival.

Through a careful and close reading of Erdrich's second novel, *The Beet Queen*, Sandra Cox argues for the subtle and complex layering of decolonizing narrative. The nontraditional familial relationships and the reconsiderations of narrative history not only refute previous criticisms of this novel but also challenge heteronormative prejudices. Her character analysis of gendered behaviors shed new light on the Ojibwe roots of this novel.

Amy T. Hamilton looks at the trope of walking through *Tracks*, *Love Medicine*, and *Four Souls*. Utilizing ideas about liminality and traditional Ojibwe means of locality and narrative, she observes that tribal migration occurs within life-sustaining areas and patterns. Hamilton also looks closely at Erdrich's major character Fleur and the consequences of her journeys.

Patrice Hollrah focuses on how the drum and storytelling in *The Painted Drum* help to heal historical trauma. The characters of this novel suffer from detribalization, boarding school abuse, poverty, and alcoholism. Hollrah shows how Erdrich, rather than submitting to despair, offers these characters hope and resilience.

Looking at multiple works, Lisa Tatonetti considers Erdrich's representations of gender, particularly two-spirit characters. Like Sandra Cox's reading of *The Beet Queen*, Tatonetti's essay contextualizes multiple characters within Erdrich's works. Most importantly, she presents a smart analysis of Agnes DeWitt/Father Damien from *The Last Report on the Miracles at Little No Horse*.

Lakota scholar Debra K. S. Barker examines history and identity in *The Plague of Doves*. She roots the historical context of the novel in representing reservation and border-town life. More importantly, she illustrates how Erdrich captures the details of contemporary American Indian life, which is full of rich experience, pop culture, and a parallel way of deciphering the world—mainstream and Native.

In a careful character analysis, Gwen N. Westerman (Dakota) considers similarities between Faye from *The Painted Drum* and Irene in *Shadow Tag*, both of whom have challenges in personal relationships. Westerman shows how Erdrich masterfully presents these characterizations of women with complicated histories and tribal identities. Ultimately, each is reconciled—Faye and her mother through tribal stories and understanding forgiveness, Irene and her daughter, Riel, through return to the tribal community and perseverance.

Joanne DiNova (Anishinaabe) considers the Anishinaabe core of *Shadow Tag* through the primary trope of image and shadow. Closely examining the language, relationships, double diary, art, and even reflections on Erdrich's own life in the novel, DiNova shows how Erdrich engages the reader's ideas and expectations beyond the text.

Applying a variety of critical methodologies, these authors together offer readings of texts that illuminate varied ways of understanding and taking account of Erdrich's lyricism, complexities, and compelling narratives. Working with any living and productive author dates most critical discussions immediately; however, Erdrich's writings presents a unique challenge as new works often revise previous writings or change understandings of the texts. As Erdrich says in the epigraph to *Tracks*, "The story comes up different every time." Thus, a volume like this cannot be comprehensive, and while the essays are suggestive, they inevitably raise further questions. For instance, while Lisa Tatonetti's essay in this volume and Patrice Hollrah's essay "Love and the Slippery Slope of Sexual Orientation: L/G/B/T/Q etc. Sensibility in *The Last Report on the Miracles at Little No Horse*" in Deborah Madsen's volume offer fine analyses of the gender issues in *Last Report*, much more work needs to be done to expand the discussion of additional ideas in that novel. Likewise, more criticism about *The Plague of Doves* and *Shadow Tag* will certainly be forthcoming. Nonetheless, the discussions in this volume are excellent beginnings, opening Erdrich's works for further discussion.

Grateful acknowledgments are due to all the writers in the project. They each show their appreciation for Erdrich and her works. Additionally, Carol Harter, director of the Black Mountain Institute, offered encouragement and a fellowship that allowed me time to complete this volume.

CAREER, LIFE, AND INFLUENCE

On Louise Erdrich

P. Jane Hafen

The writings of Louise Erdrich are multilayered and complex. While her work is recognized and honored with national prizes, it also spans a range of intricate narratives, lyrical language, and issues of contemporary indigeneity. Her characters and experiences illuminate the diversity of contemporary American Indian experiences that look back to history, observe changes and survival among Native peoples, and look forward to future generations. Her life has taken dramatic turns, as has her writing. Finding early success with her fiction, more recently her work has intensified in both its emotional depth and elaborate intertwining.

Louise Erdrich burst on the literary scene with a series of prominent prizes. After earning a bachelor's degree at Dartmouth in its first coeducational class and a master of fine arts degree at Johns Hopkins, she returned to Dartmouth as writer in residence. Her first widespread recognition came with the 1982 Nelson Algren Award for her short story "The World's Greatest Fisherman." Famously created with her husband Michael Dorris, whom she married in 1981, Erdrich's works and his were collaborative projects. She won the Pushcart Prize for "Indian Boarding School: The Runaways" in 1983. She also finished and published a poetry manuscript, which became *Jacklight* (1984). "The World's Greatest Fisherman" became the first chapter of the novel *Love Medicine* (1984).

Love Medicine thrust Erdrich into prominence. With Dorris acting as her agent, the book was published by a major New York publisher, Holt, Rinehart and Winston. The novel is a collection of stories narrated by various characters. The comparisons to William Faulkner were immediate, and Erdrich's continuing cycle of North Dakota novels establishes an epic chronicle of Ojibwe families and place exceeding Faulkner's imaginative Yoknapatawphah County. *Love Medicine* became the first novel by an American Indian writer to win the National Book Critics Circle Award and numerous other awards.

In many ways, *Love Medicine* is the foundation of Erdrich's writing. It represents the complicated nature of narrative storytelling traditions that are part of her Ojibwe heritage. There is no singular protagonist, but a tribal community presented by nine different storytellers. While Erdrich's Native background is crucial in content, language, and process, she acknowledges that she is a mix of many things. As part of the Faces of America series, she told Henry Louis Gates Jr.: "I've always valued the different people in my ancestry. It really helps me as writer. The thing about being a writer is you can't leave anybody out of your sympathies—the criminal, the rich or the poor or the downtrodden or the destitute. So that has to be all inside of you" (89). Erdrich's German grandmother appears in narrative poems, and her German grandparents' story is fictionalized in *The Master Butchers Singing Club* (2003). Erdrich has an Ivy League education and wide experience in the world at large. The characters of *Love Medicine* demonstrate this range.

Also with *Love Medicine*, Erdrich understands the fluid nature of literature. She introduces the major families and characters that will inhabit the North Dakota cycle of novels. Yet, in many ways, Erdrich grapples with a shifting landscape of understanding. First, she withdrew the original edition of *Love Medicine* and, in 1993, released a new version with added chapters, Ojibwe words and phrases, and modified language. Then, in 2009, Erdrich again revised the novel with modified language and moved one of the 1993 chapters to an appendix.

Furthermore, as the stories from *Love Medicine* continue in the other novels, Erdrich challenges what the reader assumes to be fixed. For example, *Love Medicine* begins with the death of June Morrissey in the snow after being picked up by a wildcatter. *Tales of Burning Love* (1996) starts with a breathtaking retelling of the episode from Jack Mauser, the wildcatter's point of view. *Tracks* reveals that Pauline Puyat is Marie Kashpaw's birth mother, but *The Last Report on the Miracles of Little No Horse* (2001) adds the information that Marie was unaware of that connection during their cosmic confrontation in the "Saint Marie" chapter of *Love Medicine*. Additionally, in *The Last Report*, the narrative of "Saint Marie" is revealed as Marie Kashpaw's religious confession. One of the most startling changes occurs with Father Damien, a minor character in *Tracks* (1988) who is revealed to be a woman as the primary character in *The Last Report*. Such changes illustrate the oral nature of Erdrich's writing and demand that the reader reread the first novels with a new understanding. More than shifting point of view, Erdrich creates fresh contexts to see the former story anew. Therefore, Erdrich's work is not fixed or static like most literature but evolving through the continuation of storytelling.

A closer reading of one memorable selection from *Love Medicine* (1993) illustrates the themes that will continue through Erdrich's saga. While the idea of "love medicine" is tied to reconciliation and forgiveness throughout the novel, there are also numerous episodes of survival humor, often precipitated by trickster. In the eponymous chapter, "Love Medicine," narrated by Lipsha Morrissey, Marie Kashpaw entreats Lipsha to perform a love medicine on her husband, Nector, to end his philandering and, particularly, his lasting desire for Lulu Lamartine. Lipsha conjectures a ritual combination of his gifted touch and goose hearts, since geese supposedly mate for life, a trope used earlier in the novel when Nector and Marie meet. However, through his own ineptitude, Lipsha fails to obtain the goose hearts and tries to substitute store-bought turkey hearts instead. The role of Catholicism in Ojibwe culture comes to the fore when Lipsha asks first a Catholic priest and later a nun to bless the turkey hearts. Both refuse, leading Lipsha to bless them himself. The botched ritual then triggers a sacrificial and tragic crisis, as Nector chokes to death on one of the hearts. Through Lipsha's hopeless resuscitation attempts, the scene gives way to dark comedy. Lipsha comes to realize that "it was other things that choked [Nector] as well. It didn't seem like he wanted to struggle or fight. Death came and tapped his chest, so he went just like that" (208). Lipsha's comically incongruous but accurate observations mitigate the scene's horror. Were this incident told within the Western tradition, without the Ojibwe trickster humor, Nector's death would have been seen as merely tragic. However, Lipsha's role as trickster is evident when he disregards the details of sacred ritual, undermines the hierarchical order of Catholicism, and thus courts calamity. Nector's mythic death is therefore a natural consequence of Lipsha's clumsiness. Moreover, his death is rendered ironically humorous as *Lipsha* sees Nector's life flash past him in Nector's final moments, a twist through which past, present, and future are synthesized and Lipsha's understanding is transformed. Ultimately, the forgiveness and love of a lifetime constitute the real "love medicine" that enables the tribal community to move on through storytelling.

The continuation of the North Dakota novels takes the stories forward to the dislocated Ojibwe Travers family in New Hampshire and back into tribal history of Fleur's beginnings in *The Painted Drum* (2005). Fleur Pillager is a larger-than-life character in many of the North Dakota novels. Although her character first appears in *Tracks*, she is a primary figure in *Four Souls* (2004) and a presence in the rest of the North Dakota novels. Again emphasizing orality, Erdrich never has Fleur engage in direct discourse; other characters report what she says. In a sleight of hand, some of those retellings give Fleur the major stage, especially during her Minneapolis stay in *Four Souls*. Nevertheless, the details, the conversations, the actions, are all reported by other characters, most often by Nanapush.

Nanapush is another recurring character in the North Dakota saga. As an incarnation of the Ojibwe trickster, Nanabozho, he engages in outrageous behaviors and exaggerated storytelling but also provides a moral center. He and Pauline Puyat are principal narrators of *Tracks*. While he is not a reliable narrator, he is much more trustworthy than Pauline, and his version of events carries more veracity. Nanapush is also a major character in *The Last Report*.

Erdrich often plants seeds for plot elements that may occur in subsequent novels years later. For example, two incidents receive brief mention: when Fleur returns in a white suit with a little boy and no explanation in *The Bingo Palace* (1993) and when Nanapush drinks the communion wine in *The Last Report*. Each of these seemingly minor mentions becomes significant developments in *Four Souls*. Likewise, a short story that seems completely unconnected from any novel, "The True Story of Mustache Maude," was originally published in 1984 and expanded to become an integral part of *The Plague of Doves* (2008), twenty-four years later. The development of these kernels is part of a larger narrative strategy.

Indeed, many chapters from the novels appear in previous publications as short stories. Some stories, including "The World's Greatest Fisherman" and "Fleur," won awards, and some were included in volumes of *The Best American Short Stories*. Many were published in prominent periodicals such as the *New Yorker*, and a few are anthologized in textbooks and other publications. The ability of these stories to stand independently or to be interwoven in the larger narrative of a novel speaks to Erdrich's skill in carefully polishing and condensing her language. In 2009, Erdrich collected these stories in their original forms and published them along with some new stories in *The Red Convertible: Selected and New Stories, 1978–2008*.

A substantial body of Erdrich's work is outside the North Dakota cycle. In her early writing years, Dorris said that the fiction was a collaboration, but Erdrich has said the poetry was hers alone. The collection *Jacklight* was followed by *Baptism of Desire* (1989). The second book continues the Butcher's Wife and Potchikoo narratives of the first book. Nearly twenty years after *Jacklight*, Erdrich selected poems from both books and published new ones in *Original Fire: New and Selected Poems* (2003).

The collaborative process also led Michael Dorris to turn from a strictly academic career to writing. In 1987, he wrote *A Yellow Raft in Blue Water* about a mixed African American and tribally ambiguous American Indian young girl. Erdrich wrote the foreword to Dorris's prize-winning nonfiction book *The Broken Cord* (1989). In that volume, Dorris lays out the excruciating story of a child he adopted, prior to their marriage, who was afflicted with fetal alcohol syndrome. The other two children Dorris adopted also had fetal alcohol syndrome. The intimate exposure of the Dorris-Erdrich family has led to public criticism (Couser).

Only two books appear under both Dorris and Erdrich's names. *Route 2*, a limited-edition travelogue, was published in 1991. Also at that time, they received a prominent contract to write a novel with the topic of the Columbus Quincentenary. The result was *The Crown of Columbus*. The book was not well received, although some of the creative constructions are very imaginative. It has dual narrators, a traditional mixed-blood professor, Vivian Two-star, and a stodgy non-Indian academic, Roger Williams. The novel not only addresses the colonial consequences of the Columbus voyage, but, set at Dartmouth, demonstrates many of the real-life challenges for Native academics. While plot seems to overtake the novel at times, a careful reading offers a superb rendering of decolonization.

Along with the poor critical reception of *The Crown of Columbus* and additional personal challenges, the oldest son whose life was the subject of *The Broken Cord* died in a tragic accident. As Erdrich has revealed more recently in an unusually personal interview in *The Paris Review*, after a tumultuous period, the marriage began to disintegrate. Amid accusations and divorce proceedings, Michael Dorris took his own life in 1997. The swarm of publicity around this tragic event led to Erdrich's public request for privacy for the two surviving adoptive children and Dorris and Erdrich's three biological children.

During the period between *The Crown of Columbus* and Dorris's death, Erdrich's writing took some turns. She produced a personal memoir about her writing and about being a mother in *The Blue Jay's Dance* (1995), which was slightly modified and reissued in 2010, again showing the flexibility of narrative. While there were two novelistic installments in the North Dakota cycle, *The Bingo Palace* and *Tales of Burning Love*, they are less prominent in the larger cycle. However, each dealt with the death of a major character: Fleur and Pauline Puyat/ Sister Leopolda, respectively. These novels also introduced and developed characters unique and self-contained within each book. Nevertheless, given Erdrich's propensity to reintroduce and develop seemingly minor characters, such as Dot from *Love Medicine* becoming a major figure in *The Beet Queen* (1986), the characters from *The Bingo Palace* and *Tales of Burning Love* may well resurface.

More telling in a change of direction is *The Antelope Wife* (1998), finished before Dorris's death but not appearing in print until the following year. In an epigraph, Erdrich states: "This book was written before the death of my husband. He is remembered with love by all of his family." This remarkable novel introduces a whole new set of characters, takes them off the reservation, and places them in urban Minneapolis, where Erdrich herself had relocated. There are German elements and characters in the story and obsessive and doomed relationships. Erdrich has also revised this novel for reissue in 2012.

Also during this period, Erdrich turned to new projects with a children's book, *Grandmother's Pigeon* (1996), and the first of a series of young-adult books, *The Birchbark House* (1999.) Both are grounded in Ojibwe tradition. *The Birchbark House* is significant in offering an alternative voice to the historical stereotypes and genocidal attitudes presented in mainstream young-adult literature, such as the Little House on the Prairie series. The Birchbark characters and stories continue with *A Game of Silence* (2005), *The Porcupine Year* (2008), and *Chickadee* (2012).

A bold turn in Erdrich's writing and her independence from Dorris appears most clearly in *The Last Report on the Miracles at Little No Horse*, a finalist for the National Book Award. Returning to the founding families from *Love Medicine* and *Tracks*, Erdrich offers entirely new twists on characters, events, and even metanarrative. In what is now a well-known move, Erdrich presents Father Damien from *Tracks* at the end of his life and reveals him to be a woman. Through storytelling and Ojibwe language and values, Erdrich addresses questions about gender, power, clerical authority, colonialism, love, forgiveness, context, and compassion. The fabled Nanapush meets his demise after hunting "Mooz."

Erdrich also seems to answer some critical questions about her earlier writing. For example, Father Damien writes a "History of the Puyats." This history, along with character development of young Pauline Puyat/Sister Leopolda, adds context and understanding to some of her bizarre behaviors. In fascinating endnotes, Erdrich herself becomes an author/character not unlike Argentine writer Jorge Luis Borges in "Borges y yo" ("Borges and Myself"). Placing herself in the narrative, she disclaims writing about any specific reservation and says that Little No Horse Reservation is fictional. She wraps herself in the narrative by claiming to have received, as author, communication from the pope about information disclosed in the novel. She asks, "Who is the writer? Who is the voice?" (358). However, she also gives the very last word to Nanapush, thus enfolding the novel in its own narrative and affirms the imperative for indigenous survival and language while acknowledging the interrelationship with non-Natives as well.

The Master Butchers Singing Club (2003) is a marked departure from Erdrich's previous books. Still set in North Dakota, it follows a family history similar to that of Erdrich's own German lineage. Like her paternal grandparents, Fidelis and Eva Waldvogel immigrate from Germany to the United States between the First and Second World Wars. Eva becomes ill and dies of cancer at a young age. Other characters inhabit the town and play roles in the intricate plot. Although this novel appears to keep the Ojibwe characters on the periphery, they are important representations. Cyprian Lazarre is a two-spirit character who also loves a woman. Step-and-a-Half is recharacterized from The Butcher's Wife poems, and her story leads to a shocking conclusion and personalization of a major event in American Indian history.

In the fall of 2010, Pulitzer Prize–winning playwright Marsha Norman adapted *The Master Butchers Singing Club* for the stage. Performed at the Guthrie Theater in Minneapolis, the play received local rave reviews. In a stunning restructuring, Norman places Step-and-a-Half at the center of the plot, where she functions as a Greek chorus, introducing, commenting, and narrating. She becomes a trope of many Indians in small towns near reservations; she has an omnipresence on the stage despite her silences throughout the play. Additionally, Norman incorporates the music of the singing club as well as traditional Ojibwe music, thus presenting a multigenre/multidimensional experience.

Erdrich constructs an entirely new cast of characters in the Pulitzer Prize finalist *The Plague of Doves*. Based on a true historical event in which young Ojibwe men were mistakenly accused of murdering a local white family, Erdrich shows how historical events shape and haunt a whole community of Indians, mixed-bloods, and Euro-Americans.

Shadow Tag (2010) is the most startling of all of Erdrich's novels. The tale of a disintegrating marriage, Erdrich seems to purge the consuming passion that has been a theme in many of her books. The main characters, Irene and Gil America, are mixed-bloods. Irene believes that her husband, Gil, is reading her diary, so she keeps a secret diary in a safe-deposit box. An interplay of the historical art of George Catlin and contemporary Native art by Gil reveals the decolonizing aspects of aesthetics and national narrative. Gil's paintings also unmask Irene intimately and possessively. The harrowing ending is still a tale of survival, even if only for the children who must endure and try to understand the abuse the parents inflict on each other.

Erdrich's nonfiction has been published in a variety of venues. In columns in the *New York Times* and book chapters, she has reeled out bits of personal information and political views. Most notable in these revelations is her nonfiction book *Books and Islands in Ojibwe Country* (2003). Illustrations in the book were drawn by Erdrich, like those in the young-adult fiction. She acknowledges the bookstore she owns in Minneapolis, Birchbark Books, where she also blogs. She also lists her four biological daughters, the last of whom was born while she was writing *The Last Report*.

Perhaps the most astute observations of Erdrich's work come from her own essays and interviews. For an early explication of survival and place, Erdrich penned an essay for the *New York Times*, "Where I Ought to Be: A Writer's Sense of Place." Not only does she address the role of place in her writing, but she discusses the use of popular imagery as a common touchstone. She discusses indigenous peoples and their self-awareness as survivors. In a *New York Times* editorial pleading for the release of Leonard Peltier, she reveals some of her political activism. She discusses her use of Ojibwe language in her writing in "Two Languages in Mind, but Just One in the Heart."

Erdrich's involvement in Ojibwe language revitalization is apparent in both her writing and her activism. At the end of *The Last Report*, Erdrich has Nanapush say:

> We Anishinaabeg are keepers of the names of the earth. And unless the earth is called by the names it gave us humans, won't it cease to love us? And isn't it true that if the earth stops loving us, everyone, not just the Anishinaabeg, will cease to exist? That is why we all must speak our language, nindinawemagonidok, and call everything we see by the name of its spirit. Even the chimookomanag, who are trying to destroy us, are depending upon us to remember. Mi'sago'i. (361)

This admonition for language acquisition not only appears with the inclusions of Anishinaabemowin (Ojibwe language) in Erdrich's writing but in a practical commitment to language recovery. Along with her sister Heid, Erdrich founded Wiigwaas Press in 2008. The press is devoted to publishing books in the Ojibwe language. Starting with children's books, the publishing list has grown. *Awesiinyensag*, a picture book edited by Anton Treuer and collaborators, was chosen as Minnesota's Best Read for 2011 by the Center for the Book of the Library of Congress. Additionally, Erdrich was the narrator of an Upper Midwest Emmy Award–winning Minnesota Public Television film, *First Speak-*

---

ers: Restoring the Ojibwe Language, which was originally broadcast on November 26, 2010.

Although Erdrich speaks of being of mixed heritage and acknowledges the many influences in her life, her Ojibwe heritage provides a worldview that informs those other aspects of her work. Clearly, her writings are not confined to American Indian tropes, nor are they limited to cultural and racial representations. Yet the historical events, archetypal characters, literary themes, and narrative constructions are presented through an Ojibwe lens.

Nevertheless, literary critics apply the tools of their trades, sometimes trying to wedge Erdrich's work like square pegs into round holes with the theory superseding the text. Academic literary criticism, as Gregory Wright explains in his chapter on critical review, sometimes elucidates the text and, at other times, colonizes indigenous issues even further. Biographical criticism is most tempting, given the dramatic turns in Erdrich's personal life and her Ojibwe grounding. However, to impose details of her life on her work, *The Antelope Wife* or *Shadow Tag* in particular, would be to overlook larger themes, the intensity of her writing, and her larger literary achievement. In defining tribalography as a critical approach, Choctaw writer LeAnne Howe states:

> Native stories, no matter what form they take (novel, poem, drama, memoir, film, history), seem to pull all the elements together of the storyteller's tribe, meaning the people, the land, and multiple characters and all their manifestations and revelations, and connect these in past, present, and future milieus (present and future milieus mean non-Indians). I have tried to show that tribalography comes from the Native propensity for bringing things together, for making consensus, and for symbiotically connecting one thing to another. It is a cultural bias, if you will. (42)

Erdrich's writing exemplifies Howe's model of "bringing things together" through a multiplicity of writing techniques, Indian and non-Indian characters, emphasis on the land, and survival. She shows how Native characters live and interact with modern America, all while knowing and remembering their tribal heritages. Because Erdrich can show these multilayered experiences, she speaks to a wide audience.

Tribalography is one critical methodology in reading Erdrich. Numerous literary theories have been applied to Erdrich's work. Many of those theories, as will be explained later, work to elucidate the primary texts. Others colonize those texts by having the critical ideas subsume the original writings. Some theoretical applications simply do not work. For example, a number of critics refer to events in Erdrich's writing as magic realism. In an interview in *The Paris Review*, she responds: "Their [my six brothers and sisters'] experiences make magical realism seem ho-hum. It's too bad I can't use their experiences because everyone would know who they are, but believe me, my writing comes from ordinary life." She goes on to explain that seemingly supernatural occurrences are grounded in historical and real events.

Part of what makes Erdrich's writing accessible and admired is the skill of her craft. Not only does she have the ability to create indelible characters, but the beauty of her prose resonates throughout her writing. *Tracks* has an opening that ranks among the best-known novelistic beginnings. The novel begins with Nanapush as narrator:

> We started dying before the snow, and like the snow, we continued to fall. It was surprising there were so many of us left to die. For those who survived the spotted sickness from the south, our long flight west to Nadouissioux land where we signed the treaty, and then a wind from the east, bringing exile in a storm of government papers, what descended from the north in 1912 seemed impossible.
>
> By then, we thought disaster must surely have spent its force, that disease must have claimed all of the Anishinabe that the earth could hold and bury.
>
> But the earth is limitless and so is luck and so were our people once. (1)

These opening lines establish the major premises of the novel as Nanapush recounts in a tribal, first-person plural voice the hardships and survival of his tribe. The opening prose, comparing fallen lives to descending snowflakes, condenses language. This condensation involves the complex conflation of opposites for which zeugma is a particularly apt rhetorical figure. For the snow, in falling, does what it must to come into being, whereas "we," in falling, go out of being by "dying." Sandwiched between the rhetorical complexity of the first sentence and the grammatical complexity of the third is the sparse and understated heart of the passage: "It was surprising there were so many of us left to die." The tragedy is evident, though not accusing or blaming. That this story is being told is a marker of survival and a gracefulness of language.

Other novels are typified by poetic language and have a rhythm balanced with humor and plot development. Nearly all the book reviews of *The Beet Queen* note Erdrich's poetic power, with several citing this passage:

> The baby clung like a sloth, heavy with sleep, and latched on in hunger, without waking. She drew milk down silently in one long inhalation. It was then that Celestine noticed, in the fine moonlit floss of her baby's hair, a tiny white spider making its nest.
>
> It was a delicate thing, close to transparent, with long sheer legs. It moved so quickly that it seemed to vibrate, throwing out invisible strings and catching them, weaving its own tensile strand. Celestine watched as it began to happen. A web was forming, a complicated house, that Celestine could not bring herself to destroy. (176)

Compare this with the narrative section of "Saint Clare," subtitled "My Life as a Saint," from *Baptism of Desire*:

> By morning, the strands of the nest disappear
> into each other, shaping

an emptiness within me that I make lovely
as the immature birds make the air
by defining the tunnels and the spirals
of the new sustenance. And then,
no longer hindered by the violence of their need,
they take to other trees, fling themselves
deep into the world. (34–42)

Certain fundamental ideas are common: interconnectedness, nature images, real and metaphorical mothering. The first passage, in the context of a larger novelistic narrative, inserts necessary plot connections. The second passage magnifies a singular instant. Nevertheless, the generic distinctions of novel and poem are not clear. The interwoven details of the web and nest are figurative of tribal community, familial structure (no matter how "family" is defined), the characters of the novels, and the overall connections with a living universe.

Whether from a Native American heritage or European, all Americans participate in the Indian history of this country. The American Indian shaped the imagination, justifying through negativism the violence and land theft that created America, romanticizing the tragic legacy of domination. The duality of the Noble Savage still pervades popular and high culture. Erdrich reinscribes these colonial images from her Ojibwe lens. Her very existence, her drive to tell the stories, and the compelling nature of her stories gracefully extend another opportunity for American culture to expand understanding and compassion. Through the power of language, Erdrich not only reminds readers that American Indians will continue to adapt and survive, but her works offer general society a vision of *communitas*, union through diversity, as she continues to interweave the complexities of her experiences into the twenty-first century.

Works Cited

Couser, G. Thomas. "Adoption, Disability, and Surrogacy: The Ethics of Parental Life Writing in *The Broken Cord.*" *Vulnerable Subjects: Ethics and Life Writing.* Ithaca: Cornell UP, 2004. 56–73.

Erdrich, Louise. *The Antelope Wife.* New York: Harper, 1998.

———. *Baptism of Desire: Poems.* Harper, 1989.

———. *The Beet Queen: A Novel.* New York: Holt, 1986.

———, narr. *First Speakers: Restoring the Ojibwe Language.* Prod. Dianne Steinbach and John Whitehead. Twin Cities Public Television. TPT, 26 Nov. 2010. Television.

———. *The Last Report on the Miracles at Little No Horse.* New York: Harper, 2001.

———. "Louise Erdrich, The Art of Fiction No. 208." Interview by Lisa Halliday. *The Paris Review* 195 (2010):132–66.

———. *Love Medicine.* 1984. Rev. ed. New York: Holt, 1993.

———. *Love Medicine.* 1984. Rev. ed. New York: Holt, 2009.

———. *Tracks*: New York: Holt, 1988.

———. "Two Languages in Mind, but Just One in the Heart." *New York Times* 22 May 2000: E1.

———. "Where I Ought to Be: A Writer's Sense of Place." *New York Times* 28 July 1985: 1.

Gates, Henry Louis, Jr., ed. "Louise Erdrich." *Faces of America: How 12 Extraordinary People Discovered Their Pasts.* New York: New York UP, 2010. 72–90.

Howe, LeAnne. "The Story of America: A Tribalography." *Clearing a Path: Theorizing the Past in Native American Studies.* Ed. Nancy Shoemaker. New York: Routledge, 2002. 29–48.

Treuer, Anton, et al. *Awesiinyensag.* Minneapolis: Wiigwaas, 2010.

Biography of Louise Erdrich _____

A. LaVonne Brown Ruoff

Karen Louise Erdrich is a fiction writer and poet living in Minneapolis, Minnesota. She is also the owner of Birchbark Books, an independent bookstore in that city. Although Erdrich alternated using Karen and Louise as her first name during her school years, she selected Louise as her permanent first name around 1977. Born on June 7, 1954, in Little Falls, Minnesota, Erdrich is the eldest daughter of Ralph Louis Erdrich, a German American, and Rita Joanne Gourneau, of French and Turtle Mountain Chippewa (Ojibwe) heritage. The parents of seven children, Ralph taught and Rita worked at the Wahpeton Indian School, a Bureau of American Indian Affairs (BIA) institution now called Circle of Nations-Wahpeton Indian School. A talented artist, Rita is the daughter of Patrick "Patrice" Moses Gourneau. Also known as Aun Nish E Naubay, he chaired the Turtle Mountain Chippewa Advisory Committee (1954–58) and testified before Congress opposing the proposed termination of that nation. He received the North Dakota Heritage Profile Honor Award. Louise Erdrich is an enrolled member of this band. Her paternal grandparents, Elisabeth "Liesel" Ruf and Ludwig "Louis" Friedrich Erdrich, emigrated from Germany. Ludwig, a World War I veteran of the German army, established a butcher shop in Little Falls, Minnesota. After the death of Elizabeth, Ludwig married Mary Ann Erdrich.

Ralph Erdrich introduced Louise to Shakespeare's plays, recited poetry to his children, and encouraged his daughters to write their own stories. He paid Louise a nickel for each story she wrote, and her mother sewed her collected stories into little books. According to Erdrich, "the people in our families make everything into a story" (qtd. in Schumacher 175). She attended schools in Wahpeton before entering Dartmouth College in Hanover, New Hampshire, in 1972 as a member of the first coeducational class. That year, Michael Anthony Dorris (1945–97), a Modoc, became a faculty member in the Native

American Studies program and Department of Anthropology. She and Dorris met when she took his seminar. In his class, Erdrich began to explore her own Native ancestry. At Dartmouth, she also wrote poetry, encouraged by Professor A. B. Paulson. Erdrich told Kay Bonetti, "I kept journals and diaries when I was a kid, and I started writing when I was nineteen or twenty. After college, I decided that's absolutely what I wanted to do" (78). As an undergraduate, Erdrich published a poem in *Ms. Magazine* and won both the Cox Prize for fiction and the American Academy of Poets Prize. An avid reader, Erdrich was influenced by such authors as Jane Austen, George Eliot, Willa Cather, Katherine Anne Porter, Flannery O'Connor, William Faulkner, Gabriel García Márquez, Toni Morrison, Richard Hugo, and Louise Glück.

Erdrich and Dorris became friends and corresponded after she graduated in 1976. At that time, Erdrich taught creative writing to young people through the North Dakota Poets-in-the-Schools Program. Both before and after graduation, her low-wage jobs included waitressing, weighing trucks on the interstate, selling popcorn in a movie theater, shelving books in a library, developing photographs, and writing advertising copy. In an interview for *Publisher's Weekly*, Erdrich told Miriam Berkley that she was glad she took "some really crazy jobs" because "they turned out to have been very useful experiences" (qtd. in "Louise Erdrich").

In 1978, she entered the Johns Hopkins graduate creative writing program. Her 1979 thesis was a collection of poems entitled "The Common Mercies and Run of Hearts." Subsequently, she moved to Boston, where she edited the Boston Indian Council newspaper, the *Circle* (1979–80). In an interview with Michael Schumacher for *Writers Digest*, Erdrich described the impact of this experience: "Settling into that job and becoming comfortable with an urban community—which is very different from the reservation community—gave me another reference point. There were lots of people with mixed blood, lots of people who had their own confusions. I realized that this was part of my life . . . and it was something I *wanted* to write about" (175). While

Erdrich was in Boston and Dorris was doing research in New Zealand, the two began collaborating on short stories. In 1981, she published *Imagination*, a children's textbook on writing.

Erdrich received fellowships to the writing colonies at MacDowell (1980) and Yaddo (1981). During her appointment as writer in residence at Dartmouth in 1981, her friendship with Dorris deepened into mutual love. Now director of Native American Studies, Dorris was an adoptive single father of three Lakota children: Reynold Abel (d. 1991), Jeffrey Sava, and Madeline Hannah. On October 10, 1981, Erdrich and Dorris married in Cornish, New Hampshire; during the ceremony, she also "married" his children. Subsequently, Erdrich adopted Dorris's children, and later, the couple had three biological daughters: Persia Andromeda, Pallas Antigone, and Aza Marion. Although Dorris had published prose and poems prior to his marriage to Erdrich, afterward he also wrote fiction, including *A Yellow Raft in Blue Water* (1987) and *Cloud Chamber* (1997), as well as two children's books, *Morning Girl* (1992) and *Sees Behind Trees* (1996). He is best known for *The Broken Cord: A Family's Ongoing Struggle with Fetal Alcohol Syndrome* (1989). Containing a poignant foreword by Erdrich, the book recounts his family's efforts to cope with the effects this syndrome on Abel, called Adam in the book.

After they married, Erdrich and Dorris published several short stories under the pseudonym Milou North. They jointly authored *Route 2* (1991), a travel book, and *The Crown of Columbus* (1991), a novel. In addition, they collaborated on books published under the name of whoever authored the first draft. After one of them prepared a first draft, the other would write his or her comments on it. This process continued through subsequent versions. Before the manuscript was sent to a publisher, one would read it aloud to the other as they polished the final version.

The early eighties were breakthrough years for Erdrich. In 1982, she won the first prize of the Nelson Algren Award for her short story "The World's Greatest Fisherman" as well as a fellowship from the National

Endowment for the Arts. The following year, she also won the Pushcart Prize for her poem "Indian Boarding School" and a National Magazine Fiction Award for "Scales," another short story. In 1984, Erdrich published *Jacklight*, a poetry collection. It contains humorous Potchikoo poems about the Indian trickster and narrative poems entitled "The Butcher's Wife," named Mary Kröger. Some of Kröger's characteristics are based on those of Mary Ann Erdrich, the author's step-grandmother. Erdrich explained to Laura Coltelli her shift to fiction: "I just began to realize that I wanted to be a fiction writer. . . . I have a lot more room and it's closer to the oral tradition of sitting around and telling stories" (23).

Erdrich also published *Love Medicine* in 1984. Although it was originally conceived as a collection of short stories, Dorris recognized that it was really a novel. This widely praised book won the National Book Critics Circle Award. It is the first of her novels about generations of Nanapushes, Kashpaws, Pillagers, Lamartines, and Morrisseys, who represent Ojibwe and mixed-blood families living in the fictional Argus, North Dakota, from 1912 through the 1980s. In 1993, the new expanded edition included new chapters: "Resurrection," "The Tomahawk Factory," and "Lyman's Luck." In 2009, she published a newly revised edition, which eliminated "Lyman's Luck" and transferred "The Tomahawk Factory" to the end of the book. A version of the latter was first included in an unpublished manuscript entitled "Tracks," which was quite different from the published novel of the same name.

Other novels in the North Dakota series include *The Beet Queen*, *The Bingo Palace*, *Tales of Burning Love*, *The Antelope Wife*, *The Last Report on Miracles at Little No Horse*, *Four Souls*, and *The Painted Drum*. Among the themes that inform *Love Medicine* and the other novels above are community, family and band interconnections, relationships with non-Natives, and conflicts with Catholicism and non-Native society. Here and in later novels, she uses multiple voices and nonchronological narration.

In 1985, after Erdrich received a Guggenheim Fellowship and Dorris, a Rockefeller, they moved their family to Northfield, Minnesota, for the year. There, Erdrich completed *The Beet Queen* (1986), which covers a forty-year period beginning in 1932. She puts more emphasis on non-Natives and their interconnections with those of Ojibwe ancestry. *Tracks* (1988), a prequel to *Love Medicine*, is one of Erdrich's best novels. Set in the years 1912 to 1924, it focuses on Native conflicts with Catholicism and land ownership. It also contains powerful characterizations and rollicking humor. In 1989, Erdrich returned to poetry with the publication of *Baptism of Desire*; the title alludes to a little-known tenet of the Catholic Church. It deals with spirituality and the commingling of Native and Catholic worldviews, as well as with motherhood and children. That year, Dorris resigned his professorship at Dartmouth to write full time.

In 1991, Erdrich and Dorris moved to Kalispell, Montana, and published *The Crown of Columbus*, which they jointly authored. The two central narrators are Dartmouth professors, who are lovers and parents of a baby: Roger Williams, a literary scholar, and Vivian Two-star, a mixed-blood Native, single mother of a teenage son, and anthropologist. While negotiating their own complex relationship, the two also study the impact of Columbus's voyage on the Native inhabitants in the New World. In 1993, Erdrich edited *The Best American Short Stories*, a collection of twenty stories. That year, Erdrich and Dorris first briefly moved back to their home in Cornish and then resettled in Minneapolis. Her next novel was *The Bingo Palace* (1994), which is set in Argus and covers only one year. This very funny novel describes the efforts of the Ojibwes and mixed-bloods to adjust to contemporary pressures, such as managing a bingo hall while trying to keep the tribe united.

Erdrich's first book of nonfiction was *The Blue Jay's Dance: A Birth Year* (1995), which contains essays, memories, thoughts, and recipes. She poignantly and honestly depicts the strong bond between mother and child that develops through her pregnancy and her baby's first year. In 1995, Erdrich separated from Dorris, who later committed suicide in New Hampshire on April 10, 1997.

Tales of Burning Love (1996) and subsequent novels were written without Dorris's collaboration. Set in North Dakota, *Tales* is a wonderfully comic novel that explores how women and men negotiate the distance between their points of view. It features a mixed-blood man and the strong Indian and non-Indian women he either married or romanced. *The Antelope Wife* (1998), Erdrich's next novel, includes a self-destructive husband who accidentally kills his own child. Interspersed with the narrative are tales from the Indian and European ancestors of the four main characters.

The author's later books reflect her studies of the Ojibwe language and culture, which began in the late 1990s. *The Last Report on the Miracles of Little No Horse* (2001) was a finalist for the National Book Award. The central character is Father Damien, who is a woman disguised as a man and ministers for decades to a Native parish. That year, Erdrich also gave birth to a fourth daughter, Nenaa'ikizhikok Rita "Kiizh."

The year 2003 saw the publication of three books. *The Master Butchers Singing Club*, set in North Dakota, reflects her German American heritage, connecting the lives of a German World War I veteran and his wife with those of circus performers and small-town inhabitants. It was a National Book Award finalist. Erdrich returned to poetry with the publication of *Original Fire: Selected and New Poems*. Its new poems include "The Seven Sleepers," a collection devoted to the search for the divine, and "Original Fire," a series on the journey through birth, life, loss, grief, and redemption. *Books and Islands in Ojibwe Country*, part of the National Geographic Directions series, vividly chronicles her experiences and thoughts during her trip through the lakes and islands of southern Ontario. She was accompanied by her nursing infant and an Ojibwe spiritual leader.

In *Four Souls* (2004), the new name taken by the central character, Erdrich describes the adventures of Fleur, who travels to Minneapolis to take revenge on a lumber baron who destroyed her reservation. Her arrival transforms the life of the family for whom she works. The author's next two novels depart from the focus on characters from Argus. *The Painted Drum* (2005) describes the journey of a traditional Ojibwe drum. It also explores the relationship between mothers and daughters and the strength of family. *The Plague of Doves* (2008), a Pulitzer Prize finalist, is an ambitious and moving mystery set in Pluto, North Dakota. Based on an actual case, the novel examines the impact on the townspeople to the 1911 hanging of three innocent Indians, a boy and two men.

Erdrich began a new chapter of her personal life when she married Dan Emmel on August 8, 2008, on the Turtle Mountain Reservation in North Dakota. A businessman in Minneapolis, Emmel grew up in South Dakota. A year later, Erdrich published *The Red Convertible: Selected and New Short Stories, 1978–2008*, which showcases her short fiction. In *Shadow Tag* (2010), her most personal novel, she powerfully depicts how the bitter dissolution of "an iconic marriage" destroys Irene and Gil, an artistic mixed-blood couple, as well as their children.

Erdrich has also become a highly successful writer of children's books. *Grandmother's Pigeon* (1996), a picture book for young readers, is an imaginative story of a grandmother who rides a dolphin and whale to Greenland and of how three passenger pigeons emerge from eggs she collected long ago. *The Range Eternal* (2002), also a picture book, describes how the wood-burning stove of a Turtle Mountain Ojibwe family warms them, cooks their food, and stimulates the imagination of a young girl. Three novels, designed for middle-school readers, trace the lives of Omakayas and her Ojibwe family. Set in 1847, *The Birchbark House* (1999) describes the traditional life led by Omakayas's family on an island in Lake Superior. *The Game of Silence* (2005), the sequel, is set in 1850 and depicts the changes in Ojibwe life brought about by the arrival of non-Indians. Set in 1852, *The Porcupine Year* (2009) recounts the canoe trip of twelve-year-old Omakayas and her family as they travel along the shores of Lake Superior and the rivers of northern Minnesota, seeking a new home. Erdrich illustrated all three books.

Erdrich has three books forthcoming in 2012: a substantially revised edition of *The Antelope Wife*; *Chickadee*, a story for children; and *The Round House*, a thriller written in the voice of a thirteen-year-old boy, examining how hard it is to prosecute a crime in Indian Country. In addition to writing and running her bookstore, Erdrich, along with her sisters Heid E. and Lise, conducts a summer workshop in creative writing on the Turtle Mountain Reservation. Throughout her career, Erdrich has been a prolific writer in a variety of genres. Her memorable descriptions of the lives of Ojibwes and mixed-bloods in her native North Dakota movingly depict the power and complexity of Native communities.

Works Cited

Beidler, Peter G. "Louise Erdrich." Roemer 84–100.

Berkley, Miriam. "PW Interview with Louise Erdrich." *Publishers Weekly* 15 Aug. 1986: 58–59.

Bonetti, Kay. "Louise Erdrich and Michael Dorris." *Conversations with American Novelists: The Best Interviews from the* Missouri Review. Ed. Kay Bonetti, et al. Columbia: U of Missouri P, 1997. 76–92.

Chavkin, Allan, and Nancy Feyl Chavkin, eds. *Conversations with Louise Erdrich & Michael Dorris*. Jackson: U of Mississippi P, 1994.

Coltelli, Laura. "Louise Erdrich and Michael Dorris." Chavkin 19–29.

Erdrich, Louise K. Message to the author. 11–12 Sept. 2011, 1 Nov. 2011. E-mail.

_____. Telephone interview, 26 Oct. 2011.

Hevern, Erin C. " 'Dabbler' Draws Inspiration from Family." *Daily News*. Daily News, Wahpeton, ND, 2 Nov. 2009. Web. 3 Apr. 2012.

"Louise Erdrich." *Poetry Foundation.* Poetry Foundation, 2011. Web. 3 Apr. 2012.

McNally, Amy Leigh, and Piyali Nath Dalal. "Louise Erdrich." *Voices from the Gaps: Women Writers of Color.* University of Minnesota, 27 May 1999. Web. 3 Apr. 2012.

"Patrick 'Aun Nish E Naubay' Gourneau, 1954–1958." *The History and Culture of the Turtle Mountain Band of Chippewa Leaders: Contemporary Leaders.* North Dakota Studies, n.d. Web. 3 Apr. 2012.

Roemer, Kenneth M. *Native American Writers of the United States.* Detroit: Gale, 1997.

Ruoff, A. LaVonne Brown. Afterword. *The Chippewa Landscape of Louise Erdrich.* Ed. Allan Chavkin. Tuscaloosa: U of Alabama P, 1990. 182–88.

Schumacher, Michael. "Louise Erdrich and Michael Dorris: A Marriage of Minds." *Writers Digest* June 1991: 28–31, 59. Rpt. in Chavkin 173–83.

Spillman, Robert. "Louise Erdrich: The Creative Instinct." *Salon*. Salon Media Group, 6 May 1996. Web. 3 Apr. 2012.

Wong, Hertha D. Sweet. "Michael Dorris." Roemer 65–74.

CRITICAL
CONTEXTS

Re/creating the Past: Anishinaabe History in the Novels of Louise Erdrich

Margaret Huettl

The novels of Louise Erdrich are both inherently and explicitly histori-cal. In the first pages of *Tracks*, Nanapush, representative of a genera-tion of Anishinaabe leaders who resisted white encroachment, reflects on the past fifty years. Looking back from 1912, he describes the tran-sition to the twentieth century as a period of rapid, wrenching change. He recalls, "I guided the last buffalo hunt. I saw the last bear shot. I trapped the last beaver with a pelt of more than two years' growth. I spoke aloud the words of the government treaty, and refused to sign the settlement papers that would take away our woods and lake. I axed the last birch that was older than I, and I saved the last Pillager" (2). These changes, part of the historical experience of the Anishinaabeg, provide the backdrop for Erdrich's novels.

Nanapush's reflections capture a profound sense of loss. Initially, his view of the past seems to align with the standard narrative of American history that relegates Indians to the margins as a destroyed and vanish-ing people. However, his statement actually contradicts this trajectory of inevitable decline. His words contain a sense of hope, for he "saved the last Pillager," Fleur, whom he loves as a daughter. More impor-tantly, he is telling his story to Fleur's daughter, Lulu, "the child of the invisible" Ojibwes erased by disease and mainstream history (1). Thus, Erdrich presents the Ojibwe past as a cycle of destruction and resur-gence, both on a personal and tribal level. Writing from an Anishinaabe historical perspective, she discusses the effects of allotment, land loss, Catholic missionization, boarding schools, government administration, twentieth-century wars, urban relocation, and development of reserva-tion industry and casinos. In particular, she draws on the struggle to retain land, the complications of Métis identity, and the experiences of urban Ojibwes to demonstrate the complex responses to conflict. The past century and a half contained many grim moments that seemed to threaten to destroy Indian communities, but there also exists a counter-narrative of resistance and survival. Incorporating this alternate version of history, Erdrich's novels contain both tragedy and uplift, dislocation and reintegration.

How Erdrich approaches history is important. In *The Painted Drum*, Erdrich uses Chook to express her philosophy on the past. She says that everybody's past is full of sorrows and that "you wear down these sorrows using what you have, what comes to hand. You talk them over, you live them through, you don't let them sit inside" (105). In other words, history has an active purpose for sharing, and discussing the past helps to recover the losses. Many Ojibwe historians share Erdrich's perspective on the purpose-driven nature of history. Thomas Peacock, a Canadian Ojibwe, suggests that some stories, like those of attempted "cultural obliteration" of indigenous peoples, "must be passed down through the generations in hopes that such atrocities will never happen again" (16). One reason for this pragmatic approach is that, for the Anishinaabeg, the past and the present are inextricably intertwined. Peacock cannot escape "the interconnectedness of all things" in his writings—past, present, and future—and he argues that to do so would deny the Ojibwe worldview (65). In all of her novels, Erdrich presents the past as a tangled web of connections, each event building off another. For example, at the beginning of *The Bingo Palace*, the narrator observes, "The story comes around, pushing at our brains, and soon we are trying to ravel back to the beginning, trying to put families in order and make sense of things. But we start with one person, and soon another and another follows, and still another, and we are lost in the connections" (5). Taking into account multiple perspectives, her novels sift through these tangled events of the past and provide meaning within a larger cultural and historical context.

Erdrich's reservation, though fictional, is a historical creation. She describes it as somewhere near the border between North Dakota and Canada, not far from Minnesota. It comprises prairies, lakes and sloughs, and forests, and it borders three nonreservation towns: Argus,

Pluto, and Hoopdance. The real Turtle Mountain Reservation is located in the former bison-hunting and fur-trading territory of a band of Anishinaabeg who had slowly strayed west in search of resources. Such movement was common among the Anishinaabeg, a loose confederation of family-based bands that ranged as far west as Montana and straddled the present-day Canadian border. Located in what is now North Dakota near the border with Manitoba, the variegated landscape encompasses grassy plains, forested hills, and over two hundred lakes, not unlike their original home in Wisconsin and Minnesota (Camp 19–22). Band representatives initially claimed ten million acres in the Turtle Mountains, but the United States government granted them a fraction of that space and ultimately reduced the twenty-two townships to two. The so-called Ten Cent Treaty in 1892 offered the band ten cents per acre, a total of one million dollars, for the forcibly ceded land. This settlement was grossly disproportionate to the $2.50 per acre that other Plains tribes received and helped to create the backdrop of poverty that Erdrich describes in novels such as *Tracks*, where spoiled gopher meat becomes "Indian beef" in between shipments of government food supplies (99).

Although Erdrich situates her reservation in North Dakota and is herself a registered member of the Turtle Mountain Band, her fictional community could just as easily be Lac du Flambeau on the wooded shores of Lake Superior, and the island in Lake Matchimanito could be Strawberry Island, which Anishinaabe parents warn their children is haunted by spirits. It could be White Earth in Minnesota, which tragically lost the majority of its land and lumber resources in the early twentieth century. It could be the Bad River Reservation in northern Wisconsin, where Catholic missionaries established a school for Native children, who later remembered teachers as frightening as Sister Leopolda.

The imagined reservation replicates a recognizably Ojibwe setting. Her characters view this place as their homeland, despite their relatively recent arrival and the oppressive nature of its origins. Indian nations across the country have transformed what once were essentially prisons into meaningful sources of community, identity, and power (Hoxie, *Parading through History*). As Nanapush observes in *Four Souls*, the reservation "came about in a time of desperation and upon it we will see things occur more desperate yet" (210), but the water monster lives in the lake, the bones of their ancestors are buried among the trees, and he, Lulu, Fleur, Seraph "Mooshum" Milk, Judge Antoine Bazil Coutts, and other Anishinaabeg defend it. "*Land is the only thing that lasts life to life*," as Fleur tells Lyman Lamartine when he covets her land for a new gaming hall (*Bingo Palace* 148; emphasis in orig.). For Erdrich, the land is more than an economic resource; it is the link to their historic identity as Anishinaabeg.

For many characters, the reservation becomes a site of personal revitalization. Marie Kashpaw, formerly Lazarre, leaves the convent and vicious Pauline/Sister Leopolda and finds a place on the Kashpaw allotment. Her life is by no means perfect—Nector Kashpaw, her husband, is unfaithful and occasionally drinks and gambles away their money—but she becomes part of a community. Faye Travers, born on the East Coast, visits the reservation to return a drum and begins the "wobbling steps" of coming home (*Painted Drum* 269). Sometimes the reservation is not enough. Henry Junior, for example, never regains his peace after returning from the Vietnam War, and he jumps into a flooded river and is "gone" (*Love Medicine* 154). Others, like Pauline, reject the reservation entirely. For the rest, however, Erdrich presents the reservation as the foundation of their identity. Even those who leave continue to feel its pull. For example, in *The Antelope Wife*, Windigo Dog jokes about the reservation being a trap. "Every time one of them tries to sneak off, the others pull him back," he says, but Klaus Shawano contradicts him, insisting, "My rez is very special to me. It is my place of authority" (224). Over the course of the twentieth century, reservations became homelands in a very real and concrete sense for Indian nations like the Anishinaabeg, places that inspired bitter and determined fights to protect their land and their political and cultural sovereignty. Thus, Erdrich's constant theme of returning home is more than an abstract longing. It is a historically based cultural imperative.

Erdrich's most direct engagement with history regards allotment. The struggle to protect the land influences relationships between characters and drives the plot of multiple novels. *Tracks*, for instance, draws its drama from the threat to the Kashpaw and Pillagers' homesteads, the fallout from which carries over into the other novels involving these characters. The United States pursued allotment—the carving of tribal land held in common into individual titles for individual Indians—as a solution to its "Indian problem," for most Americans viewed Indians as a barrier to development. The goal of the General Allotment Act of 1887, or Dawes Act, was assimilation. Individual ownership of land, officials believed, would transform Native Americans into self-supporting farmers who would disappear into the mass of American citizenry. At the same time, land would be opened to westward-surging settlers. Settlers quickly claimed the desired land, but Native Americans did not morph into sedentary farmers. Allotment proved to be a disaster. Altogether, Indian nations lost almost 90 million acres by the end of allotment in 1934, over 60 percent of their landholdings in 1887 (Wilkinson 43). The 40 to 160 acres allotted depending on age were insufficient to compete in an agricultural marketplace that no longer favored the yeoman farmer. More importantly, the Burke Act in 1906 accelerated the Dawes Act's effects. In theory, a twenty-five-year waiting period protected the trust status of land parcels, during which time the land remained exempt from taxes and could not be sold. The Burke Act, however, allowed the secretary of the Interior to cut this period short by granting fee patents (deeds) to any Native Americans deemed "competent" (Hoxie, *Final Promise*). In other words, the US government could revoke the trust status of Indian land whether individual allottees wanted them to or not, bestowing the rights and responsibilities of citizenship—which often meant a staggering and unfamiliar burden of taxes and an onslaught of unscrupulous speculators and loggers who snatched up land with promises of quick cash and mortgages.

For the Turtle Mountain Band, circumstances made allotment particularly dangerous. Congress delayed the ratification of the Ten Cent Treaty, which meant that the band did not receive compensation for the ten million acres they had ceded, which exacerbated poverty on the reservation. As allotment carved up their community, few had the financial resources to succeed as independent farmers. Because the reservation was too small for all its members to receive allotments, many had to take their 160 acres away from the reservation in the public domain. A high percentage of band members were mixed-bloods, who were often exempt from the twenty-five-year waiting period, and government officials altered the status of even more individuals to expedite the fee patent process. Many of the distant allottees and government-classified mixed-bloods quickly lost their land to unpaid taxes and mortgages, often returning to the dwindling reservation to squat on relatives' land. Only 10 percent of those who had fee patents thrust upon them retained their land (Camp 36). The situation on other Ojibwe reservations, such as White Earth in Minnesota, mirrored the land loss at Turtle Mountain, where corporate scheming on the part of lumber companies defrauded hundreds of Anishinaabeg of their land (Meyer). Thus, when Nanapush describes how his reservation has been "nibbled at the edges and surrounded by farmers waiting for it to go under the gavel of the auctioneer," his words carry the weight of historical experience (*Tracks* 99).

In *Tracks*, Erdrich reveals the effects of this policy on her imagined reservation. Both the Kashpaw and Pillager allotments are in danger of being lost because of unpaid taxes they did not know had been assessed. Nanapush insists, "'Trust' means they can't tax our parcels" (174). However, legislation such as the Burke Act abrogated that protected status, and in the novel, Father Damien produces a color-coded map showing their lands in the "sharper yellow" hue that meant they owed taxes regardless of whether they were aware of it. Fleur, Nanapush, and the Kashpaws face enemies on two sides: on the one hand, logging companies and banks; on the other, fellow tribesmen, including the Lazarres, the Morrisseys, and Pukwan, a tribal police officer who profits from his alliance with the government. Although Fleur, Nanapush, and Margaret and Eli Kashpaw work to pay the taxes, peeling cranberry bark until it piles up around their legs, one day they wake up to the "faint thump of steel axes" and logging already underway on Fleur's land (206). John James Mauser has already purchased Fleur's land, and her trees are disappearing, for Margaret, lacking the money to save either parcel completely, directs all their earnings to pay off her family's land. The government agent simply says that "a lumber company offered a good price" and that "the government is obliged to take an offer of that sort when taxes are unpaid" (207). Like at White Earth, logging interests accelerated the impact of allotment without fair compensation (Meyer). Further threats to the tribal land base came from Anishinaabe council members themselves, as other novels show. When Nector is chairman, the tribe decides to sell land held in common to a tomahawk factory, despite the fact that Lulu's family has been using the land for several generations. In *Four Souls*, Margaret sells Nector's land for an even smaller investment, a linoleum floor. As Father Damien's color-coded map demonstrates, profit-driven corporations stood ready to "sweep the marks of the boundaries off our map like a pattern of straws" (*Tracks* 8). Allotment initiated a cycle of land loss that continued unabated through the middle of the twentieth century.

Erdrich recognizes the assimilative motives behind government practices. It was not simply that the Ojibwes were supposed to become farmers, but that they "were supposed to learn to farm in the chimookomaan way, using toothed machines and clumsy, big horses to pull them" (*Four Souls* 79). Nanapush attributes Margaret's sudden desire for a linoleum floor to her time at boarding school and her learned desire for material comfort. Likewise, Erdrich implies that the Lazarres and Morrisseys supported allotment precisely because they had ties to the white community. She uses Nanapush to critique this system. The purpose of the allotment agent, he says, is "to make it easier for us to sell our land to white people," not to help the Anishinaabeg navigate bureaucratic red tape or to make sure bankers and business enter into fair deals (*Four Souls* 79). Land loss is so difficult to fight, Erdrich suggests, because authorities acted as though "there was no adversary, no betrayer, no one to fight" (*Tracks* 207). These bureaucrats present it as a natural, inevitable process. Meanwhile, they pass law after law without consulting Native Americans, trapping the Ojibwes in "a landscape of webs" (79). Nanapush voices Erdrich's suspicions about the corruption underlying the guise of legal procedure. "How much of that good price, that illegal late fee perhaps, splashed into your pockets? How much is stored in the walls of my old cabin, which you gave Lazarres? How much cash did you stuff into the mattress of Bernadette?" he demands of the agent after logging begins on Fleur's land but not Margaret's, indicating a web of corruption that essentially amounts to what Erdrich elsewhere calls the "great thievery" (*Tracks* 208; *Plague of Doves* 84). Nanapush and Erdrich are justified in their suspicions. In *Four Souls*, Erdrich makes it clear that Mauser bribed Agent Jewett Parker Tatro for access to the trees. A similar instance occurred at Bad River in Wisconsin, where the Stearns Lumber Company held a monopoly over timber contracts and thereby, in the words of Bad River historian Patty Loew, secured "a stranglehold on the tribal economy" (73). Stearns was aided by Indian agent Samuel Campbell, who pocketed at least thirty thousand dollars of tribal timber revenue and consistently facilitated contracts up three times less than market value (75).

Although she considers the decisions of individuals, Erdrich leaves no doubt that allotment devastated the Anishinaabeg. The sense of loss permeates each of her novels set on the reservation. Losing her land, the culmination of personal tragedies including the death of her baby, nearly destroys Fleur, though her desire for revenge at times masks her grief. John James Mauser's house, built from the swindled lumber, gives physical form to her sense of bereavement, leaking "beads of thin sap—as though recalling growth and life on the land belonging to Fleur Pillager and the shores of Matchimanito, beyond" (*Four Souls*

9). The loss of land cuts so deep across the Anishinaabe community that it "was lodged inside of them forever," becoming the burden of each subsequent generation (*Plague of Doves* 85). She condemns allotment as a form of organized cultural destruction. It is no coincidence, Nanapush concludes, that bankers offered mortgages "just as the first of us had failed at growing or herding or plowing the fields" (*Four Souls* 79). He links these policies directly to the extermination of Native Americans, as foreclosure notices followed mortgage papers and people were reduced to begging until even begging was outlawed and the Anishinaabeg were left to starve, thus "becoming a solved problem." "Who worries about the dead?" he wonders, linking the land policies in the reader's mind beyond mere dispossession to extermination (80).

Despite the devastation, however, Erdrich provides her own Anishinaabe interpretation of this period that does not make loss allotment's only legacy. Through characters who resist allotment, Erdrich develops a strain of resistance and resurgence. For instance, Lulu refuses to leave the tribal land on which she is squatting when the council sells it to a tomahawk factory. She calls all monetary settlements "*merde*" and stubbornly refuses "to move one foot farther west" until Nector accidentally burns down her house (*Love Medicine* 223). In the end, she receives a new home on a different plot of tribal land "rightfully repurchased from a white farmer," where "wives and children, in-laws, cousins, all collected there in trailers and more old car hulks. Box elder trees and oak scrub were planted and grew up. We even had a gooseberry patch. It became a regular nest of Lamartines" (227, 228). Lulu and her relatives renew their strength as a community on this reclaimed land. Thus, Erdrich reaffirms the reservation as a viable homeland, able to recover from being carved into pieces if the land is restored.

Mauser voices what has long been the dominant view: that Indian people like the Ojibwes were disappearing anyway, and allotment only hurried this process along. Although he is eventually married to Fleur and knows she would kill him to recover her land, he dismisses reservations as "ruined spots" with no hope of restoration. "There's nothing left!" he insists, voicing the stereotype of the Vanishing Indian (*Four Souls* 127). Erdrich, however, discounts his dismissal, and his own wife proves him wrong. She returns to the reservation, wearing the suit and driving the car his money paid for and accompanied by their son. Mauser himself has lost the land to Tatro, but, with the help of her son, Fleur wins it back from him in a game of cards. Nanapush captures the sense of disintegration and reintegration after the restoration of the Pillager land when he reflects that, over the course of the Ojibwe past, "I see that we have come out of it with something, at least. This scrap of earth" (210). Calling the reservation an *ishkonigan*, or leftover, recalls the significant losses of the past century, but he ends with a positive message for modern Anishinaabeg. "We've got this," he says, "and as long as we can hold on to it we will be some sort of people" (210).

Through the historical figure of Louis Riel, Erdrich deals with issues of Métis (mixed-blood) identity and cultural resistance. She casts Riel, whom she calls a "poet" and "a visionary hero of our people," as a symbol of both loss and renewal (*Shadow Tag* 41; *Plague of Doves* 21). Erdrich portrays his struggle as "an issue of rights" that has affected all Anishinaabeg since (*Plague of Doves* 33). Louis David Riel was born in 1844 in the Red River settlement, a largely Métis community, in a region of Canada controlled by the Hudson Bay Company. He led two insurrections against the Canadian authorities to demand a self-governing Métis nation and consequent land rights. The first rebellion in 1869 led to the creation of Manitoba as a province with equal status to other Canadian provinces. The call for protections for Métis and Indian land claims, however, was left unanswered, and Riel was exiled to the United States because the Métis provisional government had executed a Canadian official for crimes against their new nation (Stanley).

By the time Riel returned to Canada in the 1880s, he had been elected to parliament three times (although his exile made it impossible to serve), earned his American citizenship, taught at a mission school, and written poems about everything from his sister to his enemies to his dreams of a sovereign Métis homeland (Campbell). Most dramatically, perhaps, he proclaimed himself the "prophet of the New World," recounting visions of the Métis and their Native relatives as God's chosen people and demanding not only self-government in political affairs but also a separate Métis-run Catholic church. Many of his American allies believed him insane and had him confined to a mental hospital, but his prophetic visions hardly seem far-fetched from Erdrich's Anishinaabe perspective, which allows for not only human actors but other-than-human agents as well (Benton-Banai, Peacock). When the Canadian government refused to accept their demands for land title, Riel and his fellow leaders, including Gabriel Dumont, seized the Saskatchewan provincial capital, Batoche, and its religious leaders. The North-West Rebellion, as the 1885 insurrection came to be known, ended when the Canadian government used all possible force to suppress Riel and his followers, and Riel was put on trial for treason. Although an insanity plea might have spared his life, Riel staunchly refused to demean the sanctity of his mission and died faithful to his cause (Flanagan 190; Stanley).

When Mooshum and his brother Shamengwa tell the Catholic priest about Riel in *The Plague of Doves*, their discussion captures a sense of what has been lost. "Things would have been different all around" had Riel and his followers succeeded (30). As it is, Riel's failure sent his supporters, which include the brothers' parents, into diaspora. Their parents lost their farm, which meant that Mooshum and Shamengwa lost their land as well, and "the heart was out of them. They lost a baby, settled into a despondent subsistence, and were crushed when they heard Riel was tried and hanged" (21). Shamengwa describes how Riel's loss left his parents "broken," no longer "whole people" (33). The younger generations seem to live out fragments of Riel's legacy, for "history works itself out in the living" (243). Evelina, named after Riel's "lost love," ends up in a mental hospital like Riel, but her only visions seem to be the result of LSD, and Corwin Peace, descended from one of Riel's guides, trades drugs in "a banged up Chevy Nova with hubcaps missing and back end dragging" rather than sitting "high on a bale of buffalo robes or beaver skins" (198). Corwin's uncle Billy Peace, once described as "artistic," carries on Riel's visions and becomes almost "supernatural," but his prophecies become grotesque and violent (154). Marn, his wife, has visions of her own, which she fulfills when she poisons her abusive husband. The descendants of Riel's band living on Erdrich's fictional reservation seem irrevocably damaged by the trauma of their collective past. The 1911 hanging of three Indian men certainly factors into this legacy, but Mooshum links this event to the downfall of Riel as well, speaking from his own shattered position of guilt when he suggests, "our people would not have been hanged" had Riel succeeded (34). Both acts of violence against Anishinaabe men seem to parallel one another, echoing the marginalized position of tribal members. History has become so tangled that cause and effect become difficult to discern, and unraveling the past to escape its web seems impossible.

In the same conversation with the priest where they describe how Riel's failure damaged them forever, Mooshum and Shamengwa also suggest the possibilities of recovery. They imagine a special Métis brand of Catholicism, and they delight in tormenting their priest with stories about how in the new "mixed-blood Catholicism," clerics may marry and how Riel's hell "did not last forever, nor was it even very hot" (22, 30–31). They draw on this cultural hero to triumph over the priest, a representative of colonizing institutions. Riel inspires them to toast, "To our nation! To our people!" and "Land!" (33). Thus, Erdrich uses his familiar legacy to find expression for contemporary Anishinaabe desires for land and sovereignty.

In *Shadow Tag*, one of the children is named Riel in honor of Métis heritage. Other names similarly reference indigenous leaders. For instance, Riel's younger brother, Stoney, is named after Stone Child or Rocky Boy, who chose diplomatic resistance in his struggle to secure a reservation for his band of Ojibwes and Crees in Montana. Similarly,

Shawnee in *The Painted Drum* is named for the prophet Tenskwatawa, who helped Tecumseh lead his pan-Indian war against the United States and is related to the Ojibwes through common Lenape ancestors. Referencing leaders such as Riel, Stone Child, Tenskwatawa, and Cree leader Poundmaker, who joined the North-West Rebellion, creates the impression that "it's always the same story" (Peacock 46; *Shadow Tag* 41). The government denies Indians "working their land for years" the right to that land. Nevertheless, by naming young characters after these heroes of Native resistance, Erdrich entrusts future generations with the task of continuing their ancestors' mission and refusing to accept that their "visions of an Indian nation died in the bloody snow at a place called Batoche" (41). The girl Riel reenacts his legacy by learning how to be an "old-time Indian" and developing a plan to "take away [her father's] power" (63). Like her namesake, she fails in her mission and the cycle of domestic abuse leads to her parents' drowning. Erdrich, however, allows her to succeed in other ways. She avoids the pitfalls of drugs that trap her older brother, graduates from the University of Minnesota, and is strong enough to tell her family's story.

As a Métis, Riel carries additional resonance in Erdrich's work. Métis refers to those of mixed Indian and European descent, especially the children of French fur traders and Cree, Anishinaabe, and other northern Native women. Over time, these mixed-race offspring developed a sense of community and nationalism distinct from both Euro-Americans and Indians. They both saw themselves and were seen as outsiders, singled out in treaties for separate treatment and benefits. Riel defined himself as a champion of the Métis nation, and his struggles for land against the Canadian government made him a champion of Native rights more generally. Most of Riel's biographers overlook his connection to his Anishinaabe brethren and instead emphasize his ties to French Catholicism or laud him as the founder of a bilingual Canadian province. Erdrich, however, reclaims his Ojibwe identity by locating the heirs of his legacy on the reservation. He is the visionary of "our people," says Mooshum. Ultimately, the remnants of Riel's band scattered as settlers encroached on their land, exactly as Riel had feared. A significant number relocated to Turtle Mountain and were legally incorporated into the tribe, connections that Erdrich ascribes to several families in *The Plague of Doves*. Historians often depict Métis as working against Native interests or at least as having their interests in competition with one another (Camp; Meyer). This antithetical relationship seems at work elsewhere in Erdrich's work, with the Morrisseys and Lazarres eternally feuding with the Pillagers and Kashpaws. By showing how their descendants have become enmeshed in the reservation community for good or ill, Erdrich suggests that they received a new beginning and hints at the possibility of further renewal in the future.

Just as Erdrich recalls the Métis from the marginalization of mainstream history, she also incorporates the experience of urban Ojibwes. *The Antelope Wife* takes place in Minneapolis, a city with a thriving Native community and a particularly strong Ojibwe presence (Shoemaker). Scattered throughout her other novels, individuals such as Lipsha Morrissey, Beverly "Hat" Lamartine, and Gerry Nanapush leave the reservation in search of work. Beverly sees the Twin Cities as the site of "great relocation opportunities for Indians with a certain amount of stick-to-it-iveness and pride" (*Love Medicine* 77). Starting in the 1950s, the United States government took a similar view. As part of its program of termination, the Bureau of Indian Affairs (BIA) encouraged individuals and families to migrate to the cities. Of course, Native Americans had been doing so for years. Students left home to attend college, workers followed jobs during World War I and World War II, and those who lost their allotments sometimes had no choice but to relocate. Now, however, the government offered monetary incentives and promised support, both of which often proved inadequate. The majority of Indians who relocated returned to the reservation. Those who stayed behind had to rely on one another for support, and new, often pan-Indian communities developed and familiarized urban landscapes. Cities such as Chicago, Oakland, and Phoenix opened Indian community centers as early as 1947, and by the 1970s, Minneapolis had a large Native community of its own (Fixico). These communities were often so self-contained that Lipsha's assertion that, upon arriving in Minneapolis, he "just started following the Indians whenever I saw one, and eventually ended up where I belonged" is entirely plausible (*Love Medicine* 248).

According to Carol Miller, Native authors often portray cities as "places of risk, separation, disillusion, and dissolution" (31). Erdrich falls in with a second group, those who see the urban experience as formative—an opportunity to reforge identity and reaffirm connections to one's Native community. She interprets the history of relocation along the same pattern as allotment and Métis resistance. Living in the city is often a traumatic experience for her characters, but through their struggles, they renew themselves as individuals and members of a broader Anishinaabe community. Her urban characters undoubtedly experience desolation. Lipsha describes the appalling conditions in the sugar-beet plant where he works, which left him "covered with a sugary chip-proof mist of chemicals, preserved, suspended, trapped like a bug in a plastic weight," a fitting metaphor for his unfulfilling life in Fargo (*Bingo Palace* 9). For Sweetheart Calico, kidnapped by Klaus Shawano, the city is like a prison that seems to drain the life of out of her so that she never speaks, but "when she opens her mouth, her eyes go black" (*Antelope Wife* 105). The city seems to drain Richard Whiteheart Beads as well. He and his wife, Rozin, lose one of their twin daughters to carbon monoxide poisoning during Richard's aborted suicide attempt. He ends up homeless, intoxicated with Listerine, and desperate for a drink of water, and finally, he kills himself in front of Rozin on the night she marries Frank Shawano.

Again, however, Erdrich follows disintegration with stories of renewal. Where her former husband dies defeated, Rozin recovers, attends law school, and marries Frank; Cally, the surviving twin, becomes sick on the reservation and returns to the city in search of her name, rather than the reverse. Gerry Nanapush emerges as a symbol of Ojibwe resistance, for "no white man has made a jail that could hold the son of Old Man Pillager" (*Love Medicine* 225), and the city offers him the opportunity to escape and continue his subversion of a legal system that has shown him no justice. Erdrich mentions that he is a member of the American Indian Movement (AIM), an organization started in 1968 in Minneapolis by Ojibwe organizers, including Dennis Banks and Clyde Bellecourt, to combat issues such as poverty, housing inequality, and police harassment that threatened urban Indians' quality of life (Smith and Warrior). Gerry Nanapush could "inspir[e] the Indian people" from an urban forum, so clearly the city did not swallow him whole (*Love Medicine* 227). Moreover, Erdrich's Minneapolis is not a white man's wasteland. Klaus is accompanied by a windigo dog, the "bad spirit of hunger and not just normal hunger but out-of-control hunger" (*Antelope Wife* 127). The windigo dog seems to fuel his addiction, but it nevertheless represents a tie to an Anishinaabe way of experiencing reality that the city does not stifle. Cally's grandmothers use the city as a hub for their social activities, bouncing around to a "funeral here, bingo there, workshop up north or on an exciting Canadian reserve" (108). The extent of the Ojibwe community is clear at Rozin and Frank Shawano's wedding and anniversary feasts, where dozens of Ojibwes come together to celebrate and eat venison sausage and fry bread. In the final scene of this strand of the narrative, Rozin and Frank's laughter becomes "part of the general roar" of their urban friends and family (236).

Erdrich strengthens the city's restorative properties by calling it Gakahbekong and reclaiming it for the Ojibwes. It does not matter how many "driveways and houses, concrete parking garages and business stores cover the city's scape," for "that same land is hunched underneath," and that land is Indian land (*Antelope Wife* 124–25). Lulu echoes this sentiment in *Love Medicine*, declaring, "Every foot and inch you're standing on, even if it's on the top of the highest skyscraper, belongs to the Indians" (221). Just as she reclaims Louis Riel for the Ojibwes, Erdrich lays claim to urban spaces as well. In fact, an underlying function of her writing seems to be reclaiming the Anishinaabe past more generally. Erdrich's stories about allotment, political resistance, Métis identity, and urban experience show both triumph and defeat, and at either extreme, they challenge the dominance of mainstream Euro-American values and understandings of the world. Offering an alternate, Anishinaabe interpretation, she concludes that the twentieth century contains "so much given for so little" (*Four Souls* 82).

Erdrich provides a broader context that enables readers to see beyond the standard narrative of destruction that relegates modern Indians to relics of the past. Freed from this static past, the Ojibwes re-emerge as agents in their own historical narratives. Nanapush, who tells stories that others have forgotten or never knew, says that all history inevitably concerns change, and "even such people as we, the Anishinaabeg, can sometimes die, or change, or change and become" (*Four Souls* 210). There is loss, and yet even "the dead buffalo . . . are plowed into newly scratched-out fields" (210). Change is dangerous and "chaos and pain" (210), but the Anishinaabeg can overcome their struggles by drawing strength from the same history that supposedly tells of their destruction.

Works Cited

Benton-Banai, Edward. *The Mishomis Book: The Voice of the Ojibway*. Minneapolis: U of Minnesota P, 1998.

Camp, Gregory S. "Working Out Their Own Salvation: The Allotment of Land in Severalty and the Turtle Mountain Chippewa Band, 1870–1920." *American Indian Culture and Research Journal* 14.2 (1990): 19–38.

Campbell, Glen, ed. *Selected Poetry of Louis Riel*. Trans. Paul Savoie. Toronto: Harper, 2000.

Child, Brenda J. *Boarding School Seasons*. Lincoln: U of Nebraska P, 1998.

Erdrich, Louise. *The Antelope Wife*. New York: Harper, 1998.

_____. *The Beet Queen*. New York: Harper, 1998.

_____. *The Bingo Palace*. New York: Harper, 1994.

_____. *Four Souls*. New York: Harper, 2004.

_____. *The Last Report on the Miracles at Little No Horse*. New York: Harper, 2001.

_____. *Love Medicine*. New York, Harper, 2009.

_____. *The Painted Drum*. New York: Harper, 2005.

_____. *The Plague of Doves*. New York: Harper, 2009.

_____. *Shadow Tag*. New York: Harper, 2010.

_____. *Tracks*. New York: Harper, 1988.

Fixico, Donald L. *The Urban Indian Experience in America*. Albuquerque: U of New Mexico P, 2000.

Flanagan, Thomas. "Louis Riel and the Dispersion of the American Métis." *Minnesota History* 49.5 (1985): 179–90.

Hickerson, Harold. *The Chippewa and Their Neighbors: A Study in Ethnohistory*. New York: Holt, 1970.

Hoxie, Frederick E. *A Final Promise: The Campaign to Assimilate the Indians, 1880–1920*. Lincoln: U of Nebraska P, 2001.

_____. *Parading through History: The Making of the Crow Nation in America, 1805–1935*. New York: Cambridge UP, 1995.

Loew, Patty. *Indian Nations of Wisconsin: Histories of Endurance and Renewal*. Madison: Wisconsin Historical Soc., 2001.

Meyer, Melissa L. *The White Earth Tragedy: Ethnicity and Dispossession at a Minnesota Anishinaabe Reservation, 1889–1920*. Lincoln: U of Nebraska P, 1994.

Miller, Carol. "Telling the Indian Urban: Representation in American Indian Fiction." *American Indians and the Urban Experience*. Ed. Susan Lobo and Kurt Peters. Lanham: Rowman, 2001. 29–46.

Peacock, Thomas. *Ojibwe Waasa Inaabidaa: We Look in All Directions*. St. Paul: Minnesota Historical Soc., 2009.

Peterson, Nancy J. "History, Postmodernism, and Louise Erdrich." *PMLA* 109.5 (1994): 982–94. m

Reid, Jennifer. *Louis Riel and the Creation of Modern Canada: Mythic Discourse and the Postcolonial State*. Albuquerque: U of New Mexico P, 2008.

Shoemaker, Nancy. "Urban Indians and Ethnic Choices: American Indian Organizations in Minneapolis, 1920–1950." *Western History Quarterly* 19 (1988): 431–47.

Smith, Paul Chaat, and Robert Allen Warrior. *Like a Hurricane: The Indian Movement from Alcatraz to Wounded Knee*. New York: Free, 1996.

Stanley, George Rancis Gilman. *Louis Riel*. Toronto: Ryerson, 1963.

Stripes, James D. "The Problem(s) of (Anishinaabe) History in the Fiction of Louise Erdrich: Voices and Context." *Wicazo Sa Review* 7 (1991): 26–33.

Warren, William W. *History of the Ojibway People*. 1885. St. Paul: Minnesota Historical Soc., 1984.

Wilkinson, Charles. *Blood Struggle: The Rise of Modern Indian Nations*. New York: Norton, 2005.

The Work of Louise Erdrich: A Survey of Critical Responses_____

Gregory A. Wright

Ojibwe novelist and poet Louise Erdrich, one of the United States' most widely read and prolific writers, entered the literary mainstream consciousness in 1984 with the publication of *Love Medicine*. Because of the commercial and critical success of this novel, Erdrich is frequently linked with American Indian writers N. Scott Momaday (Kiowa), Leslie Marmon Silko (Laguna Pueblo), Gerald Vizenor (Ojibwe), and James Welch (Blackfeet/Gros Ventre), who represent what scholar Kenneth Lincoln has termed the Native American Renaissance. She began her illustrious career by writing poetry and short stories. The skills and techniques that she developed working in these genres prepared her for the immense success that she has achieved with the novel. Her first novel, *Love Medicine*, grew out of a short story that she wrote in 1981 over the course of two days. She entered that story, "The World's Greatest Fisherman," into the Nelson Algren short-story contest and later received the 1982 Nelson Algren Award for short fiction. This story became the opening chapter of *Love Medicine*, the winner of the 1984 National Book Critics Circle Award. In the ensuing twenty-eight years, Erdrich has written at a fast, consistent pace, publishing thirteen novels, almost one novel every two years. During that same period, she has also written and published three collections of poetry, five books for young adults and children, a collection of short stories, and two works of nonfiction.

Erdrich's literary output has not gone without notice, and her work continues to receive praise. Erdrich's novels routinely grace the *New York Times*' book review list, and her short fiction can be found in the *New Yorker*, *Harper's*, *The Paris Review*, and the *Atlantic*. Her writing receives glowing reviews and garners prestigious awards. Her seventh novel, *The Last Report on the Miracles at Little No Horse*, was nominated for a National Book Award, and her eleventh novel,

The Plague of Doves, was a finalist for the Pulitzer Prize. A. LaVonne Brown Ruoff, one of the earliest and most distinguished scholars of Native American literature, believes that readers enjoy Erdrich's work for many reasons:

> Critics and scholars have highly praised [Erdrich's] skillful weaving of Ojibwe ethnohistory into her narratives, masterful use of oral tradition and multi-layered stories, powerful portrayals of characters (particularly women), hilarious humor that ranges from mock heroic battles to survival jokes, unerring depictions of popular culture, and lyrical descriptions of nature. (183)

Indeed, Erdrich instructs, entertains, and challenges her audience with her lyrical and layered prose and poetry, yet Ruoff ultimately concludes that it is Erdrich's ability to fully realize a unique tribal community that marks her writing and appeals so much to audiences. With each novel, Erdrich's "community" grows and expands both within and beyond the fictional reservation at Little No Horse.

Erdrich's work not only appeals to a general audience, but it has also attracted the attention of the academy. Students encounter her poetry and short fiction in anthologies used in literature survey, women's studies, ethnic studies, composition, and creative writing courses. Likewise, her novels are staples of American, Native American, and multiethnic literature courses. Invariably, the reading of a literary work leads to its formal critical analysis. From 1991 to 2009, fifty-six doctoral dissertations focused on Erdrich's writing. A simple search of standard library databases returns over 350 scholarly, peer-reviewed articles from a variety of publications in the United States, Canada, and Europe. The quarterly *Studies in American Indian Literatures* (*SAIL*), the preeminent journal on American Indian literatures, has dedicated three issues solely to Erdrich and her work. In addition to these scholarly articles, critical studies can be found in numerous essay collections. Furthermore, her work is the subject of ten book-length critical studies. Erdrich's novels, short stories, poetry, and young-adult fiction have provided scholars with fertile ground for various and seemingly innumerable critical approaches.

Prior to reviewing the literary criticism of Erdrich's work, or indeed that of any Native American writer, it is important to understand the current state of and direction for American Indian literary studies. Simon Ortiz (Acoma Pueblo), in his 1981 essay "Towards a National Indian Literature: Cultural Authenticity in Nationalism," recognizes the emergence of nationalism in Native American literature and argues that the insistence of sovereignty is the most authentic of Indian stories (12). In the decades since Ortiz's article, critics of Native American literature have considered how to approach texts by Native writers and which theoretical methodologies to use for reading their work. The primary focus of discussion from both Native and non-Native scholars centers on the value and validity of contemporary literary nationalism. Advocates for literary nationalism, who are sometimes called literary essentialists or separatists, assert that to best understand a Native text, the tribal culture, history, and place must be paramount. Detractors promote cosmopolitan readings that examine the aesthetic and literary qualities of the text, maintaining that the novel is not an indigenous literary form. Each side of this discussion has important and articulate arguments.

While Ortiz's essay initially argued for a "national Indian literature," Muskogee Creek/Cherokee writer Craig Womack's seminal work *Red on Red: Native American Literary Separatism* (1999) can be seen as the impetus for a discussion on the responsibility that critics have to Native literatures and the peoples from whom these works originate. Womack asserts, "Native literature, and the criticism that surrounds it, needs to see more attention devoted to tribally specific concerns" (1). He continues by insisting on a Native criticism that

emphasizes Native resistance movements against colonialism, confronts racism, discusses sovereignty and Native nationalism, seeks connections between literature and liberation struggles, and, finally, roots literature in land and culture . . . emphasizes unique Native worldviews and political realities, searches for differences as often as similarities, and attempts to find Native literature's place in Indian country, rather than Native literature's place in the canon. (11)

Because the novels, short fiction, and poetry of Native writers such as Erdrich are grounded in a tribal-specific culture and place, readings of these works should first be from a Native tribal perspective. According to P. Jane Hafen (Taos Pueblo), when critics ignore or dismiss an indigenous perspective, they "may play into a five-hundred-year history of colonialism, appropriation, and misunderstanding . . . thus creating a critical colonialism" (6). This does not mean, however, that non-Native critics should be excluded from the discussion. Rather, Cherokee scholar and critic Jace Weaver asks only that "non-Natives who study and write about Native peoples do so with respect and a sense of responsibility to Native community" (11). Indigenous peoples in the Americas have endured attempts to have their language, voices, and stories silenced. Scholars such as Womack, Hafen, and Weaver call for theoretical models that allow Native writers to define tribal identity and to claim tribal literary sovereignty.

For many non-Native critics, *Red on Red* and Weaver, Womack, and Robert Warrior's *American Literary Nationalism* (2006) represent an attack on their work with indigenous texts. Scholars who reject a Native literary nationalism argue for a more cosmopolitan approach, one that privileges Western theoretical methodologies and aesthetics. These critics note that most American Indian writers, while not living and writing in a postcolonial state, are mixed-bloods who have been educated in universities, know and understand literary devices commonly found in Euro-American literature, and write in English. According to Elvira Pulitano, who champions the cosmopolitan approach, Native texts are "by their very nature heavily heterglot and hybridized" (13). In other words, the literary productions of Native peoples lend themselves to postcolonial theoretical applications. Furthermore, Pulitano argues that "tribalcentric" nationalist readings hurt more than they help: "While Separatist sentiments appear legitimate to fervent representatives of nationalistic approaches, they become all the more dangerous as they continue to ossify Native American literary production, as well as Native identity, into a sort of museum culture" (9). Critics such as Pulitano believe that texts need to be read as narratives of peoples who are living in the present, not entrenched in the past. They contend that American Indian writers such as Erdrich display a narrative complexity in their work that goes beyond their tribal identity. Indeed, Ojibwe novelist and critic David Treuer argues, "The vast majority of thought that has been poured onto Native American literature has puddled, for the most part, on how the texts are positioned in relation to history or culture" (195). It is for this reason that Treuer proclaims, "Native American fiction does not exist," since "the most amazing thing about Native American literature is the reluctance of its creators and commentators to treat it as a literature that exists within a field of other literatures" (195, 196). For Pulitano and Treuer, Erdrich's work must be considered literature first, open to a variety of theoretical methodologies.

In an essay review in *Western American Literature*, Lisa Tatonetti addresses "an imagined divide between proponents and detractors of contemporary literary nationalism" (277) and finds that proponents of either nationalism or cosmopolitanism base their arguments on a false dichotomy. Tatonetti offers an alternative approach that embraces both the tribal concerns of nationalism and the aesthetic values of cosmopolitanism. She finds the potential for a mediating solution in Arnold Krupat's *All That Remains: Varieties of Indigenous Expressions* (2009). Krupat argues for "both/and modalities of thought [that] predominate in traditional, oral, Native communities, persist in Native writing" (xii). With this framework, Tatonetti argues that Native and non-Native scholars can bring particular insights that may illuminate American Indian writing.

Finding a middle ground between and recognizing the value of both strategies is especially important when one reads Erdrich. As the daughter of a German American father and a mixed-blood Ojibwe mother, Erdrich comes from two distinct cultural backgrounds. Her writing reflects the importance of both sides of her family. Instead of embracing one and discarding the other, Erdrich positions herself as a writer who is accessible to a diverse audience. Erdrich, when asked by an interviewer if she considered herself a Native American writer, answered, "I really don't like labels. While it is certainly true that a good part of my background . . . and a lot of the themes are Native American, I prefer to simply be a writer" (Wong 107). In another interview, Erdrich reiterated the concern she has at being marked as simply a Native American who writes Indian stories, saying, "I don't think American Indian literature should be distinguished from mainstream literature" (Coltelli 47). Despite this insistence on being viewed simply as a "writer," she also acknowledges and maintains that since she writes from a tribal perspective, her work reflects the history, language, epistemology, and aesthetics of her people: "Contemporary Native American writers have . . . a task quite different from that of other writers. . . . In the light of enormous loss, they must tell the stories of contemporary survivors while protecting and celebrating the cores of cultures left in the wake of catastrophe" (Wong 48). Critics who privilege cosmopolitan approaches point to Erdrich's insistence that she not be labeled a Native American writer as validation for its use. Meanwhile, critics who advocate indigenous tribal methodologies emphasize that Erdrich's stories are those of her people, stories that preserve cultural identity and insist on tribal sovereignty. Both cosmopolitan and nationalist theoretical practitioners find rationales for their approaches, making Erdrich's work ideal for both sides of this "imagined divide."

With this brief overview of the current discussions taking place in Native American literary studies, one can see that, in many ways, the critical responses to Erdrich's writing fall on both sides of the nationalism/cosmopolitanism divide. Readers can find critical studies that examine Erdrich's narrative style and how it resembles communal story-telling, and they can find critical studies that explore the sexual politics of her novels. Regardless the literary theory, it most likely has already been applied to Erdrich's writing.

Critical responses to Erdrich's work appear primarily in peer-reviewed academic journals. Because of her broad appeal and the various possible approaches, articles on Erdrich have appeared in *American Indian Culture & Research Journal*, *MELUS*, *Critique*, *Children's Literature Association Quarterly*, *Great Plains Quarterly*, *European Review of Native American Studies*, *Western American Literature*, and *Religion and Literature*. One of the primary journals for new scholarship on Erdrich, however, is *SAIL*, which was the first publication to devote an entire issue to *Love Medicine* in 1985. The issue provides an introduction to Erdrich and her writing, commentary on the novel by Dee Brown and Ursula K. Le Guin, short critical responses that discuss the unique use of narrative in the novel, and a review of *Jacklight*, Erdrich's first collection of poetry. As her body of work grew with the publication of two more novels, *The Beet Queen* (1986) and *Tracks* (1988), the editors of *SAIL* dedicated back-to-back issues in winter 1991 and spring 1992 to new scholarship. The critical responses in these two issues centered primarily on Erdrich's third novel, *Tracks*, with many scholars focusing on questions of narrative technique and of Ojibwe cultural identity. In "The Novel as Performance Communication in Louise Erdrich's *Tracks*," James Flavin examines Erdrich's narrative style and acknowledges the apparent incompatibility of oral storytelling with written prose. Flavin argues, however, that Erdrich is able to simulate orality by using Nanapush and Pauline as alternating narrators, who provide the reader with the same stories but told through different perspectives. Ultimately, Flavin asserts that Erdrich "focuses on language, on oral traditions and their importance to tribal culture . . . by creating a novel which utilizes a framed tale and takes as part of its subject the nature of language in the Anishinaabe culture" (11). The issue of identity is also of significance, according to

Annette Van Dyke, who, in her article "Questions of the Spirit: Blood-lines in Louise Erdrich's Chippewa Landscape," explores how Lulu Nanapush's and Marie Lazarre's "spiritual legacies" shape their identity and prepare them "to use their inherited powers to ensure continuance of the nation" (24). *SAIL* continues to publish insightful critical responses like those of Flavin and Van Dyke. Recently, the journal has published J. James Iovannone's "'Mix-ups, Messes, Confinements, and Double-Dealings': Transgendered Performances in Three Novels by Louise Erdrich" and Summer Harrison's "The Politics of Metafiction in Louise Erdrich's *Four Souls*." Academic journals like *SAIL* typically provide the most current critical responses to the works of American Indian writers and should be a primary source for theoretical treatments of Erdrich's fiction and poetry.

Full-length books, both single-authored and anthologies, also provide invaluable readings and interpretations of Erdrich's work. Published in 1999, Lorena L. Stookey's *Louise Erdrich: A Critical Companion* was the first single-authored book on Erdrich. Because of the genre and a primary audience consisting of high school and undergraduate students, her text is highly accessible. This critical companion follows the format for each book in the Critical Companions to Popular Contemporary Writers series: a biographical chapter, a chapter on the literary context of the writer and her work, and a chapter on each of the author's published novels. These chapters present overviews of the plots, characters, and major themes of Erdrich's first six novels— *Love Medicine* (1984), *The Beet Queen* (1986), *Tracks* (1988), *The Bingo Palace* (1994), *Tales of Burning Love* (1996), and *The Antelope Wife* (1998). In addition, Stookey provides an Alternative Perspective section, where she applies Western methodologies to the novels. For example, she believes that a feminist approach to *The Antelope Wife* "addresses women's experiences in a variety of ways" (140), yet the most significant contribution of a feminist reading is how it reveals that the female characters in the novel are "strong and resilient" and "represent women's power to say 'no'" (142). While Stookey's critical companion has a limited critical response, it does give readers a basic introduction to Erdrich's work and to Native American literature.

The fictional world that Erdrich creates in her novels is impressive in its immensity, detail, complexity, and coherence. Each of the novels is linked to the others through place, history, and culture. Erdrich's novels follow the histories of several families on and off the reservation of Little No Horse. Readers meet the Adares, Kashpaws, Lamartines, Lazarres, Morrisseys, and Pillagers, important families whose histories are intermingled through marriages, sexual liaisons, and adoptions. Many scholars compare Erdrich's Little No Horse to William Faulkner's Yoknapatawpha County because both writers populate their novels with hundreds of interconnected characters. Understandably, readers can easily become lost and confused while trying to trace the links between families. Scholars Peter G. Beidler and Gay Barton help readers to follow and enjoy the complexity of Erdrich's novels in *A Reader's Guide to the Novels of Louise Erdrich*. Originally published in 1999 and later revised and expanded in 2006, Beidler and Barton's guide deals only with Erdrich's novels and is intended for readers unfamiliar with them. *A Reader's Guide*, however, is also an important and convenient resource for scholars. While there have been other efforts to catalog the characters and events in the novels, Beidler and Barton's attempt succeeds because of its comprehensiveness. They have laboriously combed through each novel to determine an approximate location for the Erdrich's fictional reservation (not surprisingly Beidler and Barton place it in the same location as the actual reservation for the Turtle Mountain Band of Chippewa) and to provide chronologies of events and genealogical charts. Additionally, Beidler and Barton compile an exhaustive dictionary of characters, which further helps to clarify relationships, and a glossary of the Ojibwe words, phrases, and sentences that Erdrich uses in her work. Beidler and Barton aim "to help readers trace the patterns and connections in the seemingly chaotic vista of Erdrich's world" (6), even recommending that *A Reader's Guide* be consulted after initial reading of the novels, yet the authors fail to acknowledge that the "chaotic vista" is a mirroring of the oral storytelling tradition. Indeed, as Erdrich produces a new novel, everything that the reader thought that he or she knew about the characters, their histories, and their relationships is upended. The stories are the connection; they build, complement, and complicate each other. Like the listener, the reader must piece together bits of information in an attempt to piece together an imperfect whole. Although Beidler and Barton's guide wants to expose "patterns and connections," stories are alive and reflect the lives of storytellers. They are not relics of a time gone by. Nonetheless, Beidler and Barton's text is a valuable resource, but one that quickly becomes outdated.

Like Stookey's *Critical Companion* and Beidler and Barton's *A Reader's Guide*, Connie A. Jacobs's *The Novels of Louise Erdrich: Stories of Her People* (2001) provides a survey of Erdrich's first six novels, but she also gives readers the relevant historical and cultural underpinnings necessary for situating Erdrich's writing within a literary and pan-Indian context. Hoping to expand and push a critical discussion that has centered largely on nonindigenous concerns, Jacobs's intent for her text is to fill in "critical gaps" and to "advance a more complete picture of [Erdrich's] work within the spectrum of literary studies" (xiii, xiv). According to Jacobs, what is missing from the critical examinations of this body of work is an attention to Native American history, culture, myth, and ritual. Prior to addressing Erdrich's novels, Jacobs begins by providing a brief chronicle of Native American literature since N. Scott Momaday's *House Made of Dawn* (1968), an explanation of the function of storytelling in indigenous cultures and how orality theory helps to provide greater explication, and a short history of the Turtle Mountain Band of Chippewa. These opening chapters allow Jacobs to demonstrate how Erdrich's place in the Native American literary renaissance, role as a storyteller, and tribal background inform both her subject matter and her aesthetics. With this framework established, Jacobs appraises the characters of Fleur and Sweetheart Calico and argues that through the creation of these powerful and mythic female characters Erdrich has herself become "the maker of myths" (151). In the concluding chapter, Jacobs acknowledges that Erdrich's novels are littered with allusions to and undertones of the masculine American literary canon, but Jacobs asserts that her Native heritage is the primary source for her creative and literary impulses.

As part of the Western Writers Series published by Boise State University, P. Jane Hafen's *Reading Louise Erdrich's "Love Medicine"* (2003) provides a sound introduction to the Erdrich's first novel while simultaneously advocating an indigenous reading of the text. Direct and concise, this fifty-six-page booklet includes an introduction to Native American literary studies, a brief biography of Erdrich, a chapter-by-chapter close reading of *Love Medicine*, a review of the critical response to Erdrich's writing, and a bibliography. As noted earlier, Hafen is a firm proponent of tribal-centric readings. According to Hafen, the application of literary theories derived from traditional and Western epistemologies (e.g., postcolonialism, feminism, and cultural materialism) continues the program of colonization and denies Native sovereignty. A reading of *Love Medicine* that is situated in an Ojibwe critical tradition "shares Erdrich's imperatives of survival and celebration, of connection to Ojibwe-specific culture and place on the northern plains . . . with lyric and compelling storytelling" (6). Through this indigenous critical lens, Hafen's analysis demonstrates that *Love Medicine* is a novel of resistance, survival, and healing. For example, Hafen points to the chapters "The Plunge of the Brave" and "The Tomahawk Factory" and finds that they act as humorous plays on the popular images of Indian peoples and cultures. While the slapstick humor of "The Tomahawk Factory" is entertaining, Erdrich's larger purpose is to critique the commodification of Native identity and signs. *Reading Louise Erdrich's "Love Medicine"* is a short yet valuable resource as Hafen's tribal-specific close reading of the novel offers insights that enrich the text and deepen the reader's appreciation for it.

David Stirrup's *Louise Erdrich* (2010) is a welcome addition to the ongoing critical discussion of Erdrich's work and her place in both

American and Native American literatures. Stirrup has observed the debate over the primacy of nationalist and cosmopolitan approaches and knows that more than theory is at stake in this politically informed discussion. As a result, he borrows from many approaches to demonstrate their applicability to the entirety of Erdrich's work. He sets himself a monumental task: "Engag[ing] with the full span of that output. Drawing out historical and culturally specific readings through the theoretical methodologies offered by both indigenous and postcolonial theories; the apparatus of feminism, postmodernism, and, in a minor way, regionalism" (4). After providing context for his discussion, Stirrup begins to work his way through the body of Erdrich's work, employing both Western and Native readings of the texts. For example, he devotes a chapter to Erdrich's poetry, an area that is woefully underrepresented in the critical literature, and applies feminist and postcolonial theories to her poetics. In another chapter, Stirrup discusses both Western and Native symbols, images, and threads in the North Dakota novels. He also provides readings of Erdrich's recent novels, children's fiction, nonfiction, and *The Crown of Columbus*, the novel she coauthored with her late husband Michael Dorris. Overall, the text feels fragmented, perhaps a result of its scope, as Stirrup tries to find a middle ground. His critical approach follows the "both/and" modality of thought that Tatonetti outlines in her review of theoretical trends in Native American studies. His conclusions invariably lead to a postcolonial reading that finds Erdrich's works to be products of hybridity and syncretism.

Another valuable resource for scholars and students are collections of essays, which frequently focus on individual works, have an articulated theme, or serve a particular function. *"Love Medicine": A Casebook* (1999), edited by Hertha D. Sweet Wong, is one such collection. Wong's casebook features a compilation of some of the most important and oft-cited critical responses to Erdrich's first novel. Because *Love Medicine* lends itself to a variety of critical and theoretical approaches, Wong's stated intent is to provide readers with examples of possible applications, including cultural, historical, and reader response approaches. Wong organizes her casebook in four parts: "Contexts: History, Culture, and Storytelling," "Mixed Identities and Multiple Narratives," "Individual and Cultural Survival: Humor and Homecoming," and "Reading Self/Reading Other." Additionally, Wong includes portions of four interviews with Erdrich and Dorris. The interviews, which were conducted by Wong herself, Nancy Feyl Chavkin and Allan Chavkin, Laura Coltelli, and Joseph Bruchac, and were originally published elsewhere, allow Erdrich to speak to her own "mixed identity" and the cultural source of her storytelling techniques. Finally, Wong includes Erdrich's essay "Where I Ought to Be: A Writer's Sense of Place," originally published in the *New York Times Book Review*, and "Rose Nights, Summer Storms, Lists of Spiders and Literary Mothers," an excerpt from her nonfiction work *The Blue Jay's Dance: A Memoir of Early Motherhood* (1995). These last materials situate Erdrich's writing in a historical, geographical, tribal, and literary context.

"Love Medicine": A Casebook includes many important critical analyses of the novel by some of the most well-known and well-respected scholars in the field of Native American literary studies. Wong includes perhaps the two most frequently cited essays on *Love Medicine*: Louis Owens's "Erdrich and Dorris's Mixed-bloods and Multiple Narratives," a chapter from his book *Other Destinies: Understanding the American Indian Novel*, and Catherine Rainwater's "Reading between Worlds: Narrativity in the Fiction of Louise Erdrich," which was originally published in *American Literature* in 1990. In his essay, Owens finds that the success of *Love Medicine* is a result of Erdrich's use of "fragmented narratives and prismatic perspectives" (55), a departure from the individual point of view employed by most other Native American novelists. Instead, Erdrich formulates and privileges a communal/tribal identity as the story shifts narrators and as more details and perspectives are revealed. Owens notes that while *Love Medicine* contains the sorrow and disappointment that Native peoples feel to this day, Erdrich blunts it for the non-Native reader through her use of multiple narrators. Furthermore, Owens argues that *Love Medicine*

"does not make the white reader squirm with guilt," which ultimately leads to the novels' popularity (64). Where Owens offers a more tribal-centric reading of the novel, Rainwater uses reader response theory as a tool for negotiating the marginality inherent in a novel written by a mixed-blood about mixed-bloods. Rainwater situates Erdrich and her characters in a liminal space between cultures and contends that the reader's experience is intentionally frustrating because of conflicting cultural symbols and codes derived from both Euro-American societies and Native American cultures. The presence of competing, conflicting codes and symbols "vexes the reader's effort to decide upon an unambiguous, epistemologically consistent interpretive framework" (165). Rainwater argues that while arriving at this "hermeneutical impasse" may be discomforting (167), it forces the reader to consider alternative ways of structuring the world.

Another significant early collection of essays is *The Chippewa Landscape of Louise Erdrich* (1999), edited by Allan Chavkin, which includes eight previously unpublished critical responses by important Erdrich scholars as well as an afterword by Ruoff. The purpose for gathering these essays, according to Chavkin, is "to remove some of the obstacles to understanding Erdrich's fiction and thereby enhance the reader's enjoyment and appreciation of her subtle art" (2). To help the reader's understanding, he indicates that "the critics in this volume focus upon the Chippewa aspects of Erdrich's art not only because that is the source of her greatest originality but also because it is the source of greatest difficulty for the vast majority of non-Indian readers unfamiliar with Chippewa myth, tradition, and culture" (2). The collection's title bears out this sentiment, yet a close examination of the essays reveals that few actually address the "Chippewa landscape" or Ojibwe culture.

Instead of examining how Ojibwe culture, ritual, language, history, and geography inform Erdrich's novels, the reader finds cosmopolitan theoretical enterprises, from the carnivalesque to French feminism. In his essay "From Sacred Hoops to Bingo Palaces: Louise Erdrich's

Carnivalesque Fiction," Robert A. Morace examines Erdrich's fiction through Mikhail Bakhtin's theory of the carnivalesque and provides almost endless comparisons of her novels to the work of Faulkner, Jorge Luis Borges, Gabriel García Márquez, and Giovanni Boccaccio. William J. Scheick, in his essay "Narrative and Ethos in Erdrich's 'A Wedge of Shade,'" argues that Erdrich does not achieve a narrative interconnectedness and that the best technique for understanding her fiction comes from the fine arts—atomizing. Scheick encourages a "very close scrutiny of the building blocks of [Erdrich's] artistry" (118). In the essay "Indi'n Humor and Trickster Justice in *The Bingo Palace*," Nancy J. Peterson contends that Hélène Cixous's essay "The Laugh of Medusa" provides a possible origin and framework for Erdrich's use of humor.

As part of their Approaches to Teaching series, the Modern Language Association published *Approaches to Teaching the Works of Louise Erdrich* in 2004. The text, edited by Greg Sarris, Connie A. Jacobs, and James R. Giles, includes materials that can help teachers to improve their understanding and use of Erdrich's fiction and poetry in the classroom. This collection also offers much to readers and students of Native American literature. The editors have divided the text into two main parts, "Materials" and "Approaches." The "Materials" part is relatively short, only nine pages, and includes summaries of Erdrich's first nine novels, a brief overview of her poetry, works of nonfiction, and children's literature, and as recommendations of supplementary readings, critical studies, and audiovisual materials. The "Approaches" part is subdivided into four sections: "History and Culture," "Erdrich's Fictional World," "Pedagogical Strategies," and "Critical and Theoretical Perspectives." The editors also include four appendixes that are also of value to students: genealogical charts for all of the major families in Erdrich's North Dakota novels, two maps showing Ojibwe lands in the late 1800s and how those lands have shrunk to their current size, a chronology of important dates in the history of the Turtle Mountain Band of Chippewa, and study guides for Erdrich's first eight novels.

Sarris, Jacobs, and Giles present a collection of materials that reflect both cosmopolitan and nationalist approaches to Erdrich's work. In the text's section on critical interpretations, readers can find diverse essays on feminist theory (Vanessa Holford Diana's "Reading *The Beet Queen* from a Feminist Perspective"), gender theory (Kari J. Winter's "Gender as a Drag in *The Beet Queen*"), postcolonialism (Dee Horne's "A Postcolonial Reading of *Tracks*"), and Russian formalism (Patrick E. Houlihan's "'This Ain't Real Estate': A Bakhtinian Approach to *The Bingo Palace*"). Countering the traditional Western literary approaches, Gwen Griffin and P. Jane Hafen's essay "An Indigenous Approach to Teaching Erdrich's Works" suggests readings with a tribal context, helping students to "gain insight into the uniqueness of Ojibwe culture and awareness of Ojibwe points of view" (101). Furthermore, as Debra K. S. Barker (Lakota) indicates in her essay "Teaching the Memories of the Heart: Teaching *Tales of Burning Love*," an indigenous-centered analysis may also create a possibility for "cross-cultural understanding and community building" (124). Although the materials in the text engage pedagogical issues related to Erdrich's work, they also demonstrate how cosmopolitan and nationalist approaches both work to enrich the reader's experience and understanding of her writing, her people, and her culture.

The fifteen essays in Brajesh Sawhney's collection of criticism *Studies in the Literary Achievement of Louise Erdrich, Native American Writer* (2008) focus primarily on Erdrich's writing that has not received as much critical attention. Sawhney asserts that a collection of essays that offer "fresh approaches" to Erdrich's work is necessary and overdue (1). He points specifically to a lack of critical responses to her more recent novels—*The Last Report on the Miracles at Little No Horse* (2001), *Four Souls* (2004), *The Painted Drum* (2005)—and to her novels for young adults, *The Birchbark House* (1999) and *The Game of Silence* (2005). The contributors are a mix of seasoned Erdrich scholars, including Beidler, Van Dyke, Alan R. Velie, Thomas Matchie, and Deborah Madsen, as well as younger scholars in the field.

In addition to the essays, Sawhney includes a collection of papers from the 2007 Native American Literature Symposium on "Memorable Characters in the Fiction of Louise Erdrich." Wanting his anthology to break new ground, Sawhney endorses and privileges Western literary theories, all but ignoring the voices of Native critics, except Barker. For example, Thomas Matchie's "Flannery O'Connor and Louise Erdrich: The Function of the Grotesque in Erdrich's *Tracks*," Holly Messitt's "Vestiges from the Early American Captivity Narratives: Captivity, Land and Identity in Louise Erdrich's Fiction," and Gretchen Papazian's "Razing Little House or Re-envisionary History: Louise Erdrich's Story of the American 'Frontier,' in *The Birchbark House* and *The Game of Silence*" all position Erdrich's writing in relation to Euro-American texts and writers. In the majority of the essays in this collection, Ojibwe history, language, and culture are not essential to Erdrich's writing. They are only the backdrop for her engagement with Western literary traditions.

The most recent book-length study of Erdrich's work is *Louise Erdrich: "Tracks," "The Last Report on the Miracles of Little No Horse," "The Plague of Doves"* (2011), edited by Deborah L. Madsen. The text contains Madsen's introductions to and three critical essays on each of the novels. According to Madsen, Erdrich's "core theme is the Ojibwe concept of the 'good life'—*mino bimaadiziwin*" despite the "conditions of colonization and . . . history of physical and cultural genocide" (2). Madsen finds running themes for each section of essays. In the section on *Tracks*, the essays explore the effects of colonization on the individual, family, and tribal community. Jacobs's essay " 'I knew there was never another martyr like me': Pauline Puyat, Historical Trauma and *Tracks*," for example, takes trauma theory, particularly historical trauma, and uses it to read Pauline as a victim of historical trauma, as "Erdrich's testimony to 500 years of historical oppression for American Indians" (47). For the essays on *The Last Report on the Miracles at Little No Horse*, the consideration is in the negotiation of the liminal spaces that Father Damien/Agnes inhabits. Patrice Hollrah's essay "Love and the Slippery Slope of Sexual Orientation: L/G/B/T/Q etc. Sensibility in *The Last Report on the Miracles of Little No Horse*" is particularly strong as it explains that discussions of Agnes's/Father Damien's sexual orientation can be a "slippery slope," since Western labels (e.g., gay, bisexual, queer) do not fit. Hollrah argues persuasively that an indigenous approach to the novel reveals female characters who "engage in an endless number of possibilities, including changing gender identities and sexual orientations throughout their lives" (115). The essays on *The Plague of Doves*, according to Madsen, are responses to "Erdrich's resistance of categorization, boundary-setting and binaristic thinking" (119). In this section, Gina Valentino provides a feminist response to indigenous literary nationalism, John Gamber deconstructs the stereotype of the stoic Indian, and Catherine Rainwater uses environmental criticism to show how the novel redefines Western beliefs of personhood.

In each of the three sections of Madsen's collection, a reader finds interesting approaches to these three novels. The essays on *The Plague of Doves* are particularly important, as they constitute some of the first critical treatments of the novel. The text, however, has a decidedly cosmopolitan bent; only Hollrah and Hafen offer indigenous readings of the novels. Indeed, some essays are hostile to American Indian literary nationalism. Valentino's essay "'It All Does Come to Nothing in the End': Nationalism and Gender in Louise Erdrich's *The Plague of Doves*" is an obvious example. Valentino asserts that nationalism is largely a masculine-driven project that discourages and marginalizes feminist perspectives. She finds that the novel represents Erdrich's response to "the full danger of unchecked patriarchal Native nationalism" (129). In many ways, Hollrah's indigenous reading of *The Last Report* refutes Valentino's contention that nationalism only values masculine approaches to American Indian texts. She points to the Native concept of gender complementarity, "which holds that the important aspects of men's and women's roles complement each other and are equally valued for the contributions they bring to the community, one role not having any more importance than another" (104). Valentino's and Hollrah's discussion emphasizes the need for both cosmopolitan and tribal approaches to Erdrich's writing.

As one of most prolific authors today, Erdrich continues to write fiction and compose poetry that entertains and challenges popular and scholarly audiences. The critical landscape of Louise Erdrich's work is vast and varied, yet obvious holes remain in the body of criticism. *Shadow Tag* (2010), one of Erdrich's most recent novels, is much admired by reviewers, but the novel has not yet received the critical attention that is sure to come. Although a few critics, including Hafen, Stirrup, James Ruppert, and Dean Rader, have critically examined Erdrich's poetry, it has been largely ignored. Equally overlooked are Erdrich's young-adult novels, with only seven critical essays written on *The Birchbark House* and *The Game of Silence* combined. Finally, as this review has shown, indigenous, tribal-centric perspectives are woefully underrepresented. As Erdrich's body of work grows and evolves, the corpus of literary criticism must as well.

Works Cited

Barker, Debra K. S. "Teaching the Memories of the Heart: Teaching *Tales of Burning Love*." Sarris, Jacobs, and Giles 118–29.

Beidler, Peter G., and Gay Barton. *A Reader's Guide to the Novels of Louise Erdrich*. 2nd ed. Columbia: U of Missouri P, 2006.

Chavkin, Allan, ed. *The Chippewa Landscape of Louise Erdrich*. Tuscaloosa: U of Alabama P, 1999.

Coltelli, Laura. *Winged Words: American Indian Writers Speak*. Lincoln: U of Nebraska P, 1990.

Diana, Vanessa Holford. "Reading *The Beet Queen* from a Feminist Perspective." Sarris, Jacobs, and Giles 175–82.

Erdrich, Louise. "Where I Ought to Be: A Writer's Sense of Place." Wong 43–50.

Flavin, James. "The Novel as Performance Communication in Louise Erdrich's *Tracks*." *Studies in American Indian Literatures* 3.4 (1991): 1–12.

Gamber, John. "So, a Priest Walks into a Reservation Tragicomedy: Humor in *The Plague of Doves*." Madsen 136–51.

Griffin, Gwen, and P. Jane Hafen. "An Indigenous Approach to Teaching Erdrich's Works." Sarris, Jacobs, and Giles 95–101.

Hafen, P. Jane. *Reading Louise Erdrich's* Love Medicine. Boise: Boise State UP, 2003.

Harrison, Summer. "The Politics of Metafiction in Louise Erdrich's *Four Souls.*" *Studies in American Indian Literatures* 23.1 (2011): 38–69.

Hollrah, Patrice. "Love and the Slippery Slope of Sexual Orientation: L/G/B/T/Q etc. Sensibility in *The Last Report on the Miracles of Little No Horse.*" Madsen 98–115.

Horne, Dee. "A Postcolonial Reading of *Tracks.*" Sarris, Jacobs, and Giles 191–200.

Houlihan, Patrick E. "'This Ain't Real Estate': A Bakhtinian Approach to *The Bingo Palace.*" Sarris, Jacobs, and Giles 201–09.

Iovannone, J. James. "'Mix-ups, Messes, Confinements, and Double-Dealings': Transgendered Performances in Three Novels by Louise Erdrich." *Studies in American Indian Literatures* 21.1 (2009): 38–68.

Jacobs, Connie A. "'I knew there was never another martyr like me': Pauline Puyat, Historical Trauma and *Tracks.*" Madsen 34–47.

_____. *The Novels of Louise Erdrich: Stories of Her People.* New York: Lang, 2001.

Krupat, Arnold. *All That Remains: Varieties of Indigenous Expressions.* Lincoln: U of Nebraska P, 2009.

Madsen, Deborah L., ed. *Louise Erdrich:* Tracks, The Last Report on the Miracles at Little No Horse, The Plague of Doves. New York: Continuum, 2011.

Matchie, Thomas. "Flannery O'Connor and Louise Erdrich: The Function of the Grotesque in Erdrich's *Tracks.*" Sawhney 49–61.

Messitt, Holly. "Vestiges from the Early American Captivity Narratives: Captivity, Land and Identity in Louise Erdrich's Fiction." Sawhney 133–50.

Ortiz, Simon J. "Towards a National Indian Literature: Cultural Authenticity in Nationalism." *MELUS* 8.2 (1981): 7–12.

Owens, Louis. "Erdrich and Dorris's Mixed-bloods and Multiple Narratives." Wong 53–66.

Papazian, Gretchen. "Razing Little Houses or Re-envisionary History: Louise Erdrich's Story of the American 'Frontier,' in *The Birchbark House* and *The Game of Silence.*" Sawhney 187–211.

Pulitano, Elvira. *Toward a Native American Critical Theory.* Lincoln: U of Nebraska P, 2003.

Rader, Dean. "Sites of Unification: Teaching Erdrich's Poetry." Sarris, Jacobs, and Giles 102–13.

Rainwater, Catherine. "Haunted by Birds: An Eco-critical View of Personhood in *The Plague of Doves.*" Madsen 152–66.

_____. "Reading between Worlds: Narrativity in the Fiction of Louise Erdrich." Wong 163–78.

Ruoff, A. LaVonne Brown. Afterword. *The Chippewa Landscape of Louise Erdrich.* Tuscaloosa: U of Alabama P, 1999. 182–88.

Ruppert, James. "Identity Indexes in *Love Medicine* and 'Jacklight.'" Sarris, Jacobs, and Giles 170–74.

Sarris, Greg, Connie A. Jacobs, and James R. Giles, eds. *Approaches to Teaching the Works of Louise Erdrich.* New York: MLA, 2004.

Sawhney, Brajesh, ed. *Studies in the Literary Achievement of Louise Erdrich, Native American Writer: Fifteen Critical Essays.* Lewiston: Mellen, 2008.

Scheick, William J. "Narrative and Ethos in Erdrich's 'A Wedge of Shade.'" Chavkin 117–29.

Stirrup, David. *Louise Erdrich*. Manchester: Manchester UP, 2010.

Stookey, Lorena L. *Louise Erdrich: A Critical Companion*. Westport: Greenwood, 1999.

Tatonetti, Lisa. "The Both/And of American Literary Studies." *Western American Literature* 44.3 (2009): 277–88.

Treuer, David. *Native American Fiction: A User's Manual*. Minneapolis: Graywolf, 2006.

Valentino, Gina. " 'It All Does Come to Nothing in the End': Nationalism and Gender in Louise Erdrich's *The Plague of Doves*." Madsen 121–35.

Van Dyke, Annette. "Questions of the Spirit: Bloodlines in Louise Erdrich's Chippewa Landscape." *Studies in American Indian Literatures* 4.1 (1992): 15–27.

Weaver, Jace, Craig S. Womack, and Robert Warrior. *American Indian Literary Nationalism*. Albuquerque: U of New Mexico P, 2006.

Winter, Kari J. "Gender as a Drag in *The Beet Queen*." Sarris, Jacobs, and Giles 183–90.

Womack, Craig S. *Red on Red: Native American Literary Separatism*. Minneapolis: U of Minnesota P, 1999.

Wong, Hertha D. Sweet, ed. *Love Medicine: A Casebook*. New York: Oxford UP, 2000.

Louise Erdrich in Company: The American Writer and Her Communities_____

Thomas Austenfeld

> Let me tell you about love, that silly word you believe is about whether you like somebody. . . . Love is divine only and difficult always. . . . It is a learned application without reason or motive except that it is God.
>
> (*Paradise* 141)

I.

By reading Louise Erdrich in the company of other prominent American writers and within the canon of American texts currently taught in colleges and universities, I want to demonstrate the value of a comparative critical approach in identifying and appreciating the fundamental Americanness of Erdrich's writing. Toni Morrison and, to a lesser degree, Flannery O'Connor will serve as comparison points to a close reading of Erdrich's *The Last Report on the Miracles at Little No Horse* (2001). Key aspects of Native American history—encounter, minority status, group identification—are simultaneously key aspects of what makes American literature most genuinely American. Especially when considered from outside of the United States, Louise Erdrich is as clearly an American author as she is a Native American author.

In a time when the word "love" has attained inflationary use to the point of meaninglessness, a reminder of love's qualifications as "divine," "difficult," and "learned" takes us back into the realm of gritty and unsentimental theology. The words quoted above originate neither with a character in an Erdrich novel nor are they taken from one of Flannery O'Connor's essays; instead, they are spoken by the Reverend Pulliam, a conservative minister, on the occasion of K. D.'s and Arnette's wedding in the "Divine" chapter of Toni Morrison's *Paradise* (1998). Both O'Connor and Morrison explore religious doctrine in their fiction, often in social settings that are minoritarian and perceive themselves under pressure from the larger world outside.

Morrison's tradition-bound leaders of an all-black town in Oklahoma or O'Connor's bewildered southerners looking for spiritual grounding find themselves in America but out of touch—at times intentionally so—with mainstream America. Calibrating the community's distance from mainstream America can be an important means of self-assurance and a point of pride. Flannery O'Connor insisted that the South's anguish was not caused by its alienation from the rest of the country, "but by the fact that it is not alienated enough . . . that we are being forced out, not only our many sins but of our few virtues" ("Fiction Writer" 802–3). Some of the town fathers of Ruby in Morrison's *Paradise* are willing to "shoot the white girl first" (3) in their effort to keep total control of the town and its environs. Yet no community can define itself without a foil to define against. Pulliam's hortatory sermon on love appeals not primarily to the ethnic, racial, or social status of his congregation, but to its religious convictions and ultimately to its standing in the world, its ethics, and its humanity.

The idea of a self-defining community in voluntary separation from the larger world is as old as the idea of America itself. Pilgrims and Puritans were animated by the dream of being a chosen people, a group set apart in holiness. While the concept of individualism is perhaps ultimately the most basic aspect of American self-understanding—and individualism will always tear apart the carefully designed group, whether in life or in fiction—group identification is not only key to American sensibilities but has, if anything, become more important in recent decades. Alexis de Tocqueville described the delicate balance between self-reliance and community identification in American society as early as 1831–32:

> The citizen of the United States is taught from infancy to rely upon his own exertions in order to resist the evils and the difficulties of life; he looks upon the social authority with an eye of mistrust and anxiety, and he claims its assistance only when he is unable to do without it. This habit may be traced even in the schools, where the children in their games are wont to

submit to rules which they have themselves established, and to punish misdemeanors which they have themselves defined. The same spirit pervades every act of social life. . . . In the United States associations are established to promote the public safety, commerce, industry, morality, and religion. There is no end which the human will despairs of attaining through the combined power of individuals united into a society. (bk. 1, ch. 12, par. 2)

Ethnic and social identification has remained one of the primary determinants of Americans. Census forms offer a list of choices for Americans to identify themselves according to racial and ethnic heritage, and much literary scholarship of recent decades is unthinkable without the categories of race, class, gender, and sexual orientation. In large part, the significance of these identifications is historically determined. African Americans and Native Americans were designated as "other" by those in power and were thus forcibly disadvantaged throughout the history of their encounter with European Americans. Yet in acknowledging and rectifying race-based and historical injustices, we should not fall into the essentialist trap of allowing race or any other social category to remain a permanent separator. In paying careful attention to narrations from and by minorities, in appreciating the degree of authenticity of such narratives, we tend to overlook not just the other side of the equation, the individual who is so important to American self-understanding. We have also too often overlooked the authentic Americanness of such texts. By "Americanness" I certainly do not mean the jingoistic abuses of that term, perennially popular with political and religious fanatics. I refer instead to the long American tradition—from Thomas Jefferson to Susan Sontag—of writing about this country, about its people and its history, with an observant eye and a true pen. I am invoking a national literature that knows its practitioners united as Americans in addition to whatever else they may be and whatever other allegiances, hereditary or voluntary, they may embrace. In this American literature, Phillis Wheatley, William Apess, and Ralph Waldo Emerson are equally American.

Such an understanding of Americanness thus also puts Erdrich, Morrison, and O'Connor at the center of an American canon of literature in an attempt to appreciate their complex and fluid integration of minority and mainstream cultural facets. My own viewpoint as an Americanist from Europe is as limited as anybody else's, but the limitations are different: I try to perceive American literature as a national literature from the vantage point of geographical distance, after having studied and taught in the United States for over twenty years. Approaching Native American studies requires particular caveats, of course. From a distance, Europeans find it easy to agree to Native claims for originary possession of the American soil because little is at stake for them. Americans with European ancestors are in a more difficult position relative to this question, and few would embrace Isaac McCaslin's visionary reparation policies of relinquishing land described in Faulkner's *The Bear*.

II.

Few critics have articulated the persistent dilemma between the presumed essential identity and the postmodern socially constructed position of individuals or groups better than Satya P. Mohanty. Mohanty, in a 1993 article in *Cultural Critique*, pointed to the obvious limitations of "disputes over genuineness or authenticity" in discussing minority literatures from an essentialist point of view and the equally limited perspectives offered by a postmodernism that assumes identities to be completely constructed and thus distrusts experience (41–42). Present-day examples can easily be adduced for illustration: In the realm of religion, for example, no reasonable person would claim that President Jimmy Carter's Baptist faith and the cynical Westboro Baptist Church have anything essentially Baptist in common. The notion of an essential Baptist identity is thereby rendered absurd, though individual Baptists can, of course, situate themselves genuinely—experientially—in such an identity. On the other side of the issue, the social construction of manhood and womanhood in the United States, while constantly

undergoing change in the legal arena, the world of fiction and imagination, and the practical living conditions of women and men in the
workplace, is not sufficient to describe the gendered experience we
live, which is in large part determined by biology. Social descriptions
of sex—though not perhaps gender—will forever be insufficient to
bring theory and practice into perfect alignment; experience trumps essentialism in this case. The dilemma between essence and experience
continues.[1]

Fully aware of the impossibility of defining "American" satisfac-
torily as either social construct or experience, I want to make a claim
for Louise Erdrich's work as genuinely American literature, using
comparative methods to achieve my goal. My method therefore will
consist in circumscribing (but not thereby defining) "American" with
the help of three literary-historical parameters that bear a certain self-
evidentiary weight and, in a complementary move, looking at a specific Erdrich text side-by-side with other texts by writers who are now
"experientially" perceived by readers as having gone far beyond the
parochial social identifiers that may have initially identified them. The
edifice of comparison I am thus constructing is rather delicate and tran-
sitory, like Robert Frost's "silken tent," which "is loosely bound / By
countless silken ties of love and thought" (9–10). Our contemporary
understanding of Flannery O'Connor has left behind the critical cor-
ner she constructed in part for herself when she meditated on the fate
of "The Catholic Novelist in the Protestant South." Toni Morrison, in
turn, has shed the limitations of the label "African American writer"
precisely by enlarging what that term can encompass and by becoming
an American writer who is African American. Likewise, I suggest that
Louise Erdrich has contributed to making Native American lives part
and parcel of American life without denying their particularity. I hope
to demonstrate the merit of a comparative approach and the continuing
need to re-perform such analyses for new historical moments.

III.

Louise Erdrich has been a part of the American literary landscape long enough to carve out a secure place for herself in its topography, but a clear definition of that place is still missing. We no longer need to borrow explanatory patterns from other writers, as we did in the 1980s (then, her interconnected novels and families irresistibly suggested Faulkner); by now, Erdrich has become a writer against whom others are measured. If we want to establish the particularities of Erdrich's accomplishments, however, we still need to compare her to other writers who have succeeded similarly. The apparent paradox of a claim for uniqueness and the need for comparison is difficult to resolve but lies at the heart of all literary comparisons: We compare the similarities so that we may contrast the differences. The art of literary comparison lies in the construction of patterns that heuristically, for a certain time, allow us to see things afresh so as to advance our understanding. Looking for models suggests a derivative approach; looking for peers shows us traces of historical movement.

What does it mean to situate Erdrich as an American writer while looking from a European vantage point? Erdrich has always been an American writer, of course, but she has been claimed at times as "Native American" or "woman writer" or "trickster and magical realism" writer or "German American" writer or "Catholic novelist"[2] so strongly that her compound Americanness has been obscured. These qualifying adjectives again illustrate the paradox: Erdrich can be discovered in her similarities to other Native American, women, German American, or Catholic writers, but only at the expense of shortchanging other significant parts of her complexity. At the same time, even the adjective "American" can only mean something if it is further defined and thereby (de)limited.

Setting aside for the moment the difficulty of employing "American" not as a hemispheric designation but, in its more common, limited usage, as adjective for the United States, I want to focus on those aspects of American literature that most clearly distinguish it from European national literatures. By calling her an American writer, then, I mean to evoke for Erdrich a place within a national literature that can be seen as defined in fundamental ways by three historical and social conditions. In their totality, these three circumscribe the difference of American national literature from European national literatures. All three are both essential and abiding in their significance and yet subject to constant modification by experience: the encounter of Europeans and Native Americans, the negotiation of majority and minority groups relative to each other, and the building of communities as nodes of identification for Americans. If we denied the initiatory and lasting significance of Columbus's arrival in the New World and the conflictual narratives spawned by that encounter, we would falsify the historical record. Native American literature of the past two generations, from N. Scott Momaday through Gerald Vizenor to Sherman Alexie, has situated itself in important ways in that same conflict by evoking the contrasts between life on and off the reservation and by rethinking the place of Native culture and Native peoples within mainstream America.[3] Similarly, a full awareness of the complex history of slavery, the Civil War, the civil rights movement, and the ongoing social negotiations of any and all minority groups in the United States—whether African Americans, various ethnic and national strands of Europeans, Jews, Muslims, or more recently, Hispanic immigrants—is fundamental to a correct historical understanding of the American experience. American social policy as expressed, for example, in the national census, is linked to ethnic or racial affiliation in ways that are unthinkable in Europe. Ethnic belonging is an important part of Americans' sense of self and origin. Finally, American fiction and historical narrative is often significantly a record of the building of communities. From William Bradford's Plimouth Plantation and Nathaniel Hawthorne's Brook Farm to Edith Wharton's New York Dutch aristocrats, Willa Cather's Prairie Bohemians, John Steinbeck's Okies, and Joy Nicholson's *Tribes*

---

of Palos Verdes, the fates of fairly small communities have been a central concern of American writers. Minority writers have explored the question of community with particular panache: George Washington Cable's two sets of *Grandissimes* inhabit the complex racialized world of New Orleans; Nella Larsen's characters wonder about "passing" from one community to another; and Ralph Ellison's *Invisible Man*, a community of one, defines himself first against the prevailing communities already in existence and later joins or founds alternate communities. Significantly, these American communities are often religious in origin, again harking back to Plimouth Plantation or New Harmony, or—to suggest a contemporary instance—issuing from sectarian colleges and universities. An attention to the construction of fictional communities, together with due reference to Native/European encounters as well as minority discourses, may allow us to better define Louise Erdrich's particular status as an American writer.

In balancing identitarian qualities such as ethnicity, religion, or gender against the putative Americanness of a writer, I do not want to set up an oppositional binary. Instead, I want to suggest that identitarian qualities contribute to, but do not exhaust, a writer's character. My own critical position is thus between two possible extremes. On one hand, we have Leslie Marmon Silko, who argued in 1986 that Erdrich's *Beet Queen* was so postmodern as to have betrayed genuine (essentialist?) Native American storytelling. On the other hand, we have David Treuer, who has argued that Erdrich should be measured as a "writer" and not as a "Native American writer."[4] To me, then, Erdrich's biological and biographical qualities—woman writer, enrolled member of a Native community, part-German ancestry, Catholic upbringing—are necessary but insufficient characteristics because they are partial. Together, and only together, they feed her identity as American writer, and together they compose it in its uniqueness. Personality and identity are not a question of either/or binaries but of the proportionate accretion of multiple traits.

IV.

The forward movement of time itself is in part responsible for the changing canonical status of certain texts within American literature. When a revolution is victorious, its ideas become the norm, suddenly themselves subject to new revolutionary challenge. Upstarts become classics, marginal texts move to the center, the sting of protest lessens, and the raison d'être needs to be defined afresh. Willa Cather's Nebraska novels brought Henry James's "international theme" to a portion of America that would quickly turn from frontier to heartland. Once her Bohemians became Americans, Cather seemed less fresh, until a new generation of readers unearthed, almost simultaneously, her environmental and lesbian subtexts and reinscribed Cather into two different literary traditions and interpretive patterns. Flannery O'Connor could safely be categorized as a Catholic novelist in the 1950s, when J. F. Powers and Graham Greene supplied the models for such a designation. O'Connor seemed to have less relevance when southern women writers became a favorite object of study in the late 1970s and 1980s because her difference in ideology, biography, and subject matter from Carson McCullers, Eudora Welty, and Katherine Anne Porter was all too obvious. Scholars now read O'Connor attentively, and her focus on violence is even discussed in connection with the national discourse on terror (Hewitt and Donahoo). In 1999, Michael Nowlin called attention to the manner in which Toni Morrison had supplemented her successful fiction about African American experiences with theoretical texts, in particular, *Playing in the Dark: Whiteness and the Literary Imagination* (1993). Nowlin surmised that by "transfigur[ing] her usual subject matter, the complex world of black Americans, into a synecdoche for America," Morrison had acknowledged the particular responsibility she had taken on "as though the price for moving irreversibly from margin to center and inserting herself into an American canon dominated by white male writers was to make African American identity a national rather than tribal question" (151–52). Is the project of becoming American, then, as Nowlin claims in his reading of Morrison, "a notion of cultural pluralism grounded in racial difference" (152)? Is it true, as he further claims, that "one cannot write *American* literature ... without reinscribing the racial divide that makes blackness that literature's fundamental trope" (153)? Here, we have Louise Erdrich's predicament in a nutshell. Her humanity transcends her ethnic or tribal affiliation. Her characters are equally interesting, whether they are Native or European Americans. And they become more fully American as their fates reveal themselves to us ever closer to our historical present. Nanapush or Four Souls are now remote from mainstream American experience. Power broker Lyman Lamartine, jail breaker Gerry Nanapush, or multiwived entrepreneur Jack Mauser could be people from any American neighborhood. Lipsha Morrissey, finally, may be destined to become a character of world literature as much as Huckleberry Finn.

V.

Louise Erdrich's 2001 novel, *The Last Report on the Miracles at Little No Horse*, serves as a key example of my aforementioned theoretical contentions. Let us take a final look at my objects of comparison before delving into Erdrich's fictional reservation. Toni Morrison's *Paradise* describes the history of an all-black town in Oklahoma whose founding fathers, in two "installments" of settlements, Haven and Ruby, seek to find social peace in voluntary segregation and an oligarchical leadership obedient to the town's patriarchal founding traditions. Their nemesis is a nearby community of women, which mutates from an Indian school to a convent to a women's shelter. All of these latter manifestations are examples of identitarian groups that are even smaller than the black township. The escalating conflict results in a violent encounter that erupts in July 1976, around the bicentennial of the United States. Flannery O'Connor's collection of stories, *Everything that Rises Must Converge* (1965), offers vignettes of southern life, whose characters haphazardly stumble from daily inconveniences into existential questions. The subtle separations between town and country folk, believers and unbelievers, naïfs and con men, establish patterns of group membership.

O'Connor's orthodox and hard-nosed Catholicism provides the ferment within which these crises are negotiated. Louise Erdrich's *Last Report* describes individuals and communities looking for spiritual sustenance by unconventional means. By looking at the fates of these communities and the manner in which the writers suggest the significance of spiritual questions to their readers, we may see Erdrich in a context defined by Morrison and O'Connor, who both stand for something specific and yet transcend it: Morrison writes out of her African American experience but, by virtue of her Nobel Prize, she is recognized as an American (not only as African American) writer within world literature.[5] O'Connor, quirky and grotesque though she and her characters may appear, is recognized as a serious southern American writer in the Catholic tradition. Ethnicity, regional affiliation, religion, and gender thus are contributing factors to these writers' standing, but they are absorbed in the Americanness of each. Erdrich's *Last Report* is constituted in important ways through the considerations of ethnicity, region, religion, and gender, but in employing those categories with considerable (and sometimes refreshingly irreverent) playfulness, Erdrich transcends the individual categories toward an American entirety.

Without wishing to diminish the Native authenticity of Erdrich's work in any way, I want to suggest the value of reading her 2001 novel within the canonical tradition of American literature. Set on a fictional reservation and offering deeply observed descriptions of Native life along with unflinching evocations of abject poverty, *Last Report* is steeped in Catholic lore while cognizant of the charged interaction of Native and missionary cultures, abounds in rich, evocative descriptions of northern landscape, and describes religious, musical, and sexual ecstasy. It is, above all, an American novel. In the figure of Agnes/Father Damien, Erdrich has created an Adamic American hero. Self-begotten in the decisive act of slipping on the clothes of a dead priest while standing by the side of a roaring river, Agnes reinvents herself as Father Damien much as Jay Gatsby "sprang from his Platonic conception of himself" (Fitzgerald 104). As Huck Finn, quintessential American youngster, dons girl's clothes prior to his advance into the Deep South from which he will depart for the western territories (Twain 697), so young Agnes turns herself male for protection and social status while penetrating into the northern wilderness. "Call me Damien Modeste," she might have said at the beginning of her new life, as she begins a test of survival in both physical and metaphysical terms—the constant danger of starvation and the development of a Catholic theology and practice responsive to local conditions—that is no less existential than that of Ishmael in Melville's *Moby-Dick*. Like Ishmael, Father Damien will be the story's only survivor, the only one who can still offer testimony to Father Jude, the inquisitive visitor sent by the Vatican. Like Salinger's Holden Caulfield, Father Damien will find his life's consuming duty to be that of caretaking, the cure of his Native flock. I recognize that Gatsby, Huck, Ishmael, and Holden are the creations of white male novelists and that I may bend—though not intentionally misread—Erdrich's text in order to suggest a literary parentage; however, Thea Kronborg's musicianship, Alexandra Bergson's masculine clothing and vacillating gender position, and Antonia Shimerda's caring and competent motherhood and leadership of a farm would also allow us to find in Willa Cather's novels an equally rich set of precursors for Erdrich. In any case, our ability to place motifs from Erdrich's *Last Report* into different strands of American literature confirms the assertion that this text is as much to be appreciated for its American appeal as for its Native roots—and that the duality of this appreciation is complementary, not conflictual.

Last Report enacts the three parameters of encounter, minority consciousness, and group identification suggested above. Father Damien's life is patterned as an American story along the lines of motifs familiar from the American literary tradition, especially those portions of it which were sometimes interpreted as replicating biblical history and thus marking Americans as a chosen people. "All that happened began with that flow of water" (11): Farmer Berndt Vogel[6] loses part of his topsoil but gains a waif seeking food and shelter and, later, his bed. A brief period of happiness comes to an end when a bank robber known as the Actor, disguised as a priest, wounds Agnes and eventually dies, along with Berndt who has pursued them. A season or two later, another flood of biblical proportions sweeps Agnes, dressed only in "the white treble clef of her flannel nightdress" (39) out of civilization, clinging to a piano that might be Queequeg's coffin or Huck's raft. Agnes dons the garb of a drowned priest and becomes Father Damien as she lights out for the Indian territories of the Far North. Erdrich clearly intends us to read Agnes as comprehending her fate in tropological terms—that is, as the unfolding of certain patterns designed by a higher power, perhaps God, and decipherable in certain key events in her life, much as Puritan divines did:

> Now and then Agnes recalled a tiny portion of her encounter with the Actor, and she came to understand it as a sure prefigurement and sign of what was to come. The Actor had influenced the quality of Father Damien's disguise, for when Agnes was held by that rope-tough arm against the car door she'd felt remote enough, from blood loss, to marvel at and assess the Actor's change in personality from priest to robber. (76)[7]

Agnes's acculturation to the reservation at Little No Horse replicates metonymically the outlines of Native American history after the encounter with Europeans. Famine, land loss, decimation by influenza, internal fighting over the correct response to government and land agents' demands, the arrival of a priest who is in turn feared, ridiculed, and welcomed but who sufficiently dedicated to try and preserve his flock's language and grammar, and even unsuccessful attempts to right the wrongs of governmental rapaciousness—all these are examples of stories repeated countless times over the course of the past centuries as European Americans inexorably moved westward. Father Damien confesses to his inquisitor that he has long abandoned his belief in the redemptive quality of conversion: He stayed on the reservation "out of duty to the practical desperation of the situation" (239).

Erdrich wears her deep knowledge of Catholicism lightly but slyly in this novel. Her early book of poetry, *Baptism of Desire* (1989), manifested her profound knowledge of some fairly obscure points of Catholic doctrine, among them the eponymous baptism of desire, which one can obtain with full sacramental validity even if no rite of baptism has been performed. At the same time, the very notion of "desire" has obvious connotations of erotic desire, particularly coming from an author who writes as lyrically about sex as Erdrich does. In a similar mingling of orthodoxy and subversion, Agnes arrives on the reservation on the feast of Saint Dismas, "the first day of her existence as Father Damien, the first day of the great lie that was her life" (*Last Report* 61). Saint Dismas, the "good thief" crucified next to Jesus and promised entry into paradise by the dying Savior, was never canonized by the Catholic Church but is venerated in some localities ("Dismas"). His feast day is March 25, which is, ironically, also the feast day of the Annunciation—that is, the day on which Mary is told by the angel that she will be the mother of Christ, the beginning of the great mystery of the incarnation. We see Father Damien in this novel performing the work of God as obediently as Mary, who called herself "the Lord's handmaiden." Occasionally we see Damien celebrating Mass, the central sacrament of his faith, but more often we see him hearing confession, through which he is made privy to knowledge about rapes, trauma, stillborn children, gruesome murders, assaults, pretended piety, and many more frailties of the human body and spirit. The secrecy and mystery surrounding the sacrament of confession is at the tropological foundation of this novel of disguise and dissimulation, in which almost nobody is what he or she seems to be. Nonetheless, in true American fashion, everyone is allowed to be what he or she wants to be.

While Dismas is not a saint, Damien certainly is. He is a Belgian priest (1840–89), who—beatified in 1995 and canonized in 2009, after the appearance of the novel—served in a lepers' colony in Hawaii and eventually died of leprosy himself. Known also as apostle to the outcast, he prefigures the fate that Erdrich constructs for Father Damien, who ministers to Native Americans sequestered on a reservation ("De Veuster"). To round out the roster of significant names, the Catholic calendar recognizes several saints called Agnes, but Agnes of Rome is most likely the model upon which Erdrich builds her central protagonist. This particular saint is iconographically represented with a lamb ("Agnes"). As Father Damien denies his body and sacrifices himself for his flock, though not unto death, the suggestion of an *agnus Dei*, "lamb of God," is implied in Erdrich's choice of this name.

Erdrich describes the reservation perfectly in terms of a human community that seeks to give itself shape: "It was a place of shifting allegiances, new feuds and old animosities, a place of clan teasing, jealousy, comfort, and love" (75). Agnes is defined by her community so much that the orthodoxy of her belief is challenged. She discovers that Ojibwe worship practices are "compatible with the teachings of Christ" (49) and begins "to address the trinity as four and to include the spirit of each direction" (182). She quickly sets aside gender restrictions, celibacy taboos, and conventional expectations, finding her ministry deepened by her brief but intense sexual experience with an apprentice priest and the peculiar combination of active and contemplative life that this community demands. In a somewhat alienated form, Agnes's story is an inverted captivity narrative. She makes herself captive of two conditions—male disguise and priestly accoutrements—which define her and also allow her certain safe modes of living.

The conclusion of the consensual, fulfilling sexual relationship with the apprentice priest pushes Agnes to answer two questions about her core identity in response to Father Gregory's challenges. Agnes has nothing to say when Gregory asserts, "You are a *woman*" (206), as if brushing away the biological fact that has enabled the two of them to have their relationship. She nevertheless answers with conviction, "I am a priest" (206), confirming thereby that her chosen identity— the position within the group to which she ministers she has taken *by choice*—is now the irrevocable portion of her identity. In true American fashion, she herself has been changed by the community to discover her genuine vocation.

As Agnes's passion for her calling finds material expression in a new church, so her spirituality, like that of Reverend Pulliam, is centered in a sermon she gives to the snakes that live in the church. It is a sermon on the great Christian—and human—topic of love. The transformation of the protagonist's identity is completed in the metamorphosis from Agnes's soft sensuality of sexual love into Damien's preaching of the indefinable love that responds to God's call: "What is the whole of our existence . . . but the sound of an appalling love?" (226). Like Pulliam, though not in the service of social conservatism but in the service of his Native congregation, he continues, "Or is God's love, perhaps, something very different from what we think we know?" (227). Whereas Pulliam offers declarative definitions of love with certainty, Damien articulates the questions at his core in the form of submission to his calling, another form of love: "If I am loved . . . it is a merciless and exacting love against which I have no defense. If I am not loved, then I am being pitilessly manipulated by a force I cannot withstand, either, and so it is all the same. I must do what I must do. Go in peace" (227). Submission to service within a community has given Agnes/Damien the reason for continuing to live. S/he builds a life out of experience and essence together. The cultural syncretism of Native and Catholic lives is enlarged by the manner in which the plot of the novel is inscribed into the American literary tradition. The success of that cultural and literary negotiation seems to me to be the real miracle at Little No Horse.

Notes

1. Mohanty's interpretation of Toni Morrison's *Beloved* turns into an interesting deconstruction of the epistemic assumptions held by "experientialists" and "postmodernists" (my terms) alike and makes for fascinating reading. Mohanty's 1993 article appeared before the "memory boom" of the 1990s, continuing to this day, flooded the book market with experiential narratives that seemed to shift the tide momentarily away from the hegemony of postmodern analytical thought that had held sway throughout the 1980s.

2. See, for example, Couser, Austenfeld, and Quinlan.
3. See, for example, Momaday's *The Way to Rainy Mountain* (1969), Vizenor's *The Trickster of Liberty* (1988), or Alexie's *Reservation Blues* (1995).
4. Says Treuer, critically: "Because Erdrich happens to be Ojibwe, her novels are interpreted as expressions of Ojibwe world-view, not as literary creations" (qtd. in Kennedy 49). A moment later, the interviewer, Virginia Kennedy, suggests a position that Treuer does not fully accept: "Your perspective is that Native writers like Silko and Erdrich write, communicating bits and pieces of their respective cultures to define their cultural experience for people who have no other way of 'knowing' it; they are coming to 'us,' rather than making us work harder to come to them, so to speak" (52). Treuer also elegantly dismisses critical concern with ethnicity even more radically than I suggested in cautioning against false essentialism: "DNA is absolutely the most important thing to most critics, and that is what is killing our genre" (qtd. in Kennedy 49). In his *Native American Fiction: A User's Manual*, Treuer actually makes very interesting arguments that place Erdrich in company with Flaubert and notes that "Erdrich's ability to find that one thing that can stand in for all the rest is almost unequalled and only surpassed by Toni Morrison's symbolic strokes" (35, 38–39).
5. According to the Nobel Prize Committee, Morrison was awarded the 1993 Nobel Prize as one "who in novels characterized by visionary force and poetic import, gives life to an essential aspect of American reality." I read "essential" in this context as meaning "basic," "central," or "undeniable." The committee was probably not taking a stance on the question of philosophical essentialism.
6. Vogel's name and origin suggest relationships of this figure with another Swabian, Fidelis Waldvogel, protagonist of *The Master Butchers Singing Club* (2003).
7. The town fathers of Ruby have an identical sense of tropological fulfillment in guiding the fate of their town.

Works Cited

"Agnes." *The Oxford Dictionary of Saints*. Ed. David Hugh Farmer. 5th ed. Oxford UP, 2003.

Austenfeld, Thomas. "German Heritage and Culture in Louise Erdrich's *The Master Butchers Singing Club*." *Great Plains Quarterly* 26.1 (2006): 3–11.

Couser, Thomas G. "Tracing the Trickster: Nanapush, Ojibwe Oral Tradition, and *Tracks*." *Approaches to Teaching the Works of Louise Erdrich*. Ed. Greg Sarris, Connie A. Jacobs, and James Richard Giles. New York: MLA 2004. 58–65.

"De Veuster, Damien." *The Oxford Dictionary of Saints*. Ed. David Hugh Farmer. Rev. 5th ed. Oxford UP, 2011.

"Dismas, the Good Thief." *The Oxford Dictionary of Saints*. Ed. David Hugh Farmer. 5th ed. Oxford UP, 2003.

Erdrich, Louise. *The Last Report on the Miracles at Little No Horse*. New York: Harper, 2001.

Faulkner, William. "The Bear." *Novels, 1942–1954*. New York: Library of America, 1994. 140–246.

Fitzgerald, F. Scott. *The Great Gatsby*. New York: Scribner, 2003.

Frost, Robert. "The Silken Tent." *Selected Poems of Robert Frost*. New York: Holt, 1963.

Hewitt, Avis, and Robert Donahoo, eds. *Flannery O'Connor in the Age of Terrorism: Essays on Violence and Grace*. Knoxville: U of Tennessee P, 2010.

Kennedy, Virginia. "A Conversation with David Treuer." *Studies in American Indian Literatures* 20.2 (2008): 47–63.

Mohanty, Satya P. "The Epistemic Status of Cultural Identity: On *Beloved* and the Postcolonial Condition." *Cultural Critique* 24 (1993): 41–80.

Morrison, Toni. *Paradise*. New York: Knopf, 1998.

"The Nobel Prize in Literature 1993: Toni Morrison." *Nobelprize.org*. Nobel Foundation, 2011. Web. 19 Apr. 2012.

Nowlin, Michael. "Toni Morrison's *Jazz* and the Racial Dreams of the American Writer." *American Literature* 71.1 (1999): 151–74.

O'Connor, Flannery. "The Fiction Writer and His Country." *Collected Works*. New York: Library of America, 1988. 801–6.

———. "The Catholic Novelist in the Protestant South." *Collected Works*. New York: Library of America, 1988. 853–64.

Quinlan, Eileen. "New Catholic Literature Sails in Open Sea." *National Catholic Reporter* 32.30 (1996): 31.

Tocqueville, Alexis de. "Political Associations in the United States." *Democracy in America*. Vol. 1. 1835. *Xroads*. American Studies at the University of Virginia, 1 Sept. 2009. Web. 19 Apr. 2012.

Treuer, David. *Native American Fiction: A User's Manual*. St. Paul: Graywolf, 2006.

Twain, Mark. "Adventures of Huckleberry Finn." *Mississippi Writings*. New York: Library of America, 1992. 617–912.

Zwischenraum: "The Space Between" Ecologies in Louise Erdrich's *The Painted Drum*

William Huggins

From its earliest writings, ecological criticism has shown an awareness of the potential of indigenous literatures to shine a light on the abuses of humanity on the natural world. Considering the larger ecological state of the planet—rivers dammed, air and water polluted, overdeveloped, deforested, species of wild animals being lost at a staggering rate—the work of many indigenous authors represents a worldview that directly confronts the development/progress paradigm. Some readers and critics have been drawn to these literatures, seeing their emphasis on mutually beneficial relations between people and the land as a tonic.

As beneficent as this motivation may seem, ecocritic Cheryll Glotfelty warns that "the willingness to 'revalue' nature-oriented literature has led many readers to seek wisdom in Native American texts. These well-meaning readers are often ignorant of the cultural and historical background necessary to understand this literature" (xxx). In their ecocritical reader, Glotfelty and Harold Fromm include two essays from Paula Gunn Allen (Laguna Pueblo/Sioux) and Leslie Marmon Silko (Laguna Pueblo) designed to introduce readers to the Native American perspective regarding story and the land. Allen's essay firmly states this connection:

> Traditional American Indian literature is not similar to Western literature because the basic assumptions about the universe and, therefore, the basic reality experienced by tribal peoples and by Western peoples are not the same, even at the level of folklore. This difference has confused non-Indian students for centuries. They have been unable or unwilling to accept this difference and to develop critical procedures to illuminate the materials without trivializing or otherwise invalidating them. (242)

The inclusion of a powerful essay articulating the Native American point of view in the first collection of ecocritical work makes it clear that ecological critics can work with indigenous literatures provided they approach the works with the respect they deserve.

Native American literature encourages readers to rethink common assumptions about land. Simon Ortiz (Acoma Pueblo) notes, "I think that a great deal of the environmental movement comes from Native American energies; attention that has been gained through an insistence on an ecological connection to people and lands and cultures" (qtd. in Berry and Lucerno 162). This theme of connectivity goes back to the earliest modern Native American writings, including Vine Deloria Jr.'s assertion in 1973: "It remains for us to learn once again that we are a part of nature, not a transcendent species with no responsibilities to the natural world" (3). One important fact to remember through all this indigenous ecoconnectivity is that there are more than 560 different, culturally unique tribal entities recognized by the United States. Though they share common attitudes toward nature and its nonhuman inhabitants, each tribe retains distinctions that mark their traditions, and any reader must understand these differences to appreciate truly what each individual tribal author seeks to do with his or her work.

Seen in this light, Louise Erdrich (Ojibwe) stands as the preeminent representative of Native American literature. Her works have stood the test of time, topped best-seller lists, yet also transcended their popular status by engaging critics from a wide diversity of disciplines and theoretical approaches. One of Erdrich's distinctive qualities—and it is a distinction of Native American literature, in general—is her focus on one place: the fictional Little No Horse Reservation in North Dakota. Erdrich's concentrated locus enables ecocritics to consider her body of work and the storied ecology within and around it. Every novel bursts with potential—from the water imagery of *Love Medicine* to the impact of nonnative sugar beets on the local economy in *The Beet Queen* to the powerfully sad final buffalo hunt in *The Last Report on the Miracles at Little No Horse* and Fleur's quest to regain her woodlands in

Tracks and *Four Souls*, to name but a few possibilities for study. In her thorough ecocritical survey of Erdrich's works up to 2001, Rinda West sees "the Anishinaabe novels of Louise Erdrich as a performance of the restoration of culture and land . . . restoring natural areas, restoring culture, and individuation" (160).

The Native American vision of land and landscape differs from that of the typical Euro-American. The idea of beauty, of natural landscapes, often calls to mind iconic national parks or other untrammeled natural areas, such as wilderness. Roderick Frazier Nash quotes that Chief Standing Bear of the Oglala Sioux "did not think of the great open plains, the beautiful rolling hills and the winding streams with their tangled growth as 'wild.' Only to the white man was nature a 'wilderness' and . . . the land 'infested' with 'wild animals' and 'savage' people" (xiii; ellipsis in orig.). Wilderness imposes a definition from without, by the dominant Euro-American culture. In her novels, Erdrich never refers to the undeveloped areas of the reservation as wild. Born into the culture and raised with an indigenous view of the land, to Erdrich these areas naturally contain the people and the stories, as she writes in "Where I Ought to Be":

> A writer must have a place where he or she feels this, a place to love and be irritated with. One must experience the local blights, hear the proverbs, endure the radio commercials. Through the close study of a place, its people and character, its crops, products, paranoias, dialects, and failures, we come closer to our own reality. It is difficult to impose a story on a place. But truly knowing a place provides the link between details and meaning. Location, whether it is to abandon it or draw it sharply, is where we start. (49)

Erdrich's literary legacy reflects her commitment to this specific place. The best of her novels take place in and around Little No Horse, creating a storied ecology that ties itself to the land, people, and larger Ojibwe culture. All of these elements are essential parts of a greater whole, not independent pieces. When Erdrich leaves the reservation, as in *The Crown of Columbus*, her connection to the land seems to devolve, and thus the novel becomes something less than her more powerful work, tied to the reservation she knows so well. This makes an ecocritical reading of *The Painted Drum* appropriate because for half of the novel, Erdrich goes away from Little No Horse to the forests of New England. Erdrich makes this connective leap by emphasizing the differing forest ecologies of North Dakota and New England, the ecological basis for the need to return the drum, and the role ravens and wolves play in the culture and ecology of the two regions.

Parts 1 and 4 of *The Painted Drum* take place in New England and bracket the reservation sections. Both carry the title "Revival Road," which is "named for the flat field at its southern end that once hosted a yearly revival meeting" (4). The idea of revival conjures several potential interpretations at the beginning and the end of the novel. Primarily, it serves to bring Faye Travers back into connection with her surroundings. Her mother, Elsie, does not embrace her Ojibwe heritage and makes her disdain for the reservation clear many times throughout the novel. When Faye admits to stealing the drum, Elsie says, "It is more alive than a set of human bones. . . . Of course, that is a traditional belief, not mine" (43). Yet it is through Faye's theft of the drum that both women are drawn back to Little No Horse to restore that part of their shared heritage to its rightful place, even though neither of the women practices any form of traditional Ojibwe values.

Most of the extant criticism—of which there is little to date—on *The Painted Drum* considers the psychosocial issues raised in the novel. Rinda West focuses on ecopsychological themes raised in Erdrich's novels. Though West does not touch on *The Painted Drum* specifically, her observation on character development and transformation easily works for Faye's character: "In Erdrich's work the movement away from the ego focus on narcissism, greed, or pride is a softening to love, a vulnerability that touches virtually every character" (188). This softness defines Faye. At the novel's commencement, she may as well be a piece of stone worked by her artist lover. The novel opens in a children's graveyard, where she visits her dead sister. The opening paragraphs are layered with several images of stone, from the memorial headstones that line the cemetery to the details on the gravel road, to the references to her lover, Kurt Krahe, and his artistry with the different types of rock with which he works. By novel's end, Faye reconnects with herself, healed, and Erdrich illustrates this healing with flight imagery. The freedom of air contrasts the heaviness of Faye and her stoniness when the reader first meets her.

Faye's transformation of character gets much assistance from the ravens that permeate the New England sections of the novel. Professionally, Faye and Elsie take care of the estates of the dead, which is what leads Faye to the drum in the first place. Like ravens, who pick a carcass clean, they take care of the remaining assets of an estate. Ravens fill the early and closing parts of the novel, appearing in several important scenes (15, 24, 71). Faye notes early on that "ravens are the birds I'll miss most when I die. . . . If I have a religious practice, it is the watching of these birds" (15). Davan Eyke's attempt to kill a raven sets off Kurt, who fires an arrow at the boy, though the raven Davan shot seems to be well when the shaft is pulled from its body and it walks away (16).

This scene illustrates another important connective thread between the ravens and Faye's Native American background. Ravens and wolves were likewise part of a concentrated eradication effort on the part of the early New England settlers. Bringing with them a set of religious and sociocultural biases that they did not question in a new and different land, the first European American settlers associated ravens with their darkest fears of death and evil and therefore set about eliminating them. Though not specifically an Ojibwe belief, many Native American tribes viewed the raven as "both a creator and a folk hero" (Heinrich, *Ravens in Winter* 24). Bernd Heinrich, noted wildlife biologist, further states:

In the eastern United States . . . the raven is still a symbol of the wilderness, and over large areas of Europe it has been eradicated by poisoning bait, shooting, and destroying nests. . . . Similar persecution followed the immigrants to the New World. . . . The English and German settlers loathed and feared the birds, and they were perhaps overeager to attribute the death of a sickly sheep to a raven, particularly if they found ravens feeding on the carcass. (26–27)

The persecution, clearly, was ineffective, and the ravens help pull Faye from her grief back into the larger world. Survivors themselves, the ravens flying and playing off a cliff at the novel's end literally bring Faye full circle through her grief. She wonders if the ravens "have eaten and are made of the insects and creatures that have lived off the dead in the raven's graveyard—then aren't they the spirits of the people, the children, the girls who sacrificed themselves, buried here?" (276). Thematically, this understanding of interconnectivity between all things casts a brighter light on some of the other events in the novel that lead Faye to that edge.

Faye's affair with Kurt also plays an important role in her reconnection. At the beginning of the novel, everyone on Revival Road seems to be in limbo. Kurt calls it *Zwischenraum*, the "space" or "interval between" (*Painted* 6; *Langenscheidt* 325). Faye thinks, "*Zwischenraum* is real. It is the way I see the world sometimes. Kurt has fallen into the space between his own works and is now mainly ignored" (6). The "space between" nearly defines Faye as well. Her mother is "perfectly assimilated, cold-blooded and analytical about the reservation present, and utterly dismissive of history" (59). An irony exists in Elsie's deliberate disavowal of history and willingness to profit from history's leftovers, including tribal artifacts. This early passivity and acceptance of routine could easily describe every major character in the novel, at first. Even the Eykes' dog, chained so that it could only roam in circles around the tree to which it was bound, locked in a prison of routine, is a victim of this lassitude. Suddenly, the tree to which it was tethered collapses when it dies, and the dog wanders free into the woods, yet still dragging its chain, much like Faye with her memories of her sister's death. Though now free to roam the wild woods, the dog retains the reminder of the civilization that attempted to yoke its spirit.

The liberation of the dog unleashes larger changes on Revival Road. The dog roams the nights around the small community like a new wolf, "loping on long springy wolf-legs" (22), present but mostly unseen. The linkage of the escaped dog with a wolf is worth some consideration. Though wolves and their connection with the ecology and culture of Little No Horse will be dealt with later, the role of the wolf in New England illustrates the fact that "by about 1900, the wolf had been removed from all of its ranges in the eastern half of the United States, except for the Great Lakes region" (Busch 124). The Europeans who settled New England brought with them the same great biases against wolves that they carried for ravens. The Great Lakes region has traditionally had an association with the Ojibwes, who roamed widely across the area from modern North Dakota into Ontario. The fact that wolves survived in these areas and not the eastern United States is no accident. The attitude of Native Americans enfolded wolves into the larger cultural and ecological picture.

The dog's freedom turns something loose in Davan Eyke as well, but his wildness is far less constructive. Tension rises between the boy and Kurt, which ultimately leads to the young man's death as well as that of Kurt's daughter, Kendra. These twin deaths alter Faye's relationship with the artist and lead to a freeing of her own spirit, which culminates in her theft of the drum. She seems driven to the point of a criminal act by her erratic affair with Kurt and her inability to deal with her past. She hides the liaison from her mother, though Elsie is aware of Kurt's nocturnal visits (e.g., 26). After Kendra's death, the affair intensifies for a time; Faye and Kurt "are like feral children, with no rules" (47). Faye traverses the zwischenraum between the temporary stasis of her life into motion with the theft of the drum, turning from dispassion toward passion, much like the dog when it escapes, in that "she does not appear again near the house where her nature devolved" (26). Faye's wanderings in the forest echo this sentiment, though she remains tied to her home.

One deeper connection exists between Faye and the freed dog. The fact that the dog was chained to a tree reflects Faye's attachment to and fear of the orchard behind her and Elsie's home. Until Kurt begins to work the orchard, cutting and pruning its branches, she could deny and repress the memories it holds. Kurt's insistence to do something productive and get Faye back into his life by working over the neglected orchard moves her into a position to deal with the grief of those memories.

Kurt's attempt to forcibly control her pushes Faye into the untamed woods so she does not have to confront his proposed order. Erdrich's presentation of the forests of New Hampshire resonates with authenticity: She mentions "great tender maples," an "enfolding pine," and "a white birch [that] feeds on the pulp of an old hemlock" (3, 7, 26). These are the images of a diverse and healthy forest. Her walks in the wild woods push her away from human habitations and responsibilities, letting her get back to a truer sense of self. As Faye notes, "Whenever you leave cleared land, or a path, or a road, when you step from someplace carved out, plowed, or traced by a human and pass into the woods, you must leave something of yourself behind" (25).

Faye's anger at Kurt for restoring the orchard makes sense. Bernd Heinrich notes that most apple trees "are clones that need constant pampering to stay alive" (*Trees* 128). In deliberate contrast to the wild forest in which Faye chooses to wander, the maintenance of the apple orchard has been allowed to fade because of the effort involved and the bad memories of her sister's death. The danger here comes from the monoculture the orchard represents. As Paul Greenberg states, "If there is one lesson that has been learned from terrestrial agriculture, it is that monocultures of crops are susceptible to disease and can cause undue environmental degradation" (255). The forest through which Faye walks is a signifier of ecological health; the orchard is not. Thus,

Kurt's restoration forces her to deal with the tragic event of her sister's death, which closes out part 1. Faye locks these memories out for years. She wakes, and "a breath of orchard sweetness sails, curls into my room, and I remember the days when the orchard bloomed this way every spring" (73). Kurt's project puts Faye back on the path to restoring herself, but it is the contrasting freedom of the forest that allows her to heal.

Faye's decision to return the drum to the reservation connects the different regions of the novel, an act of linking the zwischenraum between New England and North Dakota. Though once she and her mother bring the drum back to its rightful place, they become passive participants to Bernard Shaawano's narrative, listening. His tale stretches across generations to the drum's origin and construction, bringing back Fleur Pillager and expanding on her heritage in the larger Little No Horse narrative. The reservation sections of the novel also raise two important issues: the rightful place and purpose of the drum and the role of wolves at Little No Horse.

The drum's return contains much larger significance in the world outside of the novel. In 1990, the United States Congress passed the Native American Graves Protection and Repatriation Act (NAGPRA). While this act pertains mostly to "the return of the dead and the funerary objects dug up with them" (Childs 29), the context still fits *The Painted Drum* because of the larger issue of the proper place for sacred artifacts, especially considering that there are bones contained within the drum. Heid Erdrich's 2008 collection *National Monuments* deals poetically with repatriation issues, specifically in poems such as the eponymous opening work and the series on Kennewick Man. Wiley Steve Thornton (Osage/Cherokee) also writes about this issue:

After about two weeks in the city [New York], I found a job at the National Museum of the American Indian. It is a strange place to work. There are sacred objects, ceremonial objects, human remains, and medicine bundles—representations from many tribes. It was odd how non-Indians cared and knew so much about Native American objects. They seemed to feel more for the objects in their care, however, than for the actual Native people. They certainly didn't understand that some of these things were still alive with a spirit in each one. (34)

This attitude extends to the Tatros' treatment of the artifacts in their home, including the drum. Though they were incredibly stingy with themselves, they cared for the Native American pieces in their collection reverently (though not traditionally, an important distinction), dusting them, setting mousetraps to keep vermin away, and even re-wrapping them annually in fresh newspaper (38). The same could not be said of Jewett Parker Tatro's treatment of his Ojibwe charges. He amassed his collection by taking advantage of the Ojibwes who frequented his bar when they were at their lowest point. So he accepted artifacts in exchange for alcohol and fled to New Hampshire with a fortune in Native American heritage. In the long strange turnabout of history and narrative, Faye brings back at least one piece—no doubt the most important piece.

Craig Childs's 2010 book *Finders Keepers* contains many stories of the complexities of such returns. The book concerns itself with the deep complications of how Euro-American culture views ancient artifacts. In the section titled "The Destiny Jar," he tells a story about how he once stole a pot from a reading room and returned it to the ancient Salado area from which it was unearthed. After several days of hiking and climbing through challenging southwestern country, Childs asserts that he "had never done anything like it before and was . . . sure I would not do anything like it again. . . . I felt I was making more of a mess out of an already intractable situation" (37). Perhaps part of Childs's issue stems from the fact that though he loves the desert and expresses that through his activities and writing, he can make no claims to indigeneity. Faye can. When she sights the drum, "it sounds. One deep, low, resonant note" (39). While Childs looks at the dusty pots on display in a remote spot, Faye echoes the sentiments of Thornton and responds to the drum because it is not where it should be. Unlike Thornton, however, Faye can do something about the drum. Her connection "is visceral. Not a thought but a gut instinct" (40).

Erdrich never inserts ceremonial aspects of Ojibwe culture into her novels. She notes, "As in all of my books, no sacred knowledge is revealed" (*Painted* 277). Anything considered privately religious is not included. Wise non-Native critics should show the same consideration toward ceremonial aspects of Native American literature, granting privacy and respect to these traditions. Yet there is an ecological significance to the drum's construction and ultimate repatriation. Old Shaawano constructs the drum following dreams and intuition. He spends a great deal of time on the body of the drum, first camping and sleeping with the wood he uses to build it. The detail Erdrich goes into reflects the traditional way of building a drum of this kind, as cataloged by Thomas Vennum Jr. in *The Ojibwe Dance Drum*, a source Erdrich herself quotes in the author's note. True to her pledge not to reveal any "sacred knowledge," Erdrich glosses the drum's creation descriptively but skirts the edge of ceremonial significance.

Ecologically, the drum's return is essential for several reasons. First, according to Vennum's description about how drums should be cared for, the drum in its place at the Tatros' is not being treated with the respect drums deserve (61–64). Even though the Tatros kept their artifacts in good condition, there are aspects of Ojibwe tribal culture honoring the drum that are not being met. Second, the fact that Old Shaawano spends so much time with the trees before selecting one to use for the drum and tends to its cutting and shaping so delicately shows the connection the drum has to this place. In short, the land is the drum and the drum is the land. It does not belong in a dusty room in New England, no matter how well cared for, because its origin is tied to the forests of North Dakota where it was made. The bones of Shaawano's daughter also clearly tie the drum to the reservation, especially in the sense of NAGPRA mentioned earlier.

A final important ecological connector to the drum and the reservation shows in the representation of wolves on both the drum and in the novel itself. As Vennum notes, "If an Ojibwa drumhead bears any kind of symbol, it is an almost certain indication that the drum itself is put to some sacred use" (201). Though the drumhead in the novel is decorated only with a yellow stripe, tassels in the drum's tabs bear four beaded symbols, one of them "a running wolf" (39). In many ways, Erdrich's treatment of wolves in the novel's central sections may be the most fascinating ecocritical aspect of the novel.

The Ojibwe connection with wolves goes back to the earliest lore. When Original Man first walks the earth, he complains to the Creator that all the animals are paired, yet he is alone. The Creator gives him a companion, Ma-en'-gun (the wolf) (Benton-Banai 7). After roaming the world together and seeing all things under creation, the Creator says they must separate, and adds:

> 'What shall happen to one of you will also happen to the other. Each of you will be feared, respected and misunderstood by the people that will later join you on this Earth.'
>
> And so Ma-en'-gun and Original Man set off on their different journeys.
>
> This last teaching about the wolf is important to us today. What the Grandfather said to them has come true. Both the Indian and the wolf have come to be alike and have experienced the same thing. . . . Both have a Clan System and a tribe. Both have had their land taken from them. Both have been hunted for their wee-nes-se-see' (hair). And both have been pushed very close to destruction. (8)

The wolves' presence in the novel solidifies the ecological connectors already present in other aspects of the story. An essential part of his family's history and legacy, Bernard notes he has "grown up in the range of those wolves" (118). The spirit of the wolves moves him so that "when I hear the wolves . . . unrest grips me. I have to leave my house and go out walking in the night, hungry to know what I cannot know and desperate to see what will always be hidden" (118). John's brother Morris "is named for the wolf" (204), and his fidelity to Ira and her children echoes the faithfulness wolves show to their own charges. Morris tells Ira his father gave him the name "because wolves saved his life, once" (233). In another important linkage, when Shawnee leads her brother and sister to safety through three miles of snowed-in woods, "she broke the trail. Alice followed in her steps" (206). Wolves travel this way through deep snow, in single file.

Bernard tells a story about an old man who "wanted to be with the wolves and know their thoughts" (119). When young, the old man went out to decide whether or not to commit suicide, asking the wolf, "How is it that you go on living with such sorrow? How do you go on without turning around and destroying yourselves, as so many of us Anishinaabeg have done under similar circumstances?" (120). The answer the wolf gives allows the man to turn from despair back to his religious origins, "the regular, deep, violet-brown scars of a sundancer who pulled buffalo skulls" (121). Like Faye, who is pulled through her own despair by the return of the drum and the ravens that surround her, the old man reconnects with the old tales of the wolf and Original Man and chooses continuance, survival. Wolves here represent one of the primary themes running through all Native American literature, what Evelina Zuni Lucero (Isleta/Ohkay Owingeh Pueblo) states as "our presence, our present . . . a gift from the struggles of our ancestors through time, surviving beyond the horrors of conquest and the challenges of our tribes' continuance to the present day" (Berry and Lucerno 14).

Wolves play an essential role in the construction of the drum, continuing their importance in Ojibwe culture from early origin stories to the modern day. A viable wolf population currently exists in these areas, primarily spreading from the boundary waters in northern Minnesota through about 30 percent of its former range, and it is increasing (Busch 20). This range extends through traditional Anishinaabe lands but also could plausibly be large enough to extend into Little No Horse's storied ecology. A gray wolf leads Shaawano to the cedar grove where he creates the base of the drum (170).

Erdrich remains true to the essential nature of wolves in the wild except in one important instance, the attack of the pack on Anaquot's wagon. While she notes that "the story runs counter to real facts about the shyness and politic avoidance that wolves show to humans" (277), Erdrich culls the story from "the experience of an elderly man" (227). In all the wolf literature available to date, there is no mention of a healthy wolf ever attacking a human being. Rabid wolves, however, were very much a threat. Barry Lopez states in his seminal *Of Wolves and Men* that Native Americans "understood wolves in a wider context. Wolves, like grizzly bears, could, after all, kill. . . . Rabies was a real reason to fear wolves, for there were few more horrible deaths" (122–23). Erdrich's wolf pack shows no sign of rabid behavior, though.

Her presentation of the wolf attack owes more to Russian folklore and Willa Cather's *My Ántonia* than reality. In Cather's story, Peter and Pavel throw a groom and bride out of their sledge in order to survive a marauding wolf pack (38–40). Lopez writes, "Reports from Russia and Europe of wolves preying on human beings are more numerous than those from North America and there is probably some truth to them" (70). He means wolves preying on humans in individual instances, not packlike attacks: a wolf against an unarmed man, for example (71). What Erdrich does with this story resonates more with the larger theme of the novel: showing the strength of women in difficult situations. In the grand scheme of the novel, the wolf attack propels Anaquot's daughter (Fleur's sister) to make a sacrifice of herself to ensure everyone else's safety and compels her father to make the drum with part of her sacrifice within it, which ultimately comes full circle with Faye's return. The fact that the wolf attack does not conform to what is known about wolf behavior matters in an ecocritical reading because it does not stand up scientifically. S. K. Robisch urges readers to understand that "when we put a wolf in a story, the story at that point must be responsible to the wolf" (11). From an ecocritical perspective, in a novel that weaves beautifully through healthy forests and treats ravens and wolves as they appear and behave in the wild, this is the only mistake Erdrich makes.

Ultimately, the heart of Erdrich's work contains a great compassion for all things, the human and the nonhuman. At the novel's end, everything comes together again at Revival Road, which expands beyond its early compressed dynamic into the revival of a sense of connectedness, "a transformed Faye, with a new attitude that enables her to connect creatively with the outside world" (Wyatt 13). Faye's theft of the drum is an act of compassion that not only saves a life but also returns her to where she belongs. Her small act ties her into the larger idea of restoration and continuity of culture that flows through all of Erdrich's work. The wilderness background of the novel plays an important role here, as "the attempted extermination of the wolf became analogous to the extermination of whole ecosystems and of the cultures that inhabited them" (Robisch 226). By bridging that zwischenraum and letting readers conceive of a worldview in which all beings are respected for their innate rights as living beings, Native American literature can be a guide to a way to restore balance to a worldview that seems bent on its own destruction. Literary examples like *The Painted Drum* clearly show that ecological and cultural integrity remain possible even against great odds.

Works Cited

Benton-Banai, Edward. *The Mishomis Book: The Voice of the Ojibway*. St. Paul: Indian Country, 1979.

Berry Brill de Ramirez, Susan, and Evelina Zuni Lucero, eds. *Simon J. Ortiz: A Poetic Legacy of Indigenous Continuance*. Albuquerque: U of New Mexico P, 2009.

Busch, Robert H. *The Wolf Alamanc: A Celebration of Wolves and Their World, New and Revised*. Guilford: Lyons, 2007.

Cather, Willa. *My Ántonia*. Boston: Houghton, 1995.

Childs, Craig. *Finders Keepers: A Tale of Archaeological Plunder and Obsession*. New York: Little, Brown, 2010.

Deloria, Vine, Jr. *God Is Red: A Native View of Religion*. 1973. Golden: Fulcrum, 2003.

Erdrich, Louise. *The Painted Drum*. New York: Harper, 2005.

_____. "Where I Ought to Be: A Writer's Sense of Place." *Louise Erdrich's* Love Medicine: *A Casebook*. Ed. Hertha D. Sweet Wong. New York: Oxford UP, 2000.

Glotfelty, Cheryll, and Harold Fromm, eds. *The Ecocritical Reader: Landmarks in Literary Ecology*. Athens: U of Georgia P, 1996.

Greenberg, Paul. *Four Fish: The Future of the Last Wild Food*. New York: Penguin, 2010.

Heinrich, Bernd. *Ravens in Winter*. New York: Vintage, 1989.

_____. *The Trees in My Forest*. New York: Harper, 1997.

Lopez, Barry. *Of Wolves and Men*. New York: Simon, 1978.

Mech, L. David, and Luigi Boitani. *Wolves: Behavior, Ecology, and Conservation*. Chicago: U of Chicago P, 2003.

Nash, Roderick Frazier. *Wilderness and the American Mind*. 4th ed. New Haven: Yale UP, 2001.

Robisch, S. K. *Wolves and the Wolf Myth in American Literature*. Reno: U of Nevada P, 2009.

Thornton, Wiley Steve. "Indian in a Strange Land." *Genocide of the Mind: New Native American Writing*. Ed. MariJo Moore. New York: Avalon, 2003. 29–38.

Vennum, Thomas, Jr. *The Ojibwa Dance Drum: Its History and Construction*. Washington: Smithsonian Inst., 1982.

West, Rinda. *Out of the Shadow: Ecopsychology, Story, and Encounters with the Land*. Charlottesville: U of Virginia P, 2007.

Wyatt, Jean. "Storytelling, Melancholia, and Narrative Structure in Louise Erdrich's *The Painted Drum*." *MELUS* 36.1 (2011): 13–36.

"Zwischenraum." *Langenscheidt's German-English English-German Dictionary*. New York: Pocket, 1970. 325.

CRITICAL
READINGS

Louise Erdrich Anishinaabezhibiiaan _____

Margaret Noori / Giiwedinoodin

> If we call ourselves and all we see around us by our original names, will we not continue to be Anishinaabeg? Instead of reconstituted white men, instead of Indian ghosts? Do the rocks here know us, do the trees, do the waters of the lakes? Not unless they are addressed by the names they themselves told us to call them in our dreams. Every feature of the land around us spoke its name to an ancestor. . . . We Anishinaabeg are the keepers of the names of the earth. And unless the earth is called by the names it gave us humans, won't it cease to love us? And isn't it true that if the earth stops loving us, everyone . . . will cease to exist? That is why we all must speak our language, nindinawemagonidok, and call everything we see by the name of its spirit. Even the chimookomanag, who are trying to destroy us, are depending upon us to remember and to use these words. Mi'sago'i. (Erdrich, *The Last Report* 360–61)

Louise Erdrich's characters sometimes speak Anishinaabemowin and sometimes speak about Anishinaabemowin. Nanapush speaks of names found in dreams and ancient memories, words entwined with existence. To know the way words become names relates to finding a permanent place in the firmament. This is the knowledge of words Erdrich includes in her work. She writes specifically of the Anishinaabeg. Sometimes she translates such terms as *nindinawemaganidok*, "relatives," and *chimookomanag*, "long knives" or "Americans." Sometimes she leaves them standing like silent cultural sentinels in the text. Telling stories in any language is an act of hope and memory; for Erdrich, it is an act of survival. Words convey with sound and definition the history and creativity of individuals and communities. Beyond the plot, setting, and characters, readers can choose to focus more closely on Erdrich's choice of words. Within the field of literary criticism, structuralist traditions based on interpreting the symbols words represent can be useful. Sociolinguistic traditions that trace changes in language and its use reveal another dimension of meaning. This essay uses both of these traditions to show why a nationally significant American, Native American, and Anishinaabe author sometimes reaches beyond English to illustrate connections between language and culture, offering four primary reasons for her use of Anishinaabemowin. One reason is to share the sound and style of the Anishinaabe language. She writes of characters who learned Anishinaabemowin first, "whose English is forever rounded and shaped so that all of the words seem kindlier" (*Painted Drum* 69). A second reason Erdrich uses Anishinaabemowin is to teach readers important definitions and ideas. Third, she demonstrates through the conversation of her characters the importance of language to identity and continuity. Lastly, Erdrich uses Anishinaabemowin to locate bridges and barriers. There are times when two worlds blend, and there are times when they collide. Erdrich's characters do both as they move between Anishinaabe and English languages and traditions. Language can be a way to broadcast an identity or to guard secrets. Erdrich and the characters she creates do both as they weave lives mixed with Anishinaabemowin and English.

Anishinaabemowin, one of twenty-seven Algonquian languages, is the ancestral language of over two hundred communities in the United States and Canada. Now used as a single term to refer to several closely related dialects, Anishinaabemowin is the language of the Three Fires Confederacy, which consists of the Odawa, Potawatomi, and Ojibwe. The word "Anishinaabe" is sometimes used interchangeably with "Ojibwe" or "Chippewa," but most speakers today understand Odawa, Potawatomi, and Ojibwe to be ethnic communities, while "Anishinaabe" is a term for the broader cultural community. Each of the ethnic groups has its own linguistic identity and, some say, its own historic role within the confederacy. Odawa stems from the word *adaawe* (to trade). The term "Potawatomi" references the word *boodawaade*, the act of building or keeping a fire. Some say the term "Ojibwe" stems from the word *jibakwe* (to cook or roast) because the people wore moccasins that were puckered at the toe. However, it is possibly more productive to connect the initial sound of the word *jib* to such other words as *jibwa* (before) and *jiibay* (ghost), which carry implications of the past. In fact, *jibakwe* may also connect back to the concept of putting a plate out for the *jiibayag* (the ghosts), which makes sense because the role of remembering or retelling stories is the Ojibwe community role most often cited by elders. In her travel memoir, *Books and Islands in Ojibwe Country*, Erdrich herself extends this analogy connecting the term "ojibwe" to the word *ozhibii'ige*, the verb for "he or she writes" (11). The term "Anishinaabe" is a combination of the term *nishin* (good) and *aabe* (male), interpreted as "the good man" and used as a verb. For example, Erdrich herself might say, "*Nd'Anishinaabe*" (I am Anishinaabe). Adding *mo* to the end of the verb means "to speak as an Anishinaabe." Adding *win* to the word makes it a noun. This transformation may seem tangled to an English speaker, but it is a window into a world of meaning shaped by action and addition rather than presence and pronouns. *Anishinaabemowin* could be translated as "the language of the Anishinaabe" or "the way we speak as an Anishinaabe," and the slip of definition between seeing language as a noun and having a way to peel it back to a common verb is the difference between cultures.

Anishinaabemowin was the primary language in the Great Lakes until the early 1600s, when French traders and Jesuits began to explore the St. Lawrence River, seeking furs to sell and souls to save, while British settlers arrived along the Atlantic coast seeking freedom. At that time, the traders and immigrants were forced to learn the language of the natives. Alliances shifted, years passed, and by 1776, when the Declaration of Independence was written, English had become the dominant language, and the desire to speak the language of the indigenous people had dwindled. While reading Erdrich's novels, it is important to consider the way the history of indigenous people relates to the history of their culture and language. In both Canada and the United States, the relationship with Natives is one of denial and restriction of identity through numerous tactics intended to result in execution, extinction, or assimilation. Blood, land, and language can be viewed as mediums of continued warfare. As early as 1819, the Civilization Fund Act provided money to societies who would "educate" Indian students. The goal was to "civilize" Indians by getting rid of their traditions and customs, including the very words they used to communicate. The goal was to assimilate the indigenous people by teaching them to read and write English. In 1879, Captain Richard Pratt, noted for his success during the Indian Wars, was given responsibility for Indian education in the United States. Considered a forward-thinking educator willing to give Native students a chance (if they abandoned all traces of their Native roots), he opened the doors of the Carlisle boarding school to continue the work begun by early French, German, and Spanish missionaries. Eventually boarding schools and the myth of the vanishing American Indian took hold, and increasingly fewer people used indigenous languages.

Erdrich's novels often address the history of government-sponsored boarding schools. In *The Painted Drum*, young Seraphine is struck by a matron at boarding school and "the scar of speaking her language remained across her lips all of her life" (251). In *Love Medicine*, Old Rushes Bear "had let the government put Nector in school but hidden Eli, the one she couldn't part with, in the root cellar dug beneath her floor. In that way she gained a son on either side of the line. Nector came home from boarding school knowing white reading and writing, while Eli knew the woods" (19). Many years later, the family would speculate on "why or how . . . Great-uncle Eli was still sharp, while Grandpa [Nector]'s mind had left, gone wary and wild" (19). Lulu Lamartine also has memories of boarding school:

> I ran away from government school. Once, twice, too many times. I ran
> away so often that my dress was always the hot-orange shame dress and
> my furious scrubbing thinned sidewalks beneath my hands and knees to
> cracked slabs. Punished and alone, I slept in a room of echoing creaks. I
> made and tore down and remade all the dormitory beds. I lived by bells,

orders, flat voices, rough English. I missed the old language in my mother's mouth. (*Love Medicine* 68)

Through Lulu, Erdrich gives readers an Anishinaabe child's view of boarding school. She is not interested in the adult debate of the politics behind the institution or a sociologist's opinion of its effects—just the heart-wrenching reality of a child being sent away from a family, a familiar home, and a culture. Erdrich's fictional characters sum up the very real loss and anguish Anishinaabe children experienced.

Today, although over two hundred nations recognized by Canada and the United States trace their roots to the Anishinaabeg, very few communities use their ancestral language. Approximately 80 percent of all Anishinaabe speakers are over sixty-five, and no one learns Anishinaabemowin as a first or only language anymore. The language is still in use but could disappear within one generation. Traces of the language in Erdrich's work are part of literary and literal efforts to preserve and protect Anishinaabemowin. Her use of the language is a powerful demonstration of how the words, even when used sparingly or in isolation, can convey real and important differences in cultural perspectives.

A complete biography of Louise Erdrich will tell the story of a woman proud of her many ancestors and interested in their voices. Erdrich's first book, *Jacklight*, published in 1984, tells the stories of runaways, hunters, and immigrant women. She also introduces Old Man Potchikoo, whose name is a blend of the words *boochigo* (a necessary act); Wenabozho, the Anishinaabe hero-clown; and *boozhoo*, a common greeting. Through Potchikoo, she begins to trace necessary connections between stories of the past and contemporary cultural traditions. Many Anishinaabeg recognize the greeting *boozhoo*. Some of those who use the greeting learned it as a reference to Wenabozho, and a few who still know the language might use the phrase *boochigo gii Anishinaabezhibiiaan* to explain that Erdrich "had to write in Anishinaabemowin."

In her *New York Times* article "Two Languages in Mind, but Just One in the Heart," Erdrich wrote:

Ojibwemowin [Anishinaabemowin] is one of the few surviving languages that evolved to the present here in North America. The intelligence of this language is adapted as no other to the philosophy bound up in northern land, lakes, rivers, forests [and] arid plains; to the animals and their particular habits; to the shades of meaning in the very placement of stones. As a North American writer it is essential to me that I try to understand our human relationship to place in the deepest way possible, using my favorite tool, language.

Through her life and work, Erdrich reflects her support of Anishinaabemowin. In 2001, she opened Birchbark Books, where the staff greet visitors in Anishinaabemowin, Lakota, and English. According to the "Our Story" note on the website, the small, independent bookstore with an international presence was opened "to nourish and build a community based on books" and is "a locus for Indigirati—literate Indigenous people who have survived over half a millennium on this continent." To give further presence to her belief in the revitalization of Anishinaabemowin, Erdrich and her sister Heid established Wiigwaas Press in 2008. It is a nonprofit organization created to serve communities engaged in the revitalization of Native American languages for the spiritual and material health of the people. The organization works to go beyond the work of any one author to make Anishinaabemowin part of contemporary culture. This practice of support for the language is an important backdrop to her writing.

One reason Erdrich uses Anishinaabemowin is to share the sound and style of the Anishinaabe language. Basic structural differences result in different sounds. Patterns of vowels and consonants vary from one language to another, and it is easy to forget the way the music of speech varies between communities. Long words are not uncommon in Anishinaabemowin. They are built using strings of morphemes, units of meaning, and new combinations are considered ideal. Anishinaabemowin is also an agglutinative language, in which meanings are added to root words with prefixes and suffixes. For instance, "the second little naughty red bird" becomes *niizhomiiskobineshensish*. Some prefixes repeat, making a word reduplicative. To say you are really waiting a very long time, you might say *nd'baabaabiinchige*. Words have more vowels, uncommon consonant pairs called clusters, and some letters used in English are never used at all in Anishinaabemowin. There are no *r, l, f,* or *th* sounds in Anishinaabemowin. Elizabeth becomes Ezibet, Margaret is Maaganiit, and oddest of all, Ralph becomes Napa'ii. These are just a few of the structural characteristics that create the sound Erdrich shares through the use of Anishinaabemowin.

Some of the sounds Erdrich uses are Anishinaabe onomatopoeia mimicking their own definition. In *Baptism of Desire*, the poem "Owls" explains the word for "owl" is *gookookoo'oo* and tells us

> not
> even the smallest child loves the gentle sound
> of the word. Because the hairball
> of bones and vole teeth can be hidden
> under snow, to kill the man who walks over it. (9–13)

Other sounds she communicates are interjections that add flavor to any dialect. Characters commonly say *howah* when they are surprised, and old women say *oh yai* or *aaiii* when they are angry. This adds fuel to the fiery debate about whether they are swears in Anishinaabemowin. While it is true that verbs for body parts and sexual acts are not used as exclamations, there are certainly sounds that communicate surprise, anger, or disgust.

Another word with a wide range of variation is *mi'sago, mii sa igo i'iw,* or *mii'iw*. Reading Erdrich's novels, one can learn to recognize this form of voiced punctuation as the end of a sentence or story. Meaning nothing more than "right here, really," it is the marker of ending used after prayers, pleas, and speeches.

The sound of Anishinaabemowin can soothe or frighten. It can flow easily from thought to song, or it can be buried in a past too distant to be voiced. Erdrich varies her presentation of the language throughout her work, but always, she is a novelist with an ear for the sounds of a people and a place. One fine example of her skill is the scene in *The Birchbark House* when Omakayas takes a walk after losing her brother. Tuned to the details of her surroundings, she hears the song of the white-throated sparrows of spring:

> Drowsily, she whistled along with the tiny sparrows. Ingah beebeebee. Ingahbeebeebee. Those sweet, tiny, far-reaching notes were so brave. The little birds called out repeatedly in the cold dawn air, and all of a sudden Omakayas heard something new in their voices. She heard Neewo. She heard her little brother as though he still existed in the world. She heard him tell her to cheer up and live. *I'm all right*, his voice was saying, *I'm in a peaceful place. You can depend on me. I'm always here to help you, my sister.* (238–39)

"Ingah beebeebee, ingahbeebeebee" is a rhythm that could be a riff on the words *n'ga bi bi*, literally, "I will be here, here." The sounds she chooses convey an impression in Anishinaabemowin that echoes a philosophy of place and presence, an epistemology, or way of seeing the world, which is particular to the people who recognize these speech patterns, this *enewewin* (sound of the language).

A second reason Erdrich uses Anishinaabemowin in her stories is to teach readers important definitions and ideas. Sometimes her lessons are overt, while at other times she allows readers to be lost in the narrative, learning easily through the context.

In *Books and Islands in Ojibwe Country*, she explores the term for book itself, *mazina'igan*, which is a recent addition to Anishinaabemowin, related to the noun *mazinapikinigan* (rock painting) and the verb *mazinaadin* (to make an image of someone). Although *Books and Islands* is nonfiction, Erdrich introduces numerous terms in Anishinabemowin and explains their importance and often the etymology, or history of the word and the way it relates to similar terms, as in the connection between the name for sturgeon, *nameh*, which sounds so like the word for the place that fish hides, *nameh* (underneath). At other times, she clarifies the way names grow long or short, using the example of the name shared by her mother and daughter, Nenaa'ikiizhikok. She explains how it was often shortened to Kiizhikok (Sky woman) or Kiizh, which could mean warmth, sky, or place of the *giiziz* (sun).

In *The Birchbark House, The Game of Silence,* and *The Porcupine Year,* Erdrich teaches definitions through context and repetition. Her words are mostly of four types. There are the little in-between words that only use can define: *geget* (sure), *daga* (please), and *ishtay* (wow). She also teaches the verbs that shaped the life of Omakayas, a girl of the 1800s: *aadizookaan* (to tell a story), *bawa'iganakige* (to knock rice), *booni'aa* (leave it alone), *gizhawenimin* (to love someone), and *wiijiw* (to do something with someone). She includes in phrases some of the beginning and end words that can extend and clarify a meaning. At the start of a word, *n* can mean "I or mine," while *g* means "you or yours." Using *daa* at the end of a word means "let's all do it." Lastly, she uses the old names of places and beings—for instance, *Moningwanaykaning* is the Anishinaabe term for what was once known as the Island of the Golden-Breasted Woodpecker and is now called Madeline Island. The fact that her spellings have changed over time is evidence of changing trends in language revitalization and the author's own increasing knowledge of Anishinaabemowin. In Erdrich's life and literature, Anishinaabe is a living language, unlike Latin, which has long been buried in archives and texts and no longer evolves.

Other important definitions include *Gichi Manidoo*, the term for the Creator or Great Mystery, whose name appears in many of her books, including *Jacklight*, where Gichi Manidoo dreams the universe into existence using *aki* (earth), *nibi* (water), *ishkode* (fire), and *noodin* (wind) (83). By contrast, she also introduces readers to the *wiindigoog*, "greedy ones," whose name is connected to the word *wiinigad*, "foul." All cultures create their own demons, and these icy, lake-dwelling western spirits personify the parts of the landscape most frightening to people living in the woodlands surrounding the Great Lakes. By using the Ojibwe words, she transfers these distinctly Anishinaabe concepts to American readers intact, the way they would have been communicated by a native speaker or Anishinaabe storyteller.

In her book *Original Fire*, the poem "Asiniig" introduces two categories of nouns. "Stones are alive," she explains in the epigraph. "They are addressed as grandmothers and grandfathers. The universe began with a conversation between stones." In the poem, stones speak to humans, saying:

> When the original fire which formed us
> subsided,
> we thought of you.
> We allowed you to occur.
> We are still deciding whether that was
> wise. (5–10)

This idea, that some "things" treated as inanimate nouns in English could be the object of complex, animate relationships, is one of the cultural differences documented by Erdrich's use of Anishinaabemowin.

Another important idea related to cultural perspectives is represented by the word *miigwech*. Used fifteen times in three novels, the verb requires the addition of prefixes and suffixes to indicate who is thanking and who is thanked. Most often translated as "thanks," *miigwech* can also mean "you're welcome" and sometimes "amen." To be able to give thanks in Ojibwe implies the knowledge that, in Anishinaabe culture, "you're welcome" is neither welcome nor necessary. To give thanks is enough and should require no additional exchange.

Another reason Erdrich uses Anishinaabe words is to explain the importance of relations. Nanapush speaks of *nindinawemaganidok*, "relatives," in *Tracks*, *Four Souls*, and *The Last Report on the Miracles at Little No Horse*. With this word, he says, "we speak of everything that has existed in time, the known and the unknown, the unseen, the obvious, all that lived before and is living now in the worlds above and below" (*Last Report* 361).

A third reason Erdrich reaches for Anishinaabemowin is to demonstrate through the conversation of her characters the importance of language to identity and continuity. With full phrases and symbolic insertion of one word at a time, Erdrich shows how the language might have worked long ago and how it is fits fully or partially into contemporary culture.

Representations of the past are found in the Birchbark House series, and one of the foundational concepts unfolds when Omakayas says: "*Weendamawashin, daga*, Nokomis . . . tell me a story" (*Birchbark House* 132). The ending on the verb *wiindamaw* is *shin*, a reflexive ending that turns any verb back on the speaker. Anishinaabemowin weaves root verbs through phrases just as Erdrich's characters are woven through time and various narratives. The system of verb conjugation in Anishinaabemowin is as twisted as a strand of DNA, which is perhaps one reason the tangled genealogy of Erdrich's characters never surprises fluent readers. Like transitive animate prefixes and suffixes, her characters reduplicate and reassemble themselves as easily as a story moving from the past into the present. These are the ancient patterns that cling to the nature of a people, defining entire communities and causing dysfunction when suddenly and intentionally suppressed. Students today dedicate time and attention to becoming as proficient in forming verbs as they are at memorizing prayers. Having this alternate means of processing reality is a survival mechanism central to maintaining identity distinct from dominant society.

When contemporary culture has erased fluency, members of Anishinaabe communities decorate their English with as much

Anishinaabemowin as they can learn. One-word answers are often the easiest. Several of Erdrich's characters frequently use *gaawiin* (no), *enya* (yes), and *gego* (don't), and greetings including *ahneen* and *boozhoo*. The simple commands *piindigen* (come in) and *namadabin* (sit down) are used in several books. In *Shadow Tag*, Irene America, an urban, mixed-blood American Indian Movement (AIM) activist, occasionally struggles with being a contemporary American Indian wife and has forgotten most of the Ojibwe language she had once known. Despite this, she remains connected to her linguistic heritage through random phrases such as *geget igo*. Even this limited use of Anishinaabemowin conveys important information about Anishinaabe social behavior. The implication is that full fluency in the language equates with unquestionable identity. Colonization and assimilation have forced the Anishinaabeg to create these abbreviated markers of identity.

The fourth reason Erdrich uses Anishinaabemowin is to locate bridges and barriers. For hundreds of years, the Anishinaabeg, French, and British built bridges by learning one another's languages. Words were traded along with furs, tools, and techniques, exchanged freely and according to mutually established guidelines.

Language can be used to sort people by levels of cultural competency or, perhaps in the case of some of Erdrich's characters, cultural deviousness. When John James Mauser asks Fleur Pillager, "Anishinaabekwe, na?" (Are you an Anishinaabe woman?), he may or may not fully understand all that his question implies (23). Perhaps he did know the paths a Pillager might lead him to, but on the night she intends to kill him, Fleur tosses him a question of her own and is surprised by his answer. Knowing his life depends on seeing the world through her eyes, he replies, "My spirit is meant to be g'dai, your animal to do with as you wish" (*Four Souls* 46). He uses the Anishinaabe term for pet, which is synonymous with heart. His use of her language demonstrates his willingness to submit his worldview to hers, at least for a time and for a reason.

Stepping carefully across cultural bridges, many of Erdrich's characters use Anishinaabemowin to sort listeners into allies or enemies, both inside and outside the Anishishinaabe community. For example, Erdrich uses the particle *geget* (for sure) in three different novels. It functions as a subtle sound-code to determine the knowledge and perspective of a listener. An elder who answers a question with *geget* is understood as fluent and may go on to say more in the language.

Sometimes the most important questions, the most powerful words, are presented first or only in Anishinaabemowin. Consider Anaquot's innocent question directed at the woman she later learns is her lover's wife. "*Aaniin izhinikaazoyan?*" (What are you called?) takes on extra meaning (*Painted Drum* 124). Anaquot did not say, "*gd'shkitoon ina wiindamawinan gdo'nozwin?*" (Can you tell me your name?). Later, she finds out the woman is known as Ziigwan'aage, a name reminiscent of spring floods and the hunger of wolverines, which tells her a great deal about whether she is an ally or an enemy.

Cultural biases are sometimes revealed in untranslated phrases. Characters in *Four Souls* scorn "hilarious chimookomaanag doings" and the "strange frenzy for zhaaginaash stuff" (74, 76). Succumbing to the behavior and marketing of industrial capitalism is seen as negative and reinforced by using ethnic terminology that is clearly Anishinaabe. Unlike the definition of the term used for themselves, "a good human," *chimookomaan* is a military reference to "long knives," or muskets with spear tips, and *zhaaginaash* relates closely to the words for weak and joking.

While Erdrich is of a generation not given a chance to learn Anishinaabemowin as a child, she creates some characters who exercise their linguistic options with great intention. Perhaps the most vocal of these is Nanapush of the Little No Horse Reservation, who often speaks about the power of Anishinaabemowin to connect the people more accurately and fully to their place on land, in the past, and in the present. Conversely, in *Four Souls*, he explains the power of English:

Friends, relatives, nindinawemaganidok, I am Nanapush, witness of disasters, friend of folly, a man of the turtle clan, a son of old Mirage whose great deeds brought our people back to life. I am one hundred percent pure Anishinaabeg and I speak my language and the English both. But today, that English language tastes foul, tastes rancid in my mouth, for it is the language in which we are, as always, deceived. Lies are manufactured in that English language. All the treaties are written in English, are they not? In its wording our land is stolen. All the labels on the whiskey bottles are in English, do you agree? When we drink from the English bottles we piss away our minds. How can we speak English when the truth lies heavy on our Ojibwe tongues? (154)

In the Birchbark House series, Omakayas and her friends come to understand they will need to learn English if they wish to survive in the world that is changing around them. Voices like Nanapush's warn of the need to preserve the perspective of the original language to preserve Anishinaabe identity.

Louise Erdrich brings the stories of one place and one people to life on the page. In doing so, she touches on pan-tribal, even universal subjects, but her tales are made more powerful by the details. She builds her narratives using a distinctly Anishinaabe style and, by echoing traditional patterns, themes, and conscious and subconscious symbols, she contributes to a body of literature distinctly Anishinaabe. Her use of Anishinaabemowin lends veracity to her text and teaches readers that there was, and still is, a highly developed culture of the Great Lakes that cannot be completely melded into the wider landscape of America.

In her books, as is so often true in life, elders return to the "old language." When she begins to live at the Senior Citizens' home, Marie starts speaking Anishinaabemowin again, "falling back through time to the words that Lazarres had used among themselves, shucking off the Kashpaw pride yet holding to the old strengths Rushes Bear had taught her . . . having known how comfortless words of English sounded in her own ears" (*Love Medicine* 263). Although she abandoned the language in her youth, those were times of linguistic and cultural genocide. With citizenship granted in 1924 and gradual—some would say far too gradual—assertion of civil rights for indigenous North Americans, traditions and words are returning. *G'miigwetchwigo Louise, nitaazhibiigeyin, minoanishinaabezhibiiaayin sa. Chipiitzijig miinwaa nijaanisag g'bizindawigoog.* We all thank you, Louise. You write well. Your writing in Anishinaabe is so good. The elders and the children are listening.

Works Cited

Dippie, Brian. *The Vanishing American: White Attitudes and U.S. Indian Policy.* Middletown: Wesleyan UP, 1982.

Erdrich, Louise. *The Antelope Wife.* New York: Harper, 1998.

_____ . *Baptism of Desire.* New York: Harper, 1989.

_____ . *The Beet Queen.* New York: Bantam, 1986.

_____ . *The Bingo Palace.* New York: Harper, 1994.

_____ . *The Birchbark House.* New York: Hyperion, 1999.

_____ . *The Blue Jay's Dance.* New York: Harper, 1995.

_____ . *Books and Islands in Ojibwe Country.* Washington: Natl. Geographic Soc., 2003.

_____ . *Four Souls.* New York: Harper, 2004.

_____ . *The Game of Silence.* New York: Harper, 2005.

_____ . *Jacklight.* New York: Holt, 1984.

_____ . *The Last Report on the Miracles at Little No Horse.* New York: Harper, 2001.

_____ . *Love Medicine.* New York: Harper, 1993.

_____ . *The Master Butchers Singing Club.* New York: Harper, 2003.

_____ . *Original Fire.* New York: Harper, 2003.

_____ . *The Painted Drum.* New York: Harper, 2005.

_____ . *The Plague of Doves.* New York: Harper, 2008.

_____ . *The Porcupine Year.* New York: Harper, 2008.

_____ . *Shadow Tag.* New York: Harper, 2010.

_____ . *Tales of Burning Love.* New York: Harper, 1996.

_____ . *Tracks.* New York: Holt, 1988.

_____ . "Two Languages in Mind, but Just One in the Heart." *New York Times* 22 May 2000: E2.

"Our Story." *Birchkbark Books.* Birchbark Books, 2009. Web. 13 Apr. 2012.

The Relentless Throat Call: Louise Erdrich and Poetic Voice _____

Dean Rader

Most readers of this volume probably know about Louise Erdrich and her reputation as a prolific and profound fiction writer and may even be doing research on *Love Medicine* or *Tracks* for a critical paper. I want to invite readers to consider reading and writing about Erdrich's *poetry*. Of course, her novels are influential and provocative and gorgeous, but I would argue that her ability to describe a scene, detail a landscape, or profile a character comes from her interest in the lyric poem and her facility with poetic craft. While she is better known for her fiction, Erdrich has published three collections of poetry over twenty years and has authored some of the most important poems by any Native writer. This essay gives a brief timeline of Erdrich's underappreciated but significant poetic career and then attempts to make sense of her poetry by considering it in terms of persona and poetic voice.

Tracing Erdrich's Poetic Production

Like Joy Harjo, Simon Ortiz, and Leslie Marmon Silko, Erdrich established herself as a literary force in the 1980s. In fact, what many lovers of her fiction do not know is that her first book of prose, *Love Medicine*, appeared the same year as her first book of poetry, *Jacklight* (1984). Just as *Love Medicine* is one of the most important books of Native fiction, so too is *Jacklight* one of the most important books of Native poetry. Both books are written in a voice that is both elegiac and celebratory, and both consider love as a possible cure, a medicine, for the chronic maladies of the Ojibwes. *Jacklight*, however, is more overtly political, as it takes on the issue of race in more specific ways. Indeed, the temptation to reimagine or reinvent the contact zone of Indians and white settlers became a major trope of Indian poetry in the 1980s and 1990s. That poetic desire to rewrite history, to reframe through language and figuration of past transgressions, underpins much of her poetry.

Organized into four sections ("Runaways," "Hunters," "The Butcher's Wife," and "Myths"), *Jacklight* contains forty poems, most of which focus on the themes suggestive of the sections in which they appear. The only poem not to appear in one of these sections is the title poem, which begins the book set off from the rest in its own self-titled segment—a kind of proem or preface. The other sections tend to explore Native issues, particularly dealing with how to heal divisive relationships between whites and Natives, Natives and the land, and the realities of the present and the constant presence of the past. "The *Jacklight* poems," Alan Shucard observes, "tend to fall into five overlapping thematic categories: poems of Indian heritage in conflict with the dominant white culture; poems of sisterhood and family; love poems; poems peopled with the shadows of figures from her past; and mythic poems, which draw upon Native American myths and the habit of mythmaking" (109). Lyrics about Ojibwe stories and traditions merge with others that foreground non-Native figures such as Mary Rowlandson and John Wayne. Erdrich is interested in myths of all kinds—whether the cultural mythologies of Wayne and Rowlandson or the genre of American Indian myths. Indeed, the final section of *Jacklight*, entitled "Myths," consists of prose poems about the trickster figure Potchikoo, which themselves read as mini-myths. They are funny, sexual, and wildly inventive.

In 1986, Erdrich confessed that she was not going to publish any more poems. She was feeling her poetry was becoming too "personal," too intimate, and she seems to have been having some anxiety about this merging of private literary production and personal emotion. However, a few years later, her second collection of poems, *Baptism of Desire*, appeared. While it is not quite accurate to say that *Baptism of Desire* feels like it was written by a completely different person, it is fair to acknowledge how distinct the two books feel from each other. It is easy to see, for example, why Erdrich was reluctant to publish many of the poems that appear in her second collection. They are intimate, private, and perhaps for many, surprisingly *Catholic*. *Jacklight* gave some nods in this direction, but it situates itself in a specific (Ojibwe) context and makes its central themes those of Native America. In contrast, *Baptism of Desire* features more first-person poems and fewer poems that engage overtly Native themes. Much more prominent are poems that engage pregnancy, motherhood, faith, and the holy sacraments. Here, Ojibwe mythology gives way to Christian mythology, as the poet tries to navigate through mysterious interior landscapes.

Upon publication, the book received warm but meager reception, garnering only a small handful of reviews. For many reviewers, *Baptism of Desire* may have felt less revolutionary than *Jacklight* or at least more intimate. In her review, Doris Earnshaw highlights the poems' sexuality and "celebration of eros," arguing ultimately that "Erdrich is a rare phenomenon, a poet bridging several cultures who sings lovingly of her family life" (645). This claim may be true, though I wonder if this domestic reading of her work is a result of her gender. It is hard to imagine, for example, a reviewer writing of a male poet that his poems "sing lovingly of *his* family life." Then again, Erdrich herself genders these poems rather dramatically, foregrounding pregnancy and often making metaphorical connections between the speaker and the biblical figures of Eve and Mary.

In 2003, over a decade later, Erdrich released a beguiling collection of poems entitled *Original Fire: Selected and New Poems*, which collects and reorganizes most of the poems from her first two books and features a great deal of new material. Grouped thematically, the poems of *Original Fire* function as a map of Erdrich's poetics, revealing commonalities in both subject and chronology. Reading these new poems so many years after *Jacklight* and *Baptism of Desire*, it is fascinating to see how the poet's way of seeing the world has evolved. Many of the poems explore the many ways (both positively and negatively) the Ojibwe and Catholic spheres merge, such as in the fantastic poem "Rez Litany." The obsession with pregnancy that permeates *Baptism of Desire* is replaced by a series of poems on birthing and motherhood. The poet comes full circle.

Poetic Voice: Persona and Narrative

Many of the reviews of Erdrich's books call attention to her "narrative poems," so it is useful to unpack this term, as it provides a good entrée into understanding how her poems work. A narrative poem is simply a poem that tells a story. In general, it has a plot, and it often features a main character that may or may not be the poet. Classic narrative poems include Homer's *Odyssey* and Robert Frost's "Stopping by Woods on a Snowy Evening." Narrative poems tend to be more about story, plot, and character and less about figurative language, musicality, and formal experimentation, though some of the best narrative poems are also quite formal. In general, though, narrative poetry attempts to marry the best aspects of epic poetry (story, plot) with the best features of lyric poetry (compression, musical language).

Narrative poetry can be a particularly salient poetic form for Native writers because it overlaps so well with oral storytelling traditions. Part of the force of the narrative poem is its ability to capture utterance, what theorist J. L. Austin calls "performative utterances," which he describes as "statements which themselves accomplish the acts to which they refer" (qtd. in Culler 127). Prayers, sacred songs, and even incantatory language carry with them the power to alter perception and human understanding. The history and culture of narrative poetry is not quite as transformative, but, like oral narratives, it shares an emphasis on message and loaded language.

While reviewers have noted Erdrich's penchant for narrative, I have yet to come across any reading of her work that highlights her fondness for the persona poem. Persona poems, also sometimes called dramatic monologues, are poems spoken in the voice of a character that is not the author. Hugh Holman and William Harmon define a dramatic monologue as a poem in which the "character is speaking to an identifiable but silent listener at a dramatic moment in the speaker's life" (158). Probably the most famous persona poem in English, Robert Browning's "My Last Duchess," is spoken in the voice of the Duke of Ferrara. Persona poems skew toward the first person, and often they are themselves narrative poems—small monologues in which the speaker tells the audience something about himself. These poems can also be rather confessional in nature. Such gestures create intimacy and can narrow the gap between poet and audience. Many of Erdrich's most famous poems are persona poems, including "Captivity," which is spoken in the voice of Mary Rowlandson, and "Dear John Wayne," spoken, at times, in the voice of Wayne.

Fans of Erdrich's fiction will recognize her gift for storytelling and dialogue in these poems. With mini-plots and developed characters, the experience of reading these poems mirrors that of reading fiction. An interesting dilemma emerges, though, in some of the pieces in *Baptism of Desire* and *Original Fire*. In these poems in which no specific character is identified, readers tend to wonder if the speaker is Erdrich or some persona. When Erdrich writes "I," does she mean "Louise Erdrich the actual human being," or does she mean "Louise Erdrich 'the poet'"? The distinction is important.

Complicating this already complicated issue is the notion of race. Most readers tend to assume that texts written in the first person by people of color, and particularly those penned by Native authors, are narratives of actual events. Sherman Alexie writes about this phenomenon in his autobiographical essay "The Unauthorized Autobiography of Me," going so far as to complain how frequently readers (read: non-Native readers) assume the stories in his fiction and poetry are autobiography rather than literature. Since there are some factual elements in Erdrich's poems and there are many poems about motherhood (and Erdrich is a mother), there is evidence to suggest that the gap between the author's voice and the voice of the poet's persona might be very slight indeed.

For poets who, like Erdrich, rely on narrative and persona, it is helpful to read their poems through the lens of poetic voice. "Poetic voice" is hard to define, though many have tried. In a sort of how-to article for *Writer's Digest*, Laurie Zuppan correctly notes that poetic voice "has to do with the distinctive characteristics of a particular poet's work" and "is rooted in the use and repetition of specific elements—technical elements that make a poem recognizable as belonging to one poet . . . grammar and syntax, form, music, subject matter and, last, magic— the elusive connection between a reader and a poet that transcends the work." This last part—the connection between writer and reader—is profoundly important. It can determine whether someone responds to a particular work. In his lengthy study of voice, Leslie Edgerton makes the unusual but compelling argument that "readers select certain authors to read in much the same way they select their personal friends: on the basis of the 'voice' (personality) of that person" (4). So, voice is also connected to personality, both of the author and of the characters she creates.

When making sense of Erdrich's poetry then, it is helpful to keep in mind these elements of voice and personality. How would the voice of the speaker be characterized? Is it angry? Friendly? Funny? Anguished? Just as we interpret a friend's feelings based on how he might talk, so too can we begin to interpret a poem based on how it talks to us. The remainder of this essay will look at the ways Erdrich's poems talk to the reader and how their many voices help the reader enter into conversation with them.

Poetic Voice: *Jacklight*

Jacklight is a study in the persona poem. I know of few collections of poems in which there are more distinct voices than this one. The opening poem of the collection, its title poem, "Jacklight," prepares us for the ambiguity and diversity that lies ahead. Written in a first-person *plural* point-of-view, the reader is immediately put on edge and pulled in from the opening word:

> We have come to the edge of the woods,
> out of brown grass where we slept, unseen,
> out of knotted twigs, out of leaves creaked shut,
> out of hiding. (1–4)

Who is this "we"? The speaker and reader? A family? A herd? A tribe? Is the persona speaking in literal or metaphorical terms?

These are all key questions to ask, even if they do not yield easy answers. Working through the remainder of the poem, we come across the following lines in the fourth stanza: "We smell the raw steel of their gun barrels, / mink oil on leather, their tongues of sour barley. / We smell their mothers buried chin-deep in wet dirt" (16–18). The references to guns, alcohol, and trapping help us discern the poem is probably being spoken by a group of Natives, perhaps a tribe, perhaps a family. This remains unclear, but the details of the poem are less important than the address—the fact that the speaker(s) are talking directly to the reader.

We might describe the tone as direct and inclusive. The Natives are explaining a reality to us (not *them*); so in the us-versus-them dichotomy, we are part of the "us." The manner in which this information comes to us, though, is slightly different than we ourselves would probably express it. The poem features a great deal of repetition (note the anaphora of "out of") and mythical language. To be sure, we are supposed to identify these poetic elements with the speakers and their values rather than the white settlers with their guns and "minds like silver hammers" (25–26). Thus, the final stanza suggests that it is "their" turn to follow the Natives and, in so doing, are likely to get lost. While we may become a little lost in the poem, it is the poem's voice that helps us locate where we are and find our way.

Another element of poetic voice worth mentioning here is the poem's participation in the larger body of American poetic speaking. The final lines of the poem ("how deep the woods are and lightless. / How deep the woods are" [37–38]) invoke and even reference one of the most famous American poems, Robert Frost's "Stopping By Woods on a Snowy Evening." Note how similar the closing lines in Erdrich's poems are to Frost's "The woods are lovely, dark and deep" (13). What is amazing about "Jacklight" is how it simultaneously enacts the two personas of Indians and Robert Frost's famous speaker. In one poem we find, interconnected, the most unlikely pair: the voices of Indians and what is probably the most canonical American poem.

Another poem that participates in American canonicity is the famous "Dear John Wayne." Also written in the first-person plural, the "we" of this poem is slightly different from that in "Jacklight." Where "Jacklight" obviously takes place in the historical past before Erdrich was born, the setting of "Dear John Wayne" takes place during Erdrich's lifetime and could very well be at least partially autobiographical:

> August and the drive-in picture is packed.
> We lounge on the hood of the Pontiac
> surrounded by the slow-burning spirals they sell
> at the window, to vanquish the hordes of mosquitos.
> Nothing works. They break through the smoke screen for
> blood. (1–5)

Our tendency is to read the "we" in this poem as Erdrich and her friends and the "they" not as Euro-American settlers, but the nameless workers in the concession stand at the drive-in theater.

Where the poem gets tricky is when it incorporates into its monologue other elements of dialogue. Interspersed throughout the poem are curious lines in italics, clearly intended to be "spoken" lines of dialogue. Spoken by whom, though, is the question:

> His face moves over us,
> a thick cloud of vengeance, pitted
> like the land that was once flesh. Each rut,
> each scar makes a promise: *It is*
> *not over, this fight, not as long as you resist.*
> *Everything we see belongs to us.* (18–23)

Typically, italics in a poem indicate emphasis or dialogue. Here, it might be a little of both, but other elements of the poem (such as the phrase "makes a promise" and the colon) suggest we are to read these as spoken lines. What is puzzling is the absence of any obvious person to speak these passages. The first instance seems to be spoken by "ruts" and "scars" on John Wayne's face to the Indians who are watching the film. It is a bit odd to personify facial features, but it is strangely effective. The second italicizes passage indicates a different speaker because that voice speaks back to Wayne, again, in the first-person plural. I have never known if the speaker of these two sentences is the same "person" who narrates "Dear John Wayne" or if it is some different actor on the stage of the poem.

My own reading is that there are three distinct personas at work here. The main persona is the poem's speaker, which is probably "Louise Erdrich." Her narrative is interrupted by a second voice, which is the voice of Wayne. He not only speaks the italicized lines above, but these from the poem's final stanza: "*Come on, boys, we got them / where we want them, drunk, running. / They'll give us what we want, what we need*" (38–40). This mini-monologue works as a follow-up to the previous statement of removal and conquest and stands for the values of Wayne and the cowboy West. The third persona, I am less certain of, in part, because there are only two sentences (those in the third excerpted stanza above). Nonetheless, the direct address to Wayne makes me think this persona is some omniscient third-person plural community (perhaps the Ojibwes, perhaps Erdrich's specific tribe, perhaps all indigenous peoples) that speaks as a collective back to Wayne in a moment of rebuttal, defiance.

The personas are important in "Dear John Wayne" because they serve as springboards for other interesting work the poem does. For example, the poem features a unique apostrophe, a moment when the "speaker directly and often emotionally addresses a person who is dead or otherwise not physically present" (Murfin and Ray 21). What makes this apostrophe unique is Erdrich's use of canon Euro-American literary history to undercut the deceased Wayne, an icon of Euro-American culture. In a similar fashion, Erdrich also plays with the conventions of the dramatic monologue: "Dear John Wayne" is not just a persona poem but a multiple-persona poem containing both monologue and dialogue. Erdrich thereby fuses Native orality with non-Native poetics in a singularly subversive way, employing established Western literary conventions to challenge the cultural machinery that produces such icons as John Wayne.

Other persona poems, including "Captivity," "The King of Owls," "Windigo," and "The Strange People," operate somewhat more conventionally and straightforwardly. The poems are written in the first person, but the voice speaking the poem is that of another being. I say "being" and not "person" because, at times, it is unclear what we are hearing, as in the case of "The Strange People," which begins: "All night I am the doe, breathing / his name in a frozen field" (1–2). Similarly, in "Windigo," the speaker seems not quite human. An epigraph tells us that a windigo is "a flesh-eating, wintry demon with a man buried deep inside of it" (79), a terrifying concept, especially given the opening stanza:

> You knew I was coming for you, little one,
> when the kettle jumped into the fire.
> Towels flapped on the hooks,
> and the dog crept off, groaning,
> to the deepest part of the woods. (1–5)

Not too many contemporary poems can boast a first line like this one, in part because few poets could embody such bizarre figures without making the poems seem hopelessly contrived. These poems work because they straddle the fine line between human and nonhuman. They also leave a bit to the imagination. The intense subjectivity of the poems prohibits us from seeing the creatures from the outside. Also, as readers, we are the addressees—the speakers are speaking to us, so somehow we become implicated in this liminal space between worlds.

"The King of Owls" and "Captivity" also stretch the persona poem in provocative ways. The former is written from the perspective of

King Charles VI of France, while the latter, one of Erdrich's most taught and most anthologized poems, comes to us across the centuries in the voice of America's most famous captive, Mary Rowlandson. Not only do the voices of these two poems feel radically different from each other but even from the other voices in *Jacklight*'s many persona poems. King Charles, supposedly insane, begins his monologue, "They say I am excitable! / How could I not scream!" (1–2). Contrast that to Rowlandson's soft, almost contemplative tone:

> One night
> he killed a deer with a young one in her
> and gave me to eat of the fawn.
> It was so tender,
> the bones like the stems of flowers, . . . (23–27)

Functioning as a kind of counternarrative to the "real" narrative, this smart revisionist lyric offers a different perspective on this historical experience, even going so far as to suggest a sexual encounter between Rowlandson and her Native captor.

By taking on the voices of Rowlandson and King Charles, Erdrich narrativizes, fictionalizes, and characterizes the poetic moment. These new versions of old events ask the reader to reconsider how she has interpreted historical data, an interesting and important point because the "fiction" of the poems questions the reliability of historical "fact." What if Rowlandson's *actual* experience is closer to the Erdrich poem than her published narrative describes? How do we know what King Charles's voice—mad or not—actually sounded like? To what degree is interpretation also invention?

These poems also do critical work in the area of race studies. That a Native poet could inhabit the voice of a Euro-American woman and a French king calls attention to assumptions we make about identity and the lyric "I." This is particularly the case for the poems in "The Butcher's Wife" section, Erdrich's most interesting persona poem sequence.

In this cycle, Erdrich tries on the identity of Mary Kröger, a German American widow of a butcher who lived on the northern plains around the turn of the twentieth century. Through an exploration of small-town politics, lust, love lost and love sought, guilt, desire, and Catholicism, Erdrich writes her way into the daily realities of her Teutonic past. It becomes a fascinating project then to compare the history-based narrative of Mary Rowlandson to that of "Indian Boarding School: The Runaways." Is Erdrich's shift from non-Native to Native persona convincing? Why might she want to embody both ethnicities? Ultimately, it is this willingness to make *Jacklight* multiperspectivist that gives the book its broad appeal and its unique voice. It is also what makes it a particularly salient book of poems for looking closely at relations between Indians and non-Indians.

Poetic Voice: *Baptism of Desire*

Baptism of Desire never got the popular or critical traction enjoyed by *Jacklight*, in part for the same reasons the Mary Kröger sequence is overlooked. The Native-focused poems of *Jacklight* fit more easily into assumptions about what "Native American writing" is or should be, whereas poems from a Euro-American's perspective might not. Similarly, *Baptism of Desire* eschews mythological and historical content in favor of religious and spiritual concerns—notably Catholicism and its sacraments. One wonders if the reception of the book would have been different had she explored Ojibwe religious practices or New Age shamanistic spirituality rather than the less exotic and less politically correct Christian theology and hierarchy. Nevertheless, the Catholic-centric trajectory makes for some compelling reading, especially if considered through the lens of persona and poetic voice.

Take, for example, the distinctions between parts 1 and 2 versus those in part 5. The former is replete with poems written in various personas, while the latter feels like confessions from Erdrich herself. In both cases, the author tries on personas, but to be sure, the gap between author and persona is wider in the first two sections than in part 5. No one could read the intensely personal poems of that final section and *not* ask: Is the speaker of this poem Louise Erdrich?

That said, the emotions expressed in that section overlap a great deal with those expressed early in *Baptism of Desire*. Both poems evoke a sense of exploration. They are poems shrouded in darkness but seeking light. They are poems of revelation. In the four-part poem "Saint Claire," written in the voice of Claire, the speaker elucidates this very feeling when describing a sermon by Saint Francis of Assisi:

> from each widening ring a wave,
> from the waves a sea that covered the moon.
> So I was seized in total night
> and I abandoned myself in his garment
> like a fish in a net . . . (5–9)

Similarly, the following poem, "Avila," spoken from the perspective of Teresa of Avila's brother, begins with the metaphor of darkness and light: "Sister, do you remember our cave of stones, / how we entered from the white heat of afternoons, / chewed seeds, and plotted one martyrdom" (1–3). In both poems, there is a movement from darkness to light, from confusion to clarity; yet each poem retains its own specific historical characteristic. "The Visit" is a fine example of this technique. Erdrich is the author, but Mary, the mother of Jesus, is the speaker, trying to put into words the experience of the "visit" from God that left her both perplexed and pregnant:

> It was not love. No flowers or ripened figs
> were in his hands, no words
> in his mouth. There was no body
> to obstruct us from each other. (1–4)

It takes courage to enter the psyche of the mother of God. It takes courage both emotionally and poetically. To let your voice become the voice of Mary is to merge the mythical with the maternal, the poetic with the prophetic.

However, some critics claim the poetic persona is just the opposite. For them, the mask of the persona separates author and reader. They see it as a kind of costume, a performance that inhibits the reader by allowing the poet to siphon her own emotional energy into another. In *Baptism of Desire*, something else is happening, though. We see the fiction writer's desire to inhabit another being and to speak in the voice of another character, but we also see the lyric poet's desire to figure the self in language's fire.

These are the poems of the final section of *Baptism of Desire*, those written during periods of pregnancy-induced insomnia. Consider these lines from "The Fence," the opening poem of part 5:

> I'm wild for everything.
> My body is a golden armor around my unborn child's body,
> and I'll die happy, here on the ground. (3–5)

And this section from "Sunflowers":

> When I walk into their bedroom at night
> their cries fill my own mouth
> so full of accurate misery. (1–3)

Without question, the "I" speakers in these poems are different from those in previous selections from this book. The reader gets the sense that these children are not historical inventions or mythological creations, but rather Erdrich's own. Similarly, these feel like Erdrich's own emotions and reactions, though again, slightly figured to endow the lyric moment with metaphorical weight. These poems exist somewhere in the meeting place between everyday experience and poetic language. It is the persona that gives them both power and realism.

The final poem of the collection, "The Ritual," merges the historical with the personal and serves as a fine punctuation point to the collection. Drawing on the language and symbolism of Native idioms ("In the hour of the wolf, the hour of the horn"), Erdrich manages to fuse the mythical and the maternal:

> I bind the net beneath you with the tendons of my wrist.
> I call the guardian owl
> who terrifies harm. I hold the sheaf
> of lucky flowers to your forehead. (42–46)

In so doing, she writes a new kind of Native American poetry—one that maps its own landscapes on its own terms. The poet refuses to choose between Ojibwe and German, between traditional spirituality and Catholicism. She dwells in all of them, just as she dwells in each of her characters. We hear everything in her voice.

Poetic Voice: *Original Fire*

The note of collation with which Erdrich ends *Baptism of Desire* pervades *Original Fire*. The poet Donna Seaman praises Erdrich's ability to collapse many things into her work: "Erdrich grapples with both Native American and Christian beliefs, and the conflicts ignited by the friction between them, in poems of sweet gratitude, voluptuous ecstasy, cutting satire, seething grief, and fiery resolve" (195). A fine book, it provides connective tissue to a wonderful body of work.

Part of what makes the project interesting is how Erdrich recasts her own work. Except for the opening section, entitled "Jacklight," she does away with chronological organization and groups the poems by theme. So, the Potchikoo prose poems from both books are grouped together, as are the Mary Kröger poems. This latter section, called "The Butcher's Wife," is a kind of mini-version of Erdrich's novel *The Master Butchers Singing Club*. Reading the poems this way demonstrates not just how her two books of verse flow in and out of each other, but also how her books of poems and her novels merge. Nanapush appears in the Potchikoo poems, and the themes of *The Bingo Palace* run through "Rez Litany." The interplay of Ojibwe daily realities and the demands of the Catholic Church that fuel *The Last Report on the Miracles of Little No Horse* are even more prevalent in *Original Fire*.

In the book's signature poem, "Rez Litany," Erdrich juxtaposes the traditional Catholic litany with her own litany of Native transgressions. Free of stanzas, this poem appears in stichic verse, which accentuates its frenetic run-on pace:

> Saint Quantum, Martyr of Blood
> and Holy Protector of the Tribal Rolls,
> assist us in the final shredding which shall proceed
> on the Day of Judgment so we may all rain down
> in a blizzard of bum pull tabs
> and unchosen lottery tickets. . . . (30–36)

A poetic hagiographer, Erdrich invents her own saints (Pyromane, Quantum) with dark humor and righteous indignation in an attempt to shake Native America and white America out of their slumber regarding Native issues. Is Erdrich saying it would take a miracle to "save" the reservations? By trying on the voice of a Catholic priest saying mass, Erdrich endows this poem with unusual desperation. It sounds like a holy war.

The final section of *Original Fire*, entitled "Original Fire," picks up where *Baptism of Desire* leaves off by alternating among personas. One poem, "Sorrows of the Frog Woman," explores the transformative role of becoming a woman and mother through the voice of the mythical Ojibwe Frog Woman, while "Advice to Myself," a few pages later, sounds very much like a list a harried, overworked Erdrich might make. "Asiniig," the last poem of the book is a five-part meditation on the journey from birth to infinity. The epigraph to this poem tells the reader that *asin* means "stone" in the Ojibwe language and that the universe began with a conversation between two stones. That aspect of communication, of talking, of conversing, connects each of the sections of the poem. It also connects each of Erdrich's books because it helps put the speaking voice of the persona into perspective. The many voices are a way to communicate about many things to many people. Erdrich writes in the final lyric "you had best learn / how to speak to us now / without the use of signs" (sec. 6, lines 6–8). Ultimately, as in *Jacklight* and *Baptism of Desire*, the voices in these poems not only help teach us how to speak, but they also teach us how to listen.

Works Cited

Alexie, Sherman. "The Unauthorized Autobiography of Me." *New West Reader: Essays on an Ever-Evolving Frontier*. Ed. Philip Connors. New York: Avalon, 2005. 265–79.

Culler, Jonathan. *Structuralist Poetics*. Ithaca: Cornell UP, 1975.

Earnshaw, Doris. Rev. of *Baptism of Desire*, by Louise Erdrich. *World Literature Today* 64.4 (1990): 645.

Edgerton, Leslie. *Finding Your Voice: How To Put Personality in Your Writing*. Cincinnati: Writer's Digest, 2003.

Erdrich, Louise. *Baptism of Fire*. New York: Harper, 1989.

_____. *Jacklight*. New York: Holt, 1984.

_____. *Original Fire: New and Selected Poems*. New York: Harper, 2003.

Frost, Robert. "Stopping By Woods on a Snowy Evening." *Robert Frost's Poems*. Ed. Louis Untermeyer. New York: St. Martin's, 2002.

Holman, C. Hugh, and William Harmon. *A Handbook to Literature*. 5th ed. New York: Macmillan, 1986.

Murfin, Ross, and Supryia M. Ray. *The Bedford Glossary of Critical and Literary Terms*. Boston: Bedford, 1997.

Seaman, Donna. "*Original Fire: Selected and New Poems*." *Booklist* 15 Sept. 2003: 195.

Shucard, Alan. "Erdrich, (Karen) Louise." *Contemporary Women Poets*. Ed. Pamela L. Shelton. Detroit: St. James, 1998. 109–10.

Zuppan, Leslie. "Find Your Poetic Voice." *Writer's Digest*. F+W Media, 11 Feb. 2008. Web. 3 Apr. 2012.

Relative Identities: Connecting Chance and Continuance in *Love Medicine*_____

Jill Doerfler

"I like the deuce wild. I like that puny card becoming strategy." (348)
"Right and wrong were shades of meaning, not sides of a coin." (76)

Love Medicine is a dramatic soap opera–like tale of life on a fictional Anishinaabe (Chippewa/Ojibwe) reservation in North Dakota. The characters are both larger than life and entirely relatable. Just when one thread of the story seems to draw to a conclusion, another thread becomes increasingly tangled. When I read *Love Medicine* for the first time, I was struck by the diverse perspectives that Erdrich gave readers. I saw a novel that offered the reader a deep understanding of the complexity of Anishinaabe families. As scholar Greg Sarris has observed, the novel is about:

> Families bickering. Families arguing amongst themselves, drawing lines, maintaining old boundaries. Who is in. Who is not. Gossip. Jealousy. Drinking. Love. The ties that bind. The very human need to belong, to be worthy and valued. Families. Who is Indian. Who is not. Families bound by history and blood. (181)

Families have formed the very heart of Anishinaabe culture since time immemorial. Erdrich does not provide a romantic tale where everyone gets along; she is not afraid to show the messiness and, in doing so, gives readers a chance to see the Anishinaabeg as human.

Louise Erdrich's first novel, *Love Medicine*, was published in 1984; a revised and expanded version was published in 1993.[1] She revised the novel again in 2009. The 1993 version included four new chapters as well as a new section in "The Beads." In the 2009 version, Erdrich removed the chapter "Lyman's Luck" and moved "The Tomahawk Factory" to the P. S. portion of the edition. As Erdrich notes in the 2009 edition, she made these changes because she felt that they "interrupted the flow of the final quarter" (5–6). Each version of *Love Medicine* is unique, and all are equally important. Readers who read the different versions will gain important understandings about the textual history of the book, obtain insights into the complexity of the characters, and find their personal favorite. This essay focuses on the 1993 edition, and all citations hereafter refer to that edition.

The novel is set on a fictional reservation in North Dakota and covers a time span of about fifty years (1934–84). In an interview with Malcolm Jones, Erdrich explained that the novel was influenced by traditional Anishinaabe storytelling techniques, specifically the tradition of a cycle of stories focused on a central subject. This can make the novel a challenging read because readers are required to look for the "big picture" and to see the meticulously interwoven connections that hold the novel together. Another challenge to readers, as argued by Kathleen Sands, is that "there is a sort of double-think demanded by Erdrich. The incidents of the novel must be carried in the reader's mind, constantly reshuffled and reinterpreted as new events are revealed and the narrative biases of each character are exposed" (39). By providing multiple perspectives on the same event, Erdrich shows readers that there is not just one Anishinaabe perspective but many. Readers understand that there are not only divisions within Anishinaabe tribes/ nations but even within families.

It is worth noting that some have misread *Love Medicine* as a negative portrayal of the Anishinaabeg (Chavkin 91–92). This misreading stems from the images of Native peoples as vanishing victims doomed to lose their culture that predominate in popular American culture (Peterson 162–63). In fact, the characters in *Love Medicine* maintain their cultural traditions and values. In the Anishinaabe tradition, there are Seven Teachings, which were a gift from the Seven Grandfathers. These teachings are honesty, love, courage, truth, wisdom, humility, and respect, and are meant to guide Anishinaabe life. While the characters in *Love Medicine* neither lead perfect lives nor adhere perfectly to these teachings, the reader does see the characters practicing them again and again in the text. It can be difficult for non-Anishinaabeg (or non-Indians) to "see" Anishinaabe culture within the text because they do not know what it looks like. Again, the prevalence of stereotypes clouds the ability of non-Indians (and to some extent, Indians) to see contemporary Anishinaabeg as real.

Erdrich creates a rich and large cast of characters, no fewer than nine of which narrate chapters or parts of chapters. These characters are connected through an intricate web of relationships. The entangled generations of the Nanapushes, Lamartines, Kashpaws, Lazarres, and Morrisseys love, hate, fight, form alliances, laugh, gossip, and live. Their endurance and continuance is a significant challenge to the popular image of the vanishing Indian. Through encounters, both chance and conspired, they form a tribe/nation with a complex history of deep ties. Their individual stories become family stories, which then become the story of the entire nation.

Erdrich, like other American Indian writers, is stuck with a series of bad options: If her characters are alcoholics or welfare recipients, she will be critiqued for fulfilling negative stereotypes, but the characters cannot fit the romantic savage stereotype either, lest she be challenged for creating a narrative too far removed from the real experiences of the Anishinaabeg. Erdrich gives the reader a wide variety of characters that are nearly all Anishinaabe; some of them readers will love, some readers will hate, and some readers will love to hate. King Kashpaw is perhaps the most unsympathetic character. Some might say he fulfills negative stereotypes about American Indians, and, in fact, I would agree. Yet, King is a valuable character because his presence destroys some of the popular mystical romanticism that surrounds Indians. King reflects familial legacies, allowing readers sees how domestic violence passes from one generation to the next, which is all too common in contemporary life.

Erdrich's fully developed characters are liberated from traditional one-dimensional stereotypes of American Indians. As Allan Chavkin has observed, "In contrast to the ubiquitous stereotypes of Indians in film, television, and popular culture, she presents them in all their complexity and reveals their essential humanity" (2). Some characters, such as Marie and Lipsha, struggle with their identity, but they confront those questions and come to their own understanding of who they are. All readers can identify with the challenge of understanding their own family history and how it has shaped who they have become. Erdrich successfully balances a universal relatability with a distinct Anishinaabe foundation. The characters are solidly grounded in both strong cultural traditions and the land. Readers are forced to confront the fact that Anishinaabe people are diverse, dynamic, and complex, dealing with a variety of issues, including suicide, domestic abuse, marriage, love, sex, death, assimilation, political activism, imprisonment, parenting, gambling, identity crises, business ventures, and post-traumatic stress disorder (PTSD). "Traditionals," urban Indians, tribal elders, veterans, opportunists, bachelors, philanderers, tricksters, mothers, fathers, nephews, grandmothers, lovers—all figure among the major characters in *Love Medicine*.

In the remainder of this chapter, I will explore the themes of chance and continuance. I will examine some of the many chance encounters in the novel, the characters' reactions to these chances, and the effects on both the characters and their families. Despite being faced with formidable challenges, the characters demonstrate endurance and resiliency. Continuance includes an examination of how the characters defy terminal stereotypes and participate in the construction of a diversity of contemporary Anishinaabe identities.

Chance affects the lives of all the characters. The *Merriam-Webster Dictionary* defines "chance" as "something that happens unpredictably without discernible human intention or observable cause" and "the assumed impersonal purposeless determiner of unaccountable happenings." Chance has long played an important role in Anishinaabe culture. Historically, the Anishinaabeg used games of chance as a means to redistribute wealth. Lyman describes chance as a "kind of an old-time thing" (326). It is important to note that chance is not always entirely without human interference, and people can "take" a chance that is offered or choose not to participate. What people choose to do with chance makes the difference. Luck, which also plays in role in *Love Medicine*, is often seen as an outcome of chance. The characters in *Love Medicine* encounter chance time and again.

Continuance is an important theme in *Love Medicine*. According to *Merriam-Webster*, "continuance" is not only "continuation" but also "the quality of enduring" and "an adjournment of a court case to a future day." Thus, continuance can, at times, be a form of putting something on hold to be dealt with and resolved at a later time. While Erdrich gives readers resolution to some of the issues in *Love Medicine*, the reader is left with questions that are answered in *Tracks*, *The Bingo Palace*, and other novels. As already mentioned, some readers have misunderstood the text as one of victimization, but the Anishinaabeg in *Love Medicine* are not tragic, doomed victims. Instead, they endure though difficult challenges. They take chances and participate in the modern world, but they do not assimilate. Despite the loss of June, Henry Junior, and much of their land base, the individuals, families, and tribe/nation continue. For hundreds of years, Americans have been expecting that American Indians will disappear, that they cannot adapt without fully assimilating and losing their identity. Erdrich presents readers with many characters who successfully create new generations and adapt while maintaining strong Anishinaabe identities.

Indeed, *Love Medicine* begins with chance and choice. June Morrissey enters a bar and, after eating several Easter eggs, decides to take a chance with the man at the bar: "She had a feeling. The eggs were lucky. . . . He could be different" (3). June leaves with the man and, after a failed sexual encounter, decides to walk "home." Erdrich describes June's death as birth. When June exits the pick-up, "it was a shock like being born" (5). The snow starts, and June continues her journey, "the snow fell deeper . . . than it had in forty years, but June walked over it like water and came home" (7). June decides to commit suicide on Easter Sunday, a significant Christian holiday. There are several connections to Jesus in this scene. Jesus walked on water, and the phrase "walk on water" is sometimes used to reference the completion of tasks that were thought to be impossible. June walks over the snow like water and is reborn or resurrected, beginning a new life in the next world. In Christianity, Jesus rises from the dead on Easter Sunday, his resurrection meant to "save" all Christians. These connections lead to the question: Is June's death a form of salvation? There is no definitive answer, but perhaps it is the ultimate escape from, as readers learn later in the novel, a life filled with disappointment and unhappiness.[2]

There are several possible interpretations of June's suicide. Erdrich highlights both the fragility of life as well as the mystery of death. Erdrich's use of eggs in the scene is significant and provides some metaphoric insights into the layered meaning behind June's suicide, which is difficult for the reader to make sense of so early in the novel. Eggs carry a variety of meanings, often representing new life, but the eggs June peeled did not carry new life—they had been hard-boiled. The life they held was stagnated, foreshadowing June's death. Like the eggs, June wears a shell, but her shell is torn and no longer protects her life. Additionally, the term "Easter egg" is also used to reference a hidden message or surprise. June's death is also connected to Gordie Kashpaw's, which occurs in the chapter "Resurrection." Gordie, June's husband, uses alcohol both to punish himself for his mistreatment of June and to escape reality. He recalls when they first ran away to be together, which begins romantically but ends with sadness. "They kissed each other's hands and then folded them together and lay that way, like two people carved on stone caskets" (272). Like June, Gordie's death is a kind of new beginning.

The chance encounter between Nector Kashpaw and Marie Lazarre on the hill changes their lives as well as Lulu Nanapush's. Marie initially plans to "rise above" her Indian blood and take her place among the nuns and other European Americans who hold themselves above the Anishinaabeg. Marie describes her motivation: "I wanted Sister

Leopolda's heart. . . . sometimes I wanted her heart in love and admiration. Sometimes. And sometimes I wanted her heart to roast on a black stick" (48–49). Marie's decision to go to the convent was based on power, but ultimately, that power did provide the satisfaction she thought it would. She quickly abandons her plan and heads down the hill.

Meanwhile, Nector has decided that Lulu is "the one." He is on his way to sell two geese to the nuns and is distracted thinking of Lulu, "the gleam on her hair, the flash of her arm, a sly turn of hip," when he literally runs into Marie (58). His low opinion of Marie and her family causes him to stop her, they struggle, and he suddenly is "caught." He admits, "I don't want her, but I want her, and I cannot let go" (67). In Nector's hunt for love, he was "aiming" for Lulu but got Marie. Nector and Marie go on to marry and have five children, but Nector's feelings for Lulu continue and his conflicted feelings for Marie never change. Through his honesty and humility, Nector wins over the sympathies of readers who know the universal complexity of love.

Nector's actions have a significant impact on Lulu Nanapush. She was completely surprised by Nector's change of heart, and even though she does not fully admit it, readers know that her heart was broken. Despite Nanapush's warnings, she turns to Moses Pillager.[3] They develop a deep relationship that Lulu knows cannot last because Moses cannot leave his island and she cannot stay. She leaves but concedes, "I would not leave undamaged. To this day, I still hurt" (82). Lulu notes a change in her perspective after her relationship with Moses: "Nothing would look the same after loving Moses Pillager. Right and Wrong were shades of meaning, not sides of a coin" (76). This distinctly Anishinaabe worldview contrasts sharply with other cultures, such as Christianity, in which certain actions are expressly forbidden with no exceptions. In the Anishinaabe worldview, individuals must make their own choices and determine what is best; there are few, if any, absolutes.

Lulu has the courage to continue to take chances with love; she never holds back out of fear. Love is not simple for Lulu. Her tumultuous love life continues throughout the novel. Readers learn that she has nine children with several different men, and many in the community gossip about her. Lulu explains to the reader that the rumors were not true: "They used to say that Lulu Lamartine was like a cat, loving no one, only purring to get what she wanted. But that's not true" (276). Her son describes her as the kind of person who lives life unafraid of consequences. Indeed, Nanapush had advised Lulu that "the richest plan is not to have one," and she followed that advice (76). Yet, Lulu does search for love and feels that even though she has loved many, she has not been entirely successful, reflecting, "It's a sad world, though, when you can't get love right even after trying it as many times as I have" (278). Once again, readers see a character that is navigating a complex world. Lulu never gives in to the demands of others and lives her life in the moment.

It is chance that brings Nector together with Marie, and it is also chance that brings Nector back into the arms of Lulu. Despite his marriage to Marie, Nector's feelings for Lulu endure for many years. He never planned to begin an affair with her but takes the chance when it comes. As he tells it: "Seventeen tons of surplus butter on the hottest day in '52. That is what it takes to get me together with Lulu" (128). A series of chances—the broken truck, Lulu driving by in her air-conditioned car, and Nector's courage to ask for her help—set into motion the perfect opportunity for them to renew their love for each other after many years apart. Their affair lasts for five years and results in Lyman Lamartine.

Nector finally builds the courage to leave Marie when chance comes to influence his relationship with Lulu again. He is nervously and impatiently waiting for Lulu to return home when he gets distracted thinking of how Marie will react to his decision. He crumples the letter he wrote to Lulu and drops it, then, because he says, "I am so eager to smoke the next cigarette that I do not notice I have thrown down my half-smoked one still lit on the end. I throw it right into the ball of Lulu's letter" (144). The fire spreads quickly after it reaches nearby cans of gasoline. Nector stands and watches. He can feel the heat rising up "burning for Lulu, but burning her out of me" (144). He then turns away and goes home to Marie. Readers will recall that during his first encounter with Marie, Nector warns her "don't play with fire" (63). Ironically, the fire burns Lulu, both literally and figuratively.

Despite Nector's many mistakes, the attraction between him and Lulu continues. After a lengthy hiatus, they take up the affair again when they are both living at the Senior Citizens apartment complex. Marie finally tires of Nector's infidelity and calls upon Lipsha Morrissey, her favorite, who has "the touch" to mend their relationship with love medicine. Lipsha is reluctant to use "the touch" on Nector: "All in all, I could not see myself treating Grandpa with the touch, bringing him back, when the real part of him had chose to be off thinking somewhere" (234). Marie uses guilt to pressure him until eventually he agrees. Lipsha knows that love medicine is serious business and that he should really ask the Old Lady Pillager (Fleur) for help, but he chooses to take a shortcut.

Geese continue to play an important role in the relationship between Marie and Nector. Readers will recall that during their first encounter, the geese that he holds seem to have a power of their own. Nector tells how at first "the geese pull me down," then "the geese are to my advantage now," and finally, "the dead birds feel impossibly heavy. I untie them from my wrists and let them fall into the dirt" (63–64, 66). He then offers the geese to Marie. Years later, Lipsha, believing in the popular myth that geese mate for life, initially thinks that their hearts could be a key ingredient in love medicine. In fact, geese do not mate for life. Instead, studies have shown that up to 40 percent of chicks are raised by male birds that did not father them. Geese do often create a strong domestic partnership and raise offspring together, but they are not sexually exclusive ("Philandering Animals"). So, ironically, Marie and Nector's relationship mirrors the actual habits of geese, both reminding readers of the natural world and calling to mind the unnatural expectations humans often place on relationships.

Lipsha does see two geese that he thinks will be perfect for use in his love medicine recipe. He even has a chance to shoot them but misses this important opportunity. Consequently, he decides to take a shortcut. He tries to convince himself that "the real actual power to the love medicine was not the goose heart itself but the faith in the cure," even though he knew it was wrong (246). He purchases two frozen turkey hearts, blesses them himself, and delivers them to Marie. Lipsha is very relatable in this scene; readers might recall a time in their own lives when they knew they were doing something wrong but did it anyway because it was the easy choice. Erdrich effectively shows the complexity of the situation and that good people sometimes make bad choices. Upon receiving the hearts, Marie promptly eats hers and then prepares Nector's. She tries to convince Nector to eat it, and when he resists, she hits him between the shoulder blades to make him swallow. Of course, Nector does not swallow but chokes to death. Marie cannot force love down Nector's throat. Despite Nector's death, the family continues, and Lipsha even realizes that "forgiving somebody else [the Kashpaw children] made the whole thing easier to bear" (254).

Nector's death provides an opportunity for Marie and Lulu to form a friendship. Both women were excellent mothers and became increasing involved in politics after all their children grew up. Nector's death allowed them both the freedom to state their views openly and to critique both the tribal government and the US government in a way that was impossible while he was chairman. Lulu and Marie form an unlikely alliance and work together to promote traditional values and the maintenance of a vibrant, contemporary Anishinaabe culture. Lulu demonstrates that a "return to tradition" does not mean going back in time but can be done while adapting to and participating in contemporary culture. It was not a conflict that she "regularly traded in so that her car so was the latest Chevy, new and shiny" (307). Additionally, while many choose to grow out their hair and wear ribbon shirts to assert and validate their identity, Lulu "sniffed down her nose at the length and bagginess of old-time skirts. She led her gang of radicals in black spike heels and tight, low-cut dresses blooming with pink flowers" (303). Lulu's refusal to conform to expectations challenged both Indian and non-Indian stereotypes of what people who hold to traditional Anishinaabe culture look like.

Lulu and Nector are two excellent examples of how the characters in *Love Medicine* successfully resist assimilation into the dominant US culture and the rejection of Anishinaabe lifeways. The reader learns that both Nector and Lulu attend government boarding school off the reservation. Readers learn that it was on the bus to government boarding school that Lulu "cried all the tears she ever would cry in her life" because "after that they just dried up" (280–81). Erdrich does not give much detail about what life was like for Lulu and others who attended. Lulu does reveal that she ran away from the school time and again because she "missed the old language in my [her] mother's mouth" (68). She was made to wear a bright orange dress of shame, to scrub sidewalks, and to strip and remake all the dormitory beds. Beginning in the late nineteenth century and through the early twentieth century, the US government employed a system of boarding schools designed to assimilate American Indian children. They believed that, by isolating children from their families and communities, they could instill a new set of values and lifeways, which included an emphasis on Christianity. Many of the schools used strict corporal punishments. Captain Richard Henry Pratt, the founder of the Carlisle Indian Industrial School, is well known for stating that the purpose of the schools was to "kill the Indian and save the man" (qtd. in Landis), or what we would call ethnocide today. While the schools did not achieve their goal of total assimilation, they did have lasting impacts on all who attended.[4] Neither Nector nor Lulu assimilate in ways that those who ran boarding schools had hoped; they return to the reservation and create strong families that continue to follow Anishinaabe ways of life.

At first, readers are made to think that Marie is on the path to assimilation and the rejection of her Anishinaabe heritage. She is clearly ashamed of her identity when she joins the convent. Her family has a reputation as thieves, and she wants to erase her Anishinaabe heritage. She tells the reader, "They were not any lighter than me. I was going up there to pray as good as they could. Because I don't have that much Indian blood" (43). Marie surprises readers when, despite earning the respect of many of the nuns, she decides to leave the convent. However, she is still unhappy with her own identity. She decides to remake her identity through Nector: "I had decided I was going to make him into something big on this reservation. I didn't know what, not yet; I only knew . . . they would not whisper 'dirty Lazarre' when I walked down from church" (89). Here, Marie is concerned more with class and reputation than she is with heritage. Unlike Lulu, Marie craves the approval of others, especially non-Indians.

Marie never loses her desire for the approval of Sister Leopolda. Upon learning that Sister Leopolda is dying, Marie decides to visit her. Marie wants to "let her see where my devotion had gone and where it had got me. For by now I was solid class. Nector was tribal chairman. My children were well behaved, and they were educated too" (148). She tries to impress Sister Leopolda with her good wool dress, her well-behaved daughter Zelda, and her husband's position within the tribe. Sister Leopolda refuses to give Marie the approval she desires, even going so far as to tell her, "I'm sorry for you . . . now that I see you're going to suffer in hell" (155). Ultimately, Marie leaves without Sister Leopolda's validation and is forced to accept the truth: Sister Leopolda will never respect her or give her the satisfaction of her approval.

Marie is able not only to accept but to embrace her Anishinaabe identity after her mother-in-law, Rushes Bear, and Fleur save her during childbirth. Marie acknowledges that it was more than physical, "more than saving my life, she put the shape of it back in place" (104). During each of her labors, Marie had used a word to get her through; this time, the word that came was not in English. The word was *babaumawaebigowin*, and although she could not quite remember the full meaning, she knew that it was spoken in a boat. She thought she might die when she realized how the word would save her: "I understood that I was to let my body be driven by the waves, like a boat to shore, like someone swimming toward a very small light. I followed directions and that way, sometime the next afternoon, my child was born" (103). Marie's use of an Anishinaabe word to save herself, and possibly her unborn child, indicates that she is ready to see the value of her Anishinaabe heritage. Later, when Marie is living at the Senior Citizens complex, she speaks the Anishinaabe language regularly because she has seen both Catholicism and the Bureau of Indian Affairs "fail her children" and because the words of English were "comfortless" (263). By the end of the novel, Lyman even considers Marie to be part of the "traditionals" (303). Marie's transformation is motivated, in part, because she wants a better life for her children. She is focused on continuance, on the best possible future for the generations to come.

Both chance and continuance play an important role in Lyman's life as well. A chance mistake by the US government allows Lyman the opportunity to recreate himself. After his brother Henry's death, he went into a depression and used alcohol and drugs to try to escape reality. Then, by chance, "a breeze from a punched-out window flipped a paper over on the floor" (299), which Lyman could have thrown back into the large stack of unopened mail but chooses to pick up. He discovers it is a 1099 form from the Department of the Treasury. It gives him a "warm jolt" as he realizes that he is still alive on paper (300). Lyman sets to work filing papers and forming his identity. Ironically, the 1099 had been sent to him by mistake; so, as he observes, "Out of a typo, I was formed. Out of papers, I came to be" (301). Lyman goes on to create the tomahawk factory where Anishinaabeg make "museum quality" artifacts, which are actually cheap goods that fit stereotypes of what non-Indians expect "Indian" items are like.

Just when readers think that Lyman has "sold out," he undergoes a transformation. After Lyman cleans up the mess in the factory, he begins to brainstorm about new opportunities. He anticipates "some sort of Indian gaming regulatory act" and starts to imagine the possibilities of using chance itself as a way to turn the tables and create economic development on the reservation (325). He sees gaming as a way to recoup some of the wrongs perpetrated by the US government:

> They gave you worthless land to start with and then they chopped it out from under your feet. They took your kids away and stuffed the English language in their mouth. They sent your brother to hell, they shipped him back fried. The sold you booze for furs and then told you not to drink. (326)

Here, readers are given a glimpse into Lyman's contempt for the US government and its destructive policies. Lyman plans to use bingo and other games of chance to generate a significant amount of revenue, which will redistribute wealth and simultaneously serve as a kind of revenge for policies that resulted in high poverty rates for the Anishinaabeg. Lyman's plan is embodied in the popular saying "Success is the best revenge." He feels that Indians can use federal law to their advantage. Here, Erdrich foreshadows a positive future; Lyman and the Anishinaabeg are not merely passive victims of the US government but are willing to levy their assets and work to create a vibrant future. Lyman carries out this plan to "win" on the greed of non-Indians in *The Bingo Palace*. Chance will be a key to the continuance of the Anishinaabeg.

Lipsha also struggles with his identity. He has always believed that his mother never wanted him. Despite Marie's love, Lipsha has always felt unwanted and yet wondered who his parents were. Even though many in the community know, it is Lulu who has the courage to tell Lipsha the truth. Just before Lulu reveals his biological parents to him, Lipsha insists: "My real mother's Grandma Kashpaw. That's how I consider her, and why not? Seeing as my blood mother wanted to tie a rock around my neck and throw me in the slough" (334–35). Lulu tells Lipsha that his mother never threw him away but instead "watched you from a distance, and hoped that you would forgive her some day" (337). This news shocks and confuses Lipsha; initially, he steals money from Marie and runs away. Later, in an effort to find his father, he seeks out King in Minneapolis. King, Gerry Nanapush, and Lipsha end up playing cards at King's.

In the end, the Anishinaabeg win. Gerry tells King, "Society is like this card game here, cousin. We got dealt our hand before we were even born, and as we grow we have to play as best we can" (357). By chance, Gerry recognizes Lulu's signature on the cards and comes to the realization that Lipsha is his son. Using the marked deck, Lipsha deals himself a "perfect family" and wins June's car from King. In the opening chapter, June's torn shell represented the harm and hurt she experienced in her life; likewise, when Lipsha gets the car, it is damaged, with "nicks and dents in the beautiful finished skin" (360). Yet, defeat is not an option for Lipsha. He is able to repair the damage, and as he says, "A good road led on. So there was nothing to do but cross the water, and bring her home" (367). Lipsha delivers Gerry to Canada and forgives June. His forgiveness allows him to move forward. Lipsha's perfect family is far from what most would consider idyllic, but the truth enables him to respect himself.

Love Medicine ends with hope and continuance for individuals like Lipsha, Lyman, Gerry, Marie, and Lulu, as well as the promise of economic development, which will help the whole tribe/nation. Erdrich's Anishinaabeg do not vanish or lose their culture the way that many might expect. They are survivors who have the courage to take chances and the humility to admit their mistakes, boldly seek truth, and are deeply motivated by love. These Anishinaabeg are shaped by the past but look toward the future. Readers see the complexities of contemporary Anishinaabe life and come to understand the Anishinaabeg not as one-dimensional stereotypes but as multifaceted humans.

Notes

1. The novel has also won significant critical acclaim, including the 1984 National Book Critics Circle Award for fiction, the 1985 Sue Kaufman Prize for First Fiction, the 1984 Virginia McCormick Scully Award, the 1985 Los Angeles Times Book Prize for fiction, the 1985 American Book Award from the Before Columbus Foundation, and the 1985 Great Lakes Colleges Association Award for best work of fiction (Wong 4). For an analysis of the differences between the 1984 and 1993 versions of *Love Medicine*, see Chavkin 84–116.

2. Suicide is an extraordinarily difficult topic and a serious problem in many Native communities, where suicide rates are several times higher than the national average. It is important to note that I do not think Erdrich is sending a message that suicide is an acceptable answer to challenging life circumstances. Additionally, it has a deeper layered and metaphoric meaning, rather than being a reflection of either Catholic or traditional Anishinaabe spiritual beliefs. In fact, readers do not learn about June's religious beliefs. Marie, who played an important maternal role in June's life, is Catholic, but Eli, who played an important paternal role, follows traditional Anishinaabe spiritual beliefs. Many Anishinaabeg believe that, upon death, the person embarks on a four-day journey to the next world. A majority of people would argue that suicide is not an acceptable answer to dealing with difficult life challenges in either belief system.

3. Moses and Lulu's mother, Fleur, are cousins (79). Nanapush objects to the relationship between Lulu and Nanapush for a variety of reasons, and Rushes Bear insists that they are "too close a relation!" (75).

4. Excellent books on the topic include David Wallace Adams's *Education for Extinction: American Indians and the Boarding School Experience, 1875–1928* (1997) and Brenda Child's *Boarding School Seasons: American Indian Families, 1900–1940* (2000).

Works Cited

Chavkin, Allan, ed. *The Chippewa Landscape of Louise Erdrich.* Tuscaloosa: U of Alabama P, 1999.

"Continuance." *Merriam-Webster Dictionary.* Merriam-Webster, Inc., 2002. Web. 19 Apr. 2012.

Erdrich, Louise. *Love Medicine.* 1984. Rev. ed. New York: Harper, 1993.

_____. *Love Medicine.* 1984. Rev. ed. New York: Harper, 2009.

Holladay, April. "Philandering Animals, Fast Spins, Faster Circumnavigations." *USA Today.* USA Today, 26 Feb. 2005. Web. 18 Apr. 2012.

Landis, Barbara. *Carlisle Indian Industrial School (1879–1918).* Barbara Landis, 1996. Web. 18 Apr. 2012.

Peterson, Nancy. "Ind'in Humor and Trickster Justice in *The Bingo Palace*." Chavkin 161–81.

Sands, Kathleen. "*Love Medicine*: Voices and Margins." Wong 35–42.

Sarris, Greg. "Reading Louise Erdrich: *Love Medicine* as Home Medicine." Wong 179–210.

Wong, Hertha D. Sweet, ed. *Louise Erdrich's* Love Medicine: *A Casebook*. New York: Oxford UP, 2000.

"What I wished for and what I expected were two different futures": A Narratological Interpretation of Gender/Kinship Systems in *The Beet Queen*_____

Sandra Cox

In the twenty-odd years since its initial publication, Louise Erdrich's *The Beet Queen* has faced criticism for "its failure to treat the social and political dimension of Native American concerns" (Meisenholder 45). Leslie Marmon Silko writes, "In this pristine world all misery, suffering, and loss are self-generated, just as conservative Republicans have been telling us for years" (181). In accordance with this sentiment, James D. Stripes asserts that the "historic conflicts" represented in Erdrich's Indian and mixed-blood characters' experiences are "not unique to the Anishinaabeg" (28), which he sees as a reason to reject Erdrich's novel as a politicized Ojibwe text.[1] While Erdrich may not enact an Anishinaabe worldview in every detail and characterization, the syncretic potential of the novel's treatment of gender/kinship systems is, in fact, an implicit politics of identity. The novel's very structure presents an important rhetorical space for resistance to Western colonialism. Rather than fictively replacing Western structure with the singular, tribal-specific structure that Silko and Stripes seem to prefer, *The Beet Queen* presents a synthesis of dominant Western ideology and traditional Ojibwe beliefs. This liminal narrative position demonstrates how Native American identities have a continuing presence within the larger culture of the United States.

Like the worldview of the novel, the characters in *The Beet Queen* are multicultural; several even exist on the border between the two polarized cultures. The settings of the novel—Argus, North Dakota, and the Little No Horse Reservation—spatially represent the two culturally defined positions. The novel's central characters—Wallace, Celestine, and Dot—live in homes built between the town and the reservation. This borderland allows the characters and the author to choose significance from two systems of belief and reinscribe meanings from one system onto signs from the other. Rather than become embroiled in the contradictions between the two systems, which are often set in binary opposition, Erdrich's narrative strategy brings them into syncretic harmony created by the combination and permutation of two distinct structures of signification. In this mutable position, the narrative inhabits a space in which the tension between the structures can be diffused and reformulated. Rather than adjudicate between competing meanings, the novel allows those meanings fluidity and ambiguity.

In an interview with Laura Coltelli, Erdrich says that she intended for the book to "touch some universals, which is what we're talking about, Pan-Indianism. We wanted the reservation . . . to kind of ring true to people from lots of different tribes" (47). Through illuminating oppression that is, as Stripes notes, "not unique to the Anishinaabeg," Erdrich magnifies the scope of history from individual characters on and near a singular tribal reservation to expose the commonalities in the diverse experiences of colonization and cultural assimilation within a pan-Indian community.[2] Erdrich constructs a microcosm of the United States in Argus. If a singular small town stands in for the entirety of US culture, then the generalization of encoding the Little No Horse Reservation with the significance of a pan-Indian community seems justifiable. The political potential of such a symbolic move, to personalize and universalize simultaneously, is revealed in the ways Erdrich weaves cultural codes from both Western systems and Ojibwe traditions.

Through the amalgamation and transformation of Western and Ojibwe worldviews, Erdrich's novel inscribes resistance to colonialism in two specific ways. First, the synthesis of ideologies in *The Beet Queen* resists tendencies to totalize racialized and gendered identities. Second, the narrative is organized according to a synthesis of Western literary forms and Anishinaabe oral traditions. Erdrich shows readers how affinities between Natives and non-Natives, men and women, and adults and children can be reconfigured to produce families that are functional in their unorthodoxy and histories that are authentic in their plurality. The result is a testimonial novel that offers criticism of totalitarian Western ideology and presents a reparative alternative to rigid Eurocentric understandings of gender/kinship and history, one that draws on Native American traditions to underscore the problems intrinsic to the Western system.

The use of alternative gender and familial systems in *The Beet Queen* has received some critical attention.[3] Julie Barak's 1996 article "Blurs, Blends, Berdaches: Gender Mixing in the Novels of Louise Erdrich" argues that the novel's numerous "gender-mixed characters who are described either as exhibiting or in some way acting out opposite sex role mannerisms or behaviors" demonstrate "a fluidity of gender identities . . . by recreating a gender role available to [Erdrich] through her Native American background—that of the berdache" (51). In a later essay, Tara Prince-Hughes examines some of the problems with Barak's article, including its use of the word "berdache," which Prince-Hughes replaces with the less homophobic and less Eurocentric phrase "two-spirit," and its assumption that there is a singular "Native American background" that allows writers to access this special understanding of gender (6). Beyond these concerns, Prince-Hughes concurs with Barak that "*The Beet Queen* . . . depicts alternative gender characters who, to different degrees, express the two-spirit tendencies and who together build a balanced community" (1).

The two-spirit tendencies of which Prince-Hughes writes merit exploration. The construction of binary gender/kinship roles is intrinsic to Western culture; the Ojibwes of whom Erdrich writes understand gender, sexuality, and family in ways that repudiate such a binary in favor of a continuum of identities for some tribal communities. However, these understandings are just as likely to construct different but equally rigid rules regarding gender-crossing or may have allowed cross-gender performances but not homosexuality (Jacobs et al. 257). As Anishinaabe anthropologist Midnight Sun argues, a "lack of information regarding indigenous ideologies makes analysis difficult, but certain hypotheses may be made by attempting to situate native sex/gender systems in contexts specific to their societies" (45). Neither

Barak nor Prince-Hughes examines any specifically Chippewa gender structures to indicate that Erdrich's depiction of gender draws on specific tribal traditions regarding gender. The term "two-spirit" is necessarily aspecific with regard to tribal origin: An English term never translated into any Native language so as to avoid misinterpretation, it was developed in the late twentieth century as an umbrella term to describe diverse alternative gender performances in many Native American communities (Jacobs et al. 276–78). "Two-spirit," like the umbrella term "queer," expresses many sexual, social, and familial roles—from men who love men to women who live as men to sacred clowns who enact both genders fluidly to many other identities besides—and all these performances are derived from a tradition of variant expressions of gender identity within many tribal histories. "Two-spirit" is quite different from "queer" in that "queer" denotes a deviation from a rigidly defined norm, but "two-spirit" suggests a performance outside the masculine/feminine and male/female dichotomies that is not a deviation but a celebrated and useful fulfillment of a traditional Native American role (Jacobs et al. 287). Queer people may be marginal, but two-spirit people are often central to indigenous cultures.

Erdrich's novel not only enacts a vision of gender fluidity borrowed from a pan-Indian tradition, but because of the taboo nature of this gender fluidity in the society of Argus, the novel also addresses the Western binary system. By representing characters who hold allegiance to Western masculinity and femininity, as Sita Kozka and Russell Kashpaw do, the novel offers a criticism of that binary system. In representing characters who are extranormative, Erdrich's synthesis between the Western and Chippewa systems allows Wallace Pfef, Mary Adare, and Celestine James to create a functional family with a broad array of gendered behaviors. These varied gender performances serve as a model for Dot—Wallace's namesake, Mary's niece, and Celestine's daughter, whom the three parent together in a kinship system that bears little resemblance to the Western nuclear model but does not replicate exactly the Chippewa tribal system.

Erdrich's critique of the Western system is most readily apparent in her characterization of Sita, the beautiful and vain daughter of Fritzi and Pete Kozka. Sita, unlike her cousin Mary, refuses to work in the meat room of her father's butcher shop; instead, she works as a fashion model briefly and then marries, rather unhappily, twice. Sita is conventionally gendered and heterosexually oriented. In spite of the fact that Sita enacts a normative Western feminine identity, she is not allotted the mythical fairy-tale ending that enshrouds the ideology of gender in American culture.[4] In a rather perverse turn of plot, Sita dies, alone and overdressed in her front yard, and her corpse, elegantly coiffed and enrobed in bridal white, is paraded through downtown Argus before it is left to rot in the butcher shop van, while Mary and Celestine go to the crowning of the Beet Queen (297). By writing Sita's end in an absurdist parody of the Cinderella story (complete with queen and court), Erdrich shows that adherence to Western norms is no guarantee of happiness.

Erdrich develops a masculine counterpart to Sita in Russell. Her characterization of Russell is a criticism of Western masculinity. Russell is arguably the only central character in *The Beet Queen* who is identified as a full-blooded Chippewa. In analyzing Russell, Susan Meisenholder suggests that "the attempt to emulate the gender ideals of white culture results in profound dehumanization; in different ways (Sita as sex object and Russell as cannon fodder), both have social value only as bodies and receive approval only through physical sacrifice" (48). While Russell does not enact whiteness, he does enact a fantasy of masculinity that is part of the gendered narrative of colonialism. The conclusion that Russell's status as a war hero has cost him some of his Native American identity may be supported with an analysis of Russell's vision as he is dying in the parade. Russell sees his sister, Isabel, walking beside his float:

> She turned and signaled him to follow. . . . His heart slowed and numbed and seemed to grow until it pressed against his ribs. . . . "Wait for me," he called. She turned and kept walking. . . . This was the road the old-time

Chippewas talked about, the four-day road, the road of death. He'd just started out. . . . the road had gone too narrow. He stumbled. No matter how hard he called, his sister continued forward and wouldn't double back to help. (299)

Just as Russell is able to understand the significance of his vision, he is denied access to the traditional ways. Perhaps Erdrich, through the free indirect discourse of the section, is indicating that the status he achieves in the veteran's parade separates him from the traditional path of the Ojibwe warrior.[5] Russell cannot walk the four-day road alongside Isabel; instead, he dies listening to white women marvel that "he looks stuffed" as the float passes the grandstand (300). Men, particularly those from the working class or a marginalized ethnic group, are expected to prove their masculinity in wartime through sacrifice. To fulfill this ideologically implanted expectation is a sacrifice that holds social meaning; in the master narrative, the war hero, like the damsel in distress, is promised rewards for his appropriately masculine behavior. Interestingly, Russell is displayed on the veteran's float in the same parade that Sita's corpse rides in; the parallels between the two characters are rather striking. Each is dressed to convey the epitome of their gendered role (Sita as bride and Russell as war hero), but the circumstances that frame this epitomizing are ironic (Sita is dead and Russell is dying). Celestine observes Russell, her half brother, as he is elevated onto the float bearing the banner North Dakota's Most Decorated Veteran and considers that "he must wait until some statehouse official scores the other veterans, counting up their wounds on a paper tablet, and figures out who gave away the most flesh" (111). Surely, in noting her brother's pride in his sacrifice and the ridiculous ways that human pain can be quantified by an unfeeling government, Celestine sees how the militarization of masculinity is dehumanizing for the Native American man.

In addition to this rejection of constrictive Western gender parities, Erdrich presents reparative models of gender expression and familial organization without rigid roles that totalize identity and dehumanize subjects. In representing Dot's family, Erdrich uses two-spirit and queer identities to shape characters who perform personal resistance to the norms to which Sita and Russell adhere. First, Celestine James, Dot's biological mother, is not particularly feminine or maternal: "She wore tailored suits instead of dresses and carried a leather shoulderbag. Striding into the kitchen, she was handsome like a man. Her voice was low and penetrating and she smoked Viceroys" (67). However, Celestine's identity is not wholly outside the Western conception of womanhood. As Prince-Hughes notes, Celestine "also bakes and shares with Mary a love of cooking; her early behavior manifests the balance of genders that she continues to maintain as an adult" (12). In this way, she enacts a balance between the two genders, fluidly choosing behaviors from both sides of the binary and blending them together. Another way Celestine identifies her difference is through her sexuality. While she espouses no lesbian desires, Celestine does note some of her troubles in maintaining relationships with men: "I've known men. Perhaps, I think, I'm too much like them, too strong or imposing when I square my shoulders, too eager to take control" (125). The only heterosexual encounter in the novel is between Celestine and Karl Adare, Mary's effeminate brother: "[Celestine's] attraction to Karl is unique in that Karl is passive, smaller than she is and more feminine" (Prince-Hughes 13).

Celestine's mother, like the older sister who raises Celestine after their mother's death, was a Chippewa. Wallace and Mary have no Native American heritage revealed by the narrative. Prince-Hughes notes, "Since in *The Beet Queen*, most of the two-spirit characters are non-Indian, the novel suggests not only the cross-cultural occurrence of such traits, but their value to American culture as a whole" (9). Erdrich's novel suggests the multicultural existence of alternative genders and praises their values, yet Wallace and Mary do not perform as a traditional Chippewa man-woman and a warrior woman. Erdrich uses Celestine, along with Wallace and Mary as extranormative white characters, to show how both gender/kinship systems can be blended to produce a familial structure based on affinity and mutual love. This synthesis between the two-spirit tradition and the Western heterocentric nuclear family is presented in the dynamics between Dot's three co-parents.

First, Wallace identifies himself as outside normative boundaries. In his portion of the narrative, he discusses his feelings about his homosexuality: "I was queer. I don't know why, either, except that the Pfefs have always been dissatisfied. We came from over the great Ruhr Valley, perhaps even then carrying the race memory of the raw white beet" (161). Wallace's self-identification—"I was queer"—is fused in his narrative with the dissatisfaction of his ancestors, which he here elucidates as patently Western in his allusion to his Germanic origins by claiming that a "race memory" can pass this dissatisfaction through generations. If Western European traditions, like beet farming, are part of the race memory Wallace inherits, then the taboo nature of his sexual difference is as essential to his identity as occupation. Within Western society, cultural codes denigrate queer identity. Indeed, Wallace's cultural beliefs demean and discourage his queerness, but a code to integrate his alternative gender does exist in traditional Ojibwe culture. Because Wallace is not a member of that cultural community, he must suppress and hide his homosexuality, as required by the social order of Argus. Wallace achieves social acceptability through an elaborate ruse of extended mourning for his "poor dead sweetheart" (159), a framed portrait of a woman Wallace has never met. Because of this subterfuge, the closeting of his sexual proclivities does not prohibit Wallace from having satisfying relationships with other members of his community. He is perhaps the *most* nurturing and feminine influence on Dot. Wallace acts as midwife when Celestine delivers Dot in a snowstorm; he acts as her event planner, giving her a luau-themed birthday party; and in the culminating moment of the novel, he rigs a beauty pageant in hopes of raising her self-esteem. Each of these labors of love is gendered feminine, and Wallace indulges Dot, rather than restrains her. A reading suggesting that Wallace performs as a surrogate father would be troubled by how maternal his parenting style is (Storhoff 349).

In addition to her mother and Wallace, Dot has a tertiary caregiver. Dot's aunt, the sister of her estranged father, plays an important role in her life. Mary Adare's gender identity is more ambiguous than either Celestine's two-spirit performance or Wallace's queer identity. Like Celestine, Mary finds heterosexual "romance" to be more work than pleasure. In a more truncated version of Celestine's courtship with, marriage to, and estrangement from Mary's brother, Mary makes a singular attempt at slipping into the Western reproductive matrix by inviting Russell to dinner. When Russell makes it clear that he has no interest in Mary, she decides that she "would never go out of [her] way for romance again" (75). While this may seem to be a refrain of tragic spinsterhood or repressed homosexual desire, Mary is quite clear about the mixed blessing of being *sans romance*:

> I did not choose solitude. Who would? It came on me like a kind of vocation, demanding an effort that married women can't picture. Sometimes, even now, I look on the married girls the way a wild dog might look through the window at tame ones, envying the regularity of their lives but also despising the low pleasure they get from the master's touch. (69)

The "regularity" Mary envies is denied to her because she is uncomfortable in her marginal status, but the "despising" she feels for wives' dependence on their husbands marks both her difference and her independence as sources of strength as well as isolation. Mary is not the "manly-hearted woman" of Ojibwe tradition that Celestine is (Barak 52); while she certainly performs some masculinized behaviors and traits, Mary clearly is not troubled by heteronormative dictates on her sexuality in the ways that Celestine and Wallace are. Celestine displays a varied set of gendered traits that enact a balance between masculinity and femininity. Wallace identifies as queer, experiences and acts upon homosexual desires, and participates in normative culture by publicly repressing the signification of his difference. Mary's deviation from the nuclear model, as an unmarried independent woman, is signified openly; that is, Mary does not "pass" in Argus society the way Wallace does.

In spite of the fact that Mary is neither overtly homosexual like Wallace nor as markedly androgynous as Celestine, the community regards her with suspicion. Even as a child, Mary recalls this feeling of alienation: "Sita ran long legged, brightly calling, toward a group of girls. . . . I lagged far behind. It didn't bother me to walk alone" (36). Her ostracism by the girls of Argus's primary school is repeated in her isolation from her customers at the butcher shop, where Celestine has made friends and confidantes of the same folk. As a marginal figure, perhaps because of her bent for alternative spiritualism or because of her status as an impoverished orphan or because she is female and unmarried, Mary exists on the periphery; however, she is at the center of Dot's life. Her struggles with Celestine are similar to intraparental arguments about the manner of upbringing most beneficial to Dot. Mary also buys Dot the dress for her to wear in the Beet Festival pageant. The moments between Mary and Dot clearly suggest that Mary is as important in the child's life as either Celestine or Wallace.

Celestine's, Wallace's, and Mary's functions as family of origin for Dot are explicated in the complex narrative structure of the text. The characters' relationships are focused by the choices Erdrich makes in unfolding the exposition of her prose. Erdrich uses multiple first-person narrators to show the formation of bonds between Mary and Celestine, the conception and birth of Dot, the family's inauguration of Wallace, and the way they proceed, amicably but clumsily (as in most healthy families), to nurture Dot into adolescence. Sometimes Erdrich creates a varied web of first-person narratives that give the novel a polyphonic quality that renders its center ambiguous. At other points in the novel, Erdrich deploys a third-person voice to describe the characters and situations in free indirect discourse. Using multiple narrative modes, Erdrich creates a permutation of Western literary standards and Ojibwe traditions in narrative orality. In the free indirect discourse, Erdrich deploys some set conventions of the Western fiction genre. The prose is focalized clearly through a series of central characters who each contribute to the building of a linear narrative. For instance, the book begins with a brief prologue before part 1. The italicized header (in this case, *"The Branch"*) used in this prologue begins a pattern in the novel where such headers signify third-person narration. If these headers indicate a set of circumstances that concern many characters, as *"The Branch"* does, the header will direct readers' attentions to significant symbols and events in the section. In *"The Branch,"* the broken limb of a blooming tree is introduced as an image to express Karl's effeminacy, Mary's lack of sentimentality, and the fracture in their family that will begin in part 1. Other section headers for passages using free indirect discourse may be focalized through a singular character; in such cases, the character's name appears in the section title (e.g., *"Russell's Night"*). The typography of section breaks in this prose suggests a clear organizational pattern that establishes a linear plot, which might be traced objectively and chronologically through the voice of the omniscient narrator. It is also possible that the narrator is constructed to signify organization and unbiased perspectives according to the Western system of signification as a kind of narrative trick. Such a trick, which Catherine Rainwater suggests is played in *The Beet Queen* to marginalize the reader, may function to force the reader to question the assumptions that the Western literary paradigm guides her or him toward.

The third-person narrator speaks in accord with Western literary motifs; these sections provide rich descriptions of scenery, simply stated expository information, and figurative language. For example, the symbolic branch is described by the narrator as "such a large branch, from such a small tree, that blight would attack the scar where it was pulled off" (2). This image of the tree stands in for the Adare family. After losing their mother and infant brother, Karl and Mary's family tree is indeed small. The lost branch is perhaps a symbol for the estranged mother or perhaps the children themselves, who will "blight" their family tree with their failure to pair off normatively and reproduce conventionally. A judgment about the characters, situations, and events in the novel is subtextually communicated in the narration. That judgment is, of course, ideologically positioned within the Western system that regiments gender and family to such an extent that heteronormative reproduction is the only alternative to the "blight" of extranormative gendered behaviors. If the free indirect discourse is a narrative of deviance, loss, and separation, then in the first-person perspectives Erdrich creates rhetorical space for reexamining those themes from a different worldview.

In the testimonial style of the first-person confessional, prose in some sections opens up the possibility for reparative reclamations of the motifs in the Western perspective of the omniscient narrator. Through first-person storytelling in a multivocal narrative, Western ideology is challenged, revised, and altered to blend with another perspective, that of Ojibwe traditions. As Catherine Rainwater observes:

> Not only are the boundaries between nuclear and peripheral family . . . obscured, but in *The Beet Queen* there are no main characters. . . . Narrational authority or centrality shifts constantly from one narrating voice to another. These narrating characters exist on the margins of each others' lives, and often their stories do not match, because each person has only various little pieces of the whole "truth." Not even the third-person omniscient narrator . . . is a center of authority. (420)

The fact that the characters are developed through the intertextual reading of these competing narratives means that the characters are reliant upon one another to provide depth and meaning to the story told in the novel. The confessional nature of each person's narrative section is inscribed with significance only when the totality of the text serves as context to mediate meaning. This confessional narrative mode recreates the notion of stories as dynamic, living abstractions of history, which are typical of Ojibwe storytelling.[6] Stories are told in cycles, repeated through a cyclical time that can recur in different settings with distinct meanings that are socially constructed and linked together through the testimonial narrative of each storyteller.

As Karah Stokes notes, the "oral influence is demonstrated formally in the episodic form of [Erdrich's] novels and the fact that, as in traditional stories of the Anishinabe, the same characters evolve in many works . . . the events of a story will sometimes be contradicted in its retelling by another narrator" (90). For example, motifs from traditional Anishinaabe Two Sisters story cycles appear in *The Beet Queen*. Two Sisters cycles center on a pair of sisters, Oshkikwe (young woman) and Matchikwewis (bad sister), who are both much beloved to their communities, families, and one another. Though Oshkikwe and Matchikwewis are close, they often compete for the attention of the same man. Despite that competition, "they form with each other a strong bond that benefits them both and at times is more significant than their connection with the male" (Stokes 91).

In *The Beet Queen*, Celestine and Mary are not sisters, but they do share a bond that is perceptible to the other characters. Sita, the first to note the attachment between them, observes:

> Mary and Celestine smiled into each other's eyes. I could see that it was like two people meeting in a crowd, who knew each other from a long time before. And what was also odd, they looked suddenly alike. It was only when they were together. You'd never notice when they weren't. . . . It wasn't even their build. . . . It was something else, either in the way they acted or the way they talked. Maybe it was a common sort of fierceness. (32–33)

Sita sees the two as so alike that they begin, when together, to resemble one another, as sisters would. Oshkikwe and Matchikwewis may stand in for Mary and Celestine in other ways as well. Oshkikwe is modest and sexually naive; Matchikwewis is sensuous and sexually forward. Mary's passivity and the impotence of her short courtship of Russell make a similar contrast to Celestine's active and successful pursuit of Karl. As Mary—like Oshkikwe in traditional stories—becomes jealous of Karl's relationship with Celestine, more parallels between the traditional story and the novel become apparent. Karl is Mary's brother, not her husband, but her reaction to his affair with Celestine, and even to Celestine herself, is strange. After fighting about the end of her marriage to Karl, Celestine yells at Mary in the shop, "You don't know what you want. At the same time you're jealous of Karl and me, you don't want us apart" (137). Mary's inability to understand her gender difference skews the heterosexual matrix "because she has no social traditions to give meaning and context to her inclinations" (Prince-Hughes 12). While Mary does not compete with Celestine for Karl as a sexual partner, the narrator suggests that jealousy is her motivation for antagonizing Celestine. In the end, however, her allegiance to Celestine is more important than this jealousy, and she helps raise her brother and Celestine's child.

Unlike Mary, Wallace does compete with Celestine for Karl as a sexual partner in another permutation of the traditional story. If Mary, two years Celestine's junior, acts the part of the younger sister, Oshkikwe the innocent, in the story cycle just described, then Celestine, younger than Wallace, shifts from Matchikwewis to Oshkikwe when the narrative is considered with Wallace as the "bad sister." When Wallace finds Karl on Celestine's porch and Celestine scantily clad, he is grief stricken: "I squinted miserably, hating them, my teeth grinding. . . . I was in agony, almost unconscious of them, involved in my own distress" (166–67). Wallace's description of discovering Celestine with Karl is similar to the traditional story. One evening Matchikwewis and her sister look at two stars—one is very young and bright, the other is very dim and old. Matchikwewis tells Oshkikwe that she would rather marry the younger star; Oshkikwe responds that she has no preference. As they sleep beneath the heavens that night, the older star husband takes Matchikwewis as his wife and the younger takes Oshkikwe. The next day when Matchikwewis finds her sister and the young star together, she is blinded by the dawn and grief stricken. In her misery, she rejects her own husband and her sister. Oshkikwe becomes pregnant, and Matchikwewis must forgive her sister and aid her in raising the young star's child (Barnouw 47).

Like Matchikwewis, Wallace will help to raise his lover and rival's child. Like the two sisters, Wallace and Celestine's connection to one another is more important than either's attraction to Karl. The melding of the Two Sisters story into a midcentury novel suggests that blending elements of Ojibwe tradition into the dominant historical narrative may function to repair some of the hegemonic erasure that the dominant historical discourse enacts. By utilizing both Western tropes, such as free indirect discourse and structured metanarrative breaks, and Ojibwe modes of expression, such as the polyphonic narration and the adaptation of the Two Sisters story, Erdrich draws on the testimonial of those narratives according to a structure incipient in Native American traditions. The fact that she augments these narratives with the more formal free indirect discourse shows how the synthesis between literary paradigms can be more productive than the exclusive use of either. In this way, her use of narrative devices is like her use of multiple systems of gender and kinship.

The potential of the novel to add to a history that has not been recorded by either side of the colonial struggle is significant. The liminal area between these Western and Anishinaabe worldviews is developed in *The Beet Queen* with surprising political resonance. Native American nationalist scholars may take issue with Erdrich's novel because some critics read the novel as trying to "avoid that struggle [with denationalization] and present Indian populations as simply gatherings of exiles, emigrants, and refugees . . . giving support, finally, to the idea of nationalistic/tribal culture as a contradiction in terms" (Cook-Lynn 30). Erdrich confronts the idea that some populations, Indian and white, are "gatherings of exiles" and that mixed-blood identity is necessarily plotted within the kind of syncretic culture that Erdrich represents, but this does not suggest that "nationalistic/tribal culture" is a "contradiction in terms." Instead, a narrative attempt to adjudicate between total integration and absolute separatism, a mechanism for allowing subjects to speak from a discursive space that opens up avenues for multiple distinct fluid identities should be a goal of any movement that seeks to enrich the understandings of Native American literatures.

Notes

1. Silko and Stripes are not the only critics to take exception to the depoliticization of Native American themes in *The Beet Queen*. Other examples of such criticisms include a 1994 scholarly article by Dennis Walsh and Ann Braley, "The Indianness of Louise Erdrich's *The Beet Queen*: Latency as Presence," and a couple of popular source reviews: Jack Cady's "Review of *The Beet Queen*" for the *Seattle Times* and Richard Krawiec's "*Beet Queen* Wonderfully Written Despite Some Flaws" for the *Pittburgh Press*.

2. I mean here to suggest that the history, mechanisms, and ideology of colonization, assimilation, and genocide used by the United States government to oppress Native peoples necessarily creates relationships between tribal cultures. What I do not mean to suggest is that all experiences of colonization for all of the many tribal nations that lived in North America before colonial contact are the same. For clarification of the debate between tribal-specific nationalist scholars and pan-Indian activists, as well as a compelling argument for using both models to read Native American literatures to radical political ends, consult Craig Womack's *Red on Red: Native American Literary Separatism* (1999).

3. Louise Flavin, Deirdre Keenan, and Pauline Woodward's excellent articles on Erdrich's use of Native American gender and kinship systems, though not reviewed here for brevity's sake, have also informed the analysis of gender in this essay.

4. My reading of the fairy-tale motif in Sita's narration and in the free indirect discourse surrounding her is an extrapolation of Karah Stokes's discussion of two figures from other Erdrich novels, Lulu Lamartine from *Love Medicine* and Eleanor Schlick Mauser in *Tales of Burning Love*, who, as Stokes interprets the novels, offer a similar criticism of the Western system. For a more developed discussion of how fairy tales are integrated into cultural systems of meaning, see Bruno Betteheim's *The Uses of Enchantment: The Meaning and Importance of Fairy Tales* (1977).

5. Ojibwe traditions do value warriors, but the pride in bodily sacrifice espoused in Western heroic modes is not a value held by that tradition. In Anishinaabe cosmology, spirit-beings guide warriors and keep them from harm; thus, the most potent and spiritually supported warriors were not wounded in battle. For

more information, see Victoria Brehm's 1996 article "The Metamorphoses of an Ojibwa Manido" in *American Literature*.

6. Although I assert that some Ojibwe storytelling traits could be called "typical," it is necessary to acknowledge the problem of the collection, edition, and interpretation of these stories. I have made use of Victor Barnouw's *Wisconsin Chippewa Myths and Tales and Their Relation to Chippewa Life* as a primary source for the story cycle from which I contend *The Beet Queen* borrows. However, Barnouw is a white anthropologist who recorded the stories as told to him by tribal storytellers. Because Barnouw himself gained the information secondhand without benefit of understanding the tribal language in which it was originally composed, some of the story's significance has undoubtedly been lost. Several different accounts of the same story are often recorded. As an example, I make use of the story "Star Husband," told to Barnouw by Julia Badger, but other versions of the Oshkikwe and Matchikwewis tale differ from this story. Delia Oshogay tells the story "Beukowe" to Barnouw about the same two characters, and David Red Bird, identified as Ojibwe, tells a similar story, "The Foolish Girls," to Richard Erdoes and Alfonso Ortiz for their collection *American Indian Myths and Legend* (1984). All three stories have elements that contradict the others.

Works Cited

Barak, Julie. "Blurs, Blends, Berdaches: Gender Mixing in the Novels of Louise Erdrich." *Studies in American Indian Literatures* 8.3 (1996): 49–62.

Barnouw, Victor. *Wisconsin Chippewa Myths and Tales and Their Relation to Chippewa Life*. Madison: U of Wisconsin P, 1977.

Chavkin, Allan, ed. *The Chippewa Landscape of Louise Erdrich*. Tuscaloosa: U of Alabama P, 1999.

Coltelli, Laura, ed. *Winged Words: American Indian Writers Speak*. Lincoln: U of Nebraska P, 1990.

Cook-Lynn, Elizabeth. "The American Indian Fiction Writers: Cosmopolitanism, Nationalism, the Third World and First Nation Sovereignty." Ed. John Purdy and James Ruppert. *Nothing but the Truth: An Anthology of Native American Literature*. New Jersey: Prentice, 2001. 23–38.

Erdrich, Louise. *The Beet Queen*. New York: Bantam, 1986.

Flavin, Louise. "Gender Construction amid Family Dissolution in Louise Erdrich's *The Beet Queen*." *Studies in American Indian Literatures* 7.2 (1995): 17–24.

Jacobs, Sue-Ellen, Wesley Thomas, and Sabine Lang, eds. *Two-Spirit People: Native American Gender Identity, Sexuality, and Spirituality*. Urbana: U of Illinois P, 1997.

Keenan, Deirdre. "Unrestricted Territory: Gender, Two Spirits and *The Last Report on the Miracles at Little No Horse*." *American Indian Culture and Research Journal* 30.2 (2006): 1–15.

Meisenholder, Susan. "Race and Gender in Louise Erdrich's *The Beet Queen*." *ARIEL* 25.1 (1994): 45–57.

Midnight Sun. "Sex/Gender Systems in Native North America." *Living the Spirit: A Gay American Indian Anthology.* Ed. Will Roscoe. New York: St. Martin's, 1988. 32–47.

Osborne, Karen. "Swimming Upstream: Recovering the Lesbian in Native American Literature." Ed. William Spurlin. *Lesbian and Gay Studies and the Teaching of English: Positions, Pedagogies, and Cultural Politics.* Urbana: Natl. Council of Teachers of English, 2000. 191–210.

Prince-Hughes, Tara. "Worlds In and Out of Balance: Alternative Genders and Gayness in *The Almanac of the Dead* and *The Beet Queen*." *Literature and Homosexuality.* Ed. Michael J. Meyer. Amsterdam: Rodopi, 2000. 1–21.

Rainwater, Catherine. "Reading between Worlds: Narrativity in the Fiction of Louise Erdrich." *American Literature* 62.3 (1990): 405–22.

Schultz, Lydia A. "Fragments and Ojibwe Stories: Narrative Strategies in Louise Erdrich's *Love Medicine*." *College Literature* 18.3 (1991): 80–95.

Shaddock, Jennifer. "Mixed Blood Women: The Dynamic of Women's Relations in the Novels of Louise Erdrich and Leslie Silko." *Feminist Nightmares: Women at Odds.* Ed. Susan Ostrov Weisser and Jennifer Fleishner. New York: New York UP, 1994.

Silko, Leslie Marmon. "Here's an Odd Artifact for the Fairy Tale Shelf: Review of *The Beet Queen*." *Studies in American Indian Literature* 10 (1986): 178–84.

Stokes, Karah. "What About the Sweetheart?: The 'Different Shape' of Anishinabe Two Sisters Stories in Louise Erdrich's *Love Medicine* and *Tales of Burning Love*." *MELUS* 24.2 (1999): 89–105.

Storhoff, Gary. "Family Systems in Louise Erdrich's *The Beet Queen*." *Critique* 39.6 (1998): 341–53.

Stripes, James D. "The Problem(s) of (Anishinaabe) History in the Fiction of Louise Erdrich: Voices and Contexts." *Wicazo Sa Review* 7.2 (1991): 26–33.

Tanner, John. *The Falcon: A Narrative of the Captivity and Adventures of John Tanner During Thirty Year's Residence Among the Indians of the Interior of North America.* 1830. New York: Penguin, 1994.

Woodward, Pauline G. "Chance in Louise Erdrich's *The Beet Queen*: New Ways to Find a Family." *ARIEL* 26.2 (1995): 109–27.

Walking Between Worlds in Louise Erdrich's Novels_____

Amy T. Hamilton

Roads and paths weave through Louise Erdrich's North Dakota novels, connecting the reservation with nonreservation towns, schools, and convents, zigzagging through woods and around lakes, clearly demarcated and lost in vegetation. These spaces also mark the margins between worlds, liminal spaces that are not clearly one place or another but somewhere in between. Catherine Rainwater contends, "Erdrich's concern with liminality and marginality pervades all levels of her texts. It affects not only characterization but also thematic and structural features" (406). I would extend this point to suggest that liminality in the novels—a transitional or threshold state between cultures, times, or classifications—also informs the characters' material experience of land and place.[1] The roads that the characters traverse represent places that are at once metaphorically and materially marginal, intersections of story, history, and lived experience. As Erdrich's characters walk and drive the many paths in these novels, they enter a space where definitions are called into question and possible paths multiply.

Anishinaabe oral traditions recount the five-hundred-year Great Migration of the Anishinaabeg from the East Coast to Lake Superior as a significant and foundational experience. According to one version of this sacred narrative, the *migis* shell appeared and led the Anishinaabeg on a journey along inland waters, guiding them to their new homeland.[2] The route itself is "one of the defining elements of Ojibway culture," remaining central to a sacred origin story and also providing "vital clues about the actual physical landscapes through which ancestral Ojibway migrated" ("About the Project"). The migration story of the Anishinaabeg challenges the widespread stereotype that Native American peoples are limited to a single homeland, a particular point on the map. In truth, before the advent of reservations, a fixing of people in place and time, Native American groups moved freely and widely across the land. While many peoples maintained strong connection to particular places, concepts of homeland also included large swaths of space rather than restricted zones. James Clifford notes, "Tribal groups have . . . never been simply 'local': they have always been rooted and routed in particular landscapes, regional and interregional networks" (254). The long tradition of movement in Anishinaabe life includes their migration stories and their seasonal movement across a large homeland that extends far beyond the artificial boundaries of reservations.[3]

Such physical movements over land infuse Native American oral traditions. Gerald Vizenor writes, "The sovereignty of motion is mythic, material, and visionary, not mere territoriality, in the sense of colonialism and nationalism. Native transmotion is an original natural union in the stories of emergence and migration that relate humans to an environment and to the spiritual and political significance of animals and other creations" (*Fugitive* 183). The centrality of motion, Vizenor suggests, is both described by the stories and reinforced by the act of creating and transmitting those stories. The movement of the narrative, the movement within the narrative, and the physical movements across the land are bound together in storytelling.

The movement that informs Anishinaabe oral traditions and histories infuses Louise Erdrich's fiction. Laura M. Furlan argues, "As participants in the multidirectionality of cultural flows, Erdrich's Indians challenge the stasis of Indian identities and places" (58). Physical movement, Furlan contends, is a method of resistance that belies static stereotypes that restrict Native American people in place and time. Vizenor points out that mobility has always marked Native American experience: "Natives have been on the move since the creation of motion in stories; motion is the originary" (*Fugitive* 55). Further, he links mobility directly to issues of sovereignty going so far as to assert that "Native sovereignty *is* the right of motion" (*Fugitive* 182; emphasis added).

An emphasis on movement permeates Erdrich's interlocking North Dakota novels.[4] Told from the perspectives of dozens of narrators and depicting the lives of scores of people across several generations, the novels are tied together through character, location, and theme. Each novel contributes to a rich tapestry of national and tribal histories, Anishinaabe beliefs and traditions, and federal corruptions and transgressions. They are also crisscrossed with paths and roads linking peoples and places and the spaces in between. In particular, *Love Medicine, Four Souls*, and *Tracks* are filled with trails and roads, populated by characters walking to and from town and walking through the woods. In all three novels, these paths are places of possibility and danger, spaces opened up between worlds. Focusing on *Tracks*, with some attention to *Love Medicine* and *Four Souls*, this essay examines how Erdrich's paths and roads act as intersections between precolonial and postcolonial experience, establishing continuity through history and story while simultaneously exposing the lasting impact of colonialism on the physical, symbolic, and psychic movements of Erdrich's Anishinaabe characters.

Centering the Margins

Several of Erdrich's North Dakota novels begin and end with characters walking along paths and roads, drawing attention to the significance of these actions and spaces.[5] Native American literature deploys representations of marginality in complex ways. For example, Gloria Bird suggests that, in Native American literatures, issues of marginality are complicated and inverted as spaces considered "marginal" by Euro-American ideologies—such as reservations—are often considered "center/source" by Native communities (41). In highlighting roads and paths, Erdrich destabilizes notions of margins and centers—*centering* routes. For example, *Love Medicine* begins with June's movement: "June Kashpaw was walking down the clogged main street of oil boomtown Williston, North Dakota, killing time before the noon bus arrived that would take her home" (1). This opening story ends with the rich imagery of June as she "walked over [the snow] like water and came home" (7). The end of the novel echoes these images of homeward movement, this time with June's son, Lipsha, poised to drive June's car over a bridge spanning "the boundary river" (271): "I got inside. The morning was clear. A good road led on. So there was nothing to do but cross the water, and bring her home" (272). These passages emphasize repeated images of walking/crossing over water and moving homeward. Yet they both are *in motion*; we do not follow June and Lipsha home but only see them en route, crossing over symbolic boundaries of snow and bridge.

Four Souls too opens and closes with images of walking. The opening scene, in a chapter called "The Roads," follows Fleur as she walks *away* from home, in her search for John James Mauser and revenge: "Fleur took the small roads, the rutted paths through the woods traversing slough edge and heavy underbrush, trackless, unmapped, unknown and always bearing east. . . . She crossed fields and skirted lakes, pulled her cart over farmland and pasture . . . kept walking until she came to the iron road" (1). Fleur's movement away from the reservation and the allotment land she has lost takes her deep into the margin. The language Erdrich uses here to describe the land emphasizes its place outside of reservation and town: "trackless, unmapped, unknown." Moreover, her movement is along literal boundaries of "slough edge" and "skirted lakes." The chapter goes on to follow Fleur along the "iron road," the "path she had been looking for," where she "wore her makizinan to shreds" and ate dogs, mud hens, and muskrats until finally reaching her destination in the city (2).

Though Fleur's movement is away from home, while June's is toward home, in their movement on the margins, they reflect one another. When Fleur travels back to the reservation at the end of the novel, she moves in a very different way: In a "white car" and a "whiter suit," she "took the roads" (182, 184). At the close of the novel, Nanapush reflects on the changes represented by Fleur's movement, commenting, "Even our bones nourish change, and even such people as we, the Anishinaabeg, can sometimes die, or change, or change and become" (210). Nanapush draws attention to the dramatic shifts in life and experience brought about by colonialism.[6] Yet even with these differences, walking and driving in the marginal spaces ties the people to the historical movement of the Anishinaabeg and presents the possibility of adaptation. The spaces, in other words, refuse stereotypes of stasis and insist on the historical reality of movement and change.[7]

In *Tracks*, images of roads and paths fill nearly every section of the novel. Even the dead are not still, walking along the "death road," and moving through the trees along the edges of the lake. Nanapush begins the novel with a story of colonialism and movement, drawing together the desolation of illness and removal with attention to the sacred four directions of the Anishinaabe Medicine Wheel: "For those who survived the spotted sickness from the south, our long flight west to Nadouissioux land where we signed the treaty, and then a wind from the east, bringing exile in a storm of government papers, what descended from the north in 1912 seemed impossible" (1).[8]

This chapter goes on to emphasize other kinds of trail walking: Nanapush's hunting ability (2); Nanapush and Edgar Pukwan's foot journey to the Pillager cabin to see if anyone has survived the illness that devastated the community (2); their subsequent rescue of Fleur and trek back along the trail to Nanapush's house at the crossroads (4); and the spirits of Nanapush and Fleur's families as they move through the trees (6). The connections among the trails and the liminal spaces between life and death, between the Anishinaabeg and the US government, and between reservation and nonreservation are revealed in these pages. Physical movement over the trails conjures the peoples' forced movement into reservations and the devastation wrought by colonial policies, while simultaneously highlighting traditional movements across the land and the connections between people and land.

Tracks ends with the paired movement of Fleur leaving the reservation and her daughter, Lulu, returning home. Both journeys emphasize the liminal "in between" nature of the road. Fleur, having lost her land to corrupt allotment policies, takes up a handcart and walks away from home, a journey that is picked up at the beginning of *Four Souls*.

Nanapush recalls Fleur's leaving: "She looked at me, her face alight, and then she set out. I stood in the middle of the path. I watched her until the road bent, traveling south to widen, flatten, and eventually in its course meet with government school, depots, stores, the plotted squares of farms" (224). Nanapush's position "in the middle of the path" allows him an unobstructed view of Fleur's trajectory away from home to nonreservation spaces; this journey reflects the nature of the trail itself as it flattens and widens to accommodate automobile traffic and larger numbers of travelers. Fleur's movement away from community is countered with Lulu's homing movement. Gone for several years at a boarding school, Lulu is finally brought home by Nanapush's persistence. The novel ends with her emergence from "the rattling green vehicle the government sent" (226). Lulu steps down from the car and sees Nanapush and Margaret, her grandmother, across the street. Nanapush reminds her later: "You went up on your toes, and tried to walk, prim as you'd been taught. Halfway across, you could not contain yourself and sprang forward. . . . We gave against your rush like creaking oaks, held on, braced ourselves together in the fierce dry wind" (226). Lulu's refusal of the behavioral mandates of the government school is represented by her shift "halfway across" the street from prim walking to a springing run. Between the government car and Nanapush's wagon, between constrained and "natural" energy, at the end of the novel, Lulu crosses the road back to her people and returns home.

While all three novels end with a version of homecoming—Lulu in *Tracks*, Fleur in *Four Souls*, and June and Lipsha in *Love Medicine*— these endings should not be read as resolutions to the conflicted movement that swirls through the novels. The stories of these characters do not end with these homecomings but continue in subsequent novels. The characters are continually pulled back to the liminal spaces of paths and roads, spaces of conflict and power. They refuse the closure and confinement of a singular place, and both through choice and by necessity continue to move along the margins.

Tracking Historical Land Loss

Love Medicine, *Tracks*, and *Four Souls* all use the 1887 Allotment Act (Dawes Act) as a reference point—a moment when traditional land values came into direct conflict with white land values. One of the stated purposes of the Allotment Act was to break up commonly held tribal lands into allotments (parcels) assigned to individual tribal members in order to facilitate assimilation into white society. Lawmakers believed that transitioning from tribal to individual land ownership would encourage Native peoples to adopt dominant values and integrate into white society. Significantly, the act contained a provision that any land "left over" after allotment would be open for purchase by US citizens. The Allotment Act led to the loss of millions of acres of land and had a devastating impact on generations of families and communities. Billy J. Stratton and Frances Washburn argue that notions of land ownership "did not exist in American Indian cultures who considered land as an organic, communally owned entity, a source of physical survival, but also of spiritual survival. . . . These are oppositional cultural concepts of land as a commodity within European cultural concepts, and land as place within American Indian cultural concepts" (66–67). In Erdrich's North Dakota novels, the crisis precipitated by land loss and failed policies of assimilation echoes in the characters' movement over trails and roads that signify these clashes in worldviews.

Taking place between 1912 and 1924, the characters' constant movement to, from, and within the reservation in *Tracks* is closely tied to land and land loss.[9] Nanapush, one of two narrators, sets the stage for his story by noting the impact of colonialism on the community, highlighting treaties, exile, and a dwindling land base. He relates how the people's "trouble came . . . from liquor and the dollar bill. We stumbled toward the government bait, never looking down, never noticing how the land was snatched from under us at every step" (4). Even in his articulation of land loss, Nanapush employs the language of walking over the land. A few pages later, he asserts, "Starvation makes fools of anyone. In the past, some had sold their allotment land for one hundred poundweight of flour. Others, who were desperate to hold on, now urged that we get together and buy back our land, or at least pay a tax and refuse the lumbering money that would sweep the marks of our boundaries off the map like a pattern of straws" (8). Nanapush highlights not just the land loss itself, but also the attendant splintering of the community into factions. As allotment threatens to "sweep the marks of our boundaries off the map," so too does it endanger community bonds as some "fattened in the shade of the new Agent's storehouse" while others "weakened . . . as one oak went down, another and another was lost" (9).

Allotment policies and land loss initiate movement in the novel as Fleur leaves the reservation when her allotment is lost due to dishonest leveling of taxes and fees by the agent. At first, Fleur's connection to the land and her ancestors helps her fend off the grasping hands of the agent: "The Agent went out [to the Pillager land], then got lost, spent a whole night following the moving lights and lamps of people who would not answer him. . . . He asked Fleur again for money, and the next thing we heard he was living in the woods and eating roots, gambling with ghosts" (9). The agent is tricked by the wandering spirits, who continue to move through the land. The spirits of the Pillagers remain "just beyond the edges of [his] sight, they flickered, thin as needles, shadows piercing shadows" (6). Fleur's spiritual connection to the land and to the lake creature, Misshepeshu, shields her and her land from the grasp of the agent. In this liminal space where life and death, magic and real, are intertwined and even indistinguishable, Fleur is protected. Her movement along the forest paths echoes this mixing of spheres as Pauline reports, "We followed the tracks of her bare feet and saw where they changed, where the claws sprang out, the pad broadened and pressed into the dirt" (12). Here along the paths around the lake, Fleur's bear clan identity is made manifest as she becomes a bear. Through her connection to the land and traditional worldview, Fleur thrives in her home on the shore of the lake.

Fleur's movement throughout the novel is determined by her connection to the land, and the ghostly movements of spirits in the woods further tie her to place. Yet, as Lawrence William Gross argues, her powerful control begins to fracture, and "her strength temporarily fades," resulting in the loss of her land and her movement along the road to the city (53). Struggling with onerous and ultimately illegal fees and taxes, the characters in *Tracks* attempt to find ways to raise funds to save their land. In the end, they only raise enough to save one allotment. Fleur's mother-in-law, Margaret, and Margaret's son, Nector, use the funds raised by the family to pay off only their own land. Fleur's allotment land is lost. After staging a final act of rebellion by sawing through the trees so that a sudden windstorm fells them around the loggers, Fleur walks away from her land.

Connections to land also influence the movement of the characters in *Four Souls* and *Love Medicine*. In *Love Medicine*, Albertine, Nector's granddaughter and one of many narrators, tells the story of how the land had been allotted to Rushes Bear (Margaret from *Tracks*) and her children, except for Nector and Eli, who were too young to register. Her older children received allotments, "but because there was no room for them in the North Dakota wheatlands, most were deeded less-desirable parcels far off, in Montana, and had to move there or sell. The older children left" (18). The departure of these children as a direct result of the Allotment Act haunts the narrative through multiple references to other characters and narrators returning home: Nector and Lulu return home from boarding school, Marie returns from the convent, Gerry repeatedly dreams of returning home, June's spirit walks home, and Lipsha returns home with June's car. Albertine articulates the pull of the land in her narration of her own homing movement:

Driving north, I could see the earth lifting. The wind was hot and smelled of tar and the moving dust. . . . I always knew [the reservation] was coming a long way off. Even in the distance you sense hills from their opposites—pits, dried sloughs, ditches of cattails, potholes. And then the water. . . . I thought of water in the roots of trees, brown and bark smelling, cold. . . . The policy of allotment was a joke. As I was driving toward the land, looking around, I saw as usual how much of the reservation was sold to whites and lost forever. Just three miles, and I was driving down the rutted dirt road, home. (11–12)

Albertine contrasts the harsh, artificial sights and smells of the highway (tar, potholes) with the rich, comforting sights and smells of home ("bark smelling" water, tree roots, hills). She counters the devastation of being reminded "as usual" of the land lost to allotment policies with the passage's final word, "home." The highway is a liminal space, a space of conflicting meanings and possibilities, of sorrow and joy, of ugliness and beauty. Albertine draws readers' attention to the impact of allotment policies while also refusing to allow those policies to have final control over the meaning of the routes the people travel.

Marking Land and Story

The conflicting significance and experience of movement in the novels ties not only to colonial history, but also to Anishinaabe stories. Throughout the three novels, the characters counter the "official" history of the Anishinaabeg as told in history books, colonial writings, and maps, with their own sacred stories. Kelli Lyon Johnson convincingly argues that Native women authors such as Erdrich respond to attempts to universalize experience "by rejecting the imposition of European (and Euroamerican) knowledge as a paradigm for reading Native texts; by presenting their own Indigenous cultures as sources of knowledge; and by explaining and using those Indigenous knowledges as a means of asserting sovereignty for Native nations in the United States" (104). She goes on to examine indigenous mapping as a way that these authors accomplish these tasks. If mapping traditions are one way that authors reassert sacred history by replacing the imposition of Euro-American worldviews through the delimiting of land, the paths and roads throughout Erdrich's North Dakota novels perform a similar act of reclamation.

Maria DePriest notes that, according to a recent cartographic study of contemporary maps, reservations are largely represented as open space: "While on some maps, the reservation is excised—it is not there, nor is its absence indicated . . . the reservation is represented merely as a placeholder, a blank, an empty open space" (249). Reservation roads and pathways are not represented on these maps; it is as if they did not exist. Mirroring the long-standing stereotype of the "vanishing Indian"—who has been described as on his last legs almost since first contact with Europeans some five hundred years ago—the reservations themselves are erased from maps, the "official" way Europeans and Euro-Americans define and visualize land. Nanapush himself echoes this myth at the beginning of *Tracks* when he claims, "I guided the last buffalo hunt. I saw the last bear shot. I trapped the last beaver with a pelt of more than two years' growth . . . axed the last birch" (2). Yet his subsequent narration challenges readers to reject the story of the doomed Indian. In remapping the land through Nanapush and her other narrators, Erdrich reclaims the space and the people's history.

In *Tracks*, a lack of maps or "official" recognition of movement does not mean there is no Native presence. Throughout the novel, those who traverse forest paths often do not leave footprints or traces of their movement. For example, both Pauline and Nanapush tell readers that there are times when Fleur walks "without leaving tracks" (215). Further, the spirits who roam the woods remain just out of sight. When the death road walked by the spirits is revealed to Pauline and Fleur following the death of Fleur's newborn baby, Pauline marvels, "I had been everywhere on the reservation, but never before on this road, which was strange because it was so wide and so furiously trodden that the snow was beaten to a rigid ice" (159). Pauline's wonder at the existence of a wide, well-traveled road that she has never seen before further challenges the limiting Euro-American vision that cannot perceive Anishinaabe worldview clearly and so attempts to erase it completely. The road, like the Anishinaabeg themselves, has always been there, even if Pauline has been unable (or unwilling) to see it.

As Johnson argues, "Non-Native mappings continue to exploit Native lands, to erase Native knowledges, and eliminate Native peoples" (111). In other words, not only does Erdrich insist on remapping the blank spaces of the physical land, she also includes an alternate mapping system that acknowledges those roads and footprints that may not be detectable with ordinary Western vision. The Anishinaabe land is transformed from a blank space on the map to a complexly traveled and peopled land, a three-dimensional map more complex than any Western map could capture.

In the process of reclaiming indigenous movements and spaces, the characters move along paths and roads not only as a means of traveling from one location to another, but also as a way of asserting purposeful, ceremonial movement. For instance, when Margaret and Nanapush have been attacked and shamed by Clarence Morrissey and Boy Lazarre in *Tracks*, Fleur responds first by shaving her head in solidarity with Margaret and then by "walk[ing] the four streets" of the reservation town, "once in each direction" (119). In doing so, she is enacting the four sections of the sacred Anishinaabe Medicine Wheel.[10] Walking along the streets, Fleur connects the modern roads with traditional belief systems, drawing together two ways of organizing and understanding the world. The four roads become the permeable margin between present and past, modern and traditional. DePriest argues that Fleur "expresses the fluidity of a symbolic and practical system of intersections in which human and non-human, life and death, temporal and spiritual, singular and plural, are linked and sometimes even blended" (255). Just as she is linked to the woods peopled with spirits, so too is she connected to the Anishinaabe traditional beliefs and practices. When she walks the four roads of the town, she draws on these identities and insists on the continual presence of the Anishinaabeg in a land that has never been empty or blank.

Fleur is not the only character in *Tracks* who Erdrich links to traditional stories. Nanapush is strongly linked to the Anishinaabe trickster figure, Nanabozho.[11] Throughout the novel, Nanapush functions as a trickster and storyteller, shaping and influencing the narrative. In a passage that most clearly reflects Nanapush's spiritual power and traditional role, he facilitates Eli's successful moose hunt. Emphasizing the steps of ceremony, Nanapush uses a piece of coal to blacken his face. He relates that he then "placed my otter bag upon my chest, my rattle near. I began to sing slowly, calling on my helpers, until the words came from my mouth but were not mine, until the rattle started, the song sang itself, and there, in the deep bright drifts, I saw the tracks of Eli's snowshoes clearly" (101).[12] Nanapush's ceremony allows him to access Eli's consciousness as "the song picked up and stopped him until he understood . . . that everything around him was perfect for killing moose" (101). Nanapush changes Eli's movement from "wandering" to "walk[ing] carefully" (101) and guides him through the woods to a successful shot—"my song directed [Eli's bullet] to fly true" (103). Nanapush continues to sing and guide Eli, encouraging him to butcher and transport the meat correctly, avoiding souring the meat and moving too quickly and freezing to death. Nanapush relates, "I took the drum from beneath my bed and beat out footsteps for Eli to hear and follow. Each time he speeded I slowed him down. I strengthened the rhythm whenever he faltered. . . . In that way, he returned" (104). The rhythm of the drum merges with the rhythm of Eli's footfalls. As Eli follows the path Nanapush lays out for him, he walks along the margin between the physical world and the world of spirits, and on that margin, the worlds blur and blend.

As characters linked to traditional lifeways, Fleur and Nanapush draw attention to the complexity of the roads and paths the people walk daily. Rather than simply utilitarian routes from one place to another, these spaces become limens, or borders, where multiple possibilities are manifest. Victor and Edith Turner argue, "Liminality is not only *transition* but also *potentiality*, not only 'going to be' but also 'what may be'" (3; emphasis theirs). For Nanapush and Fleur, the roads and paths become places of both opportunity and memory, creating alternative pasts, presents, and futures for the people crossing over them.

Story Routes

The movement in Erdrich's novels transcends the physical movements of the characters and affects the readers as well, keeping them off balance. Kathleen Sands suggests that Erdrich's reader is "forced to shift position, turn, ponder, and finally integrate the story into a coherent whole by recognizing the indestructible connections between the characters and events of the narrative(s)" (12). When I teach Louise Erdrich's novels in my undergraduate classrooms, my students struggle with the circular and referential structure of her writing. They have trouble keeping track of the different characters and their relationships to one another. We construct elaborate genealogies and endless lists (our own "maps") to help us navigate the world she has created. Invariably, by the end of the semester, most of the students have come to appreciate the rich communities Erdrich creates, and they recognize that what they once saw as "unnecessary" confusion is central to the world of her novels. What community, after all, is *not* complicated? What families are *not* confusing when you work back through their genealogical connections? In addition to presenting real, complicated communities, Erdrich is also grappling with colonial and cultural histories that offer conflicting views of the land and the people. Erdrich draws our attention to the shifting grounds of "story," "reality," and "identity," by allowing multiple community narrators to tell their own versions of their stories. What emerges is a landscape continually made and remade through the language of storytelling.

Roads, trails, and paths mark out the movement of these stories; as we follow characters along their travels, we encounter diverse stories that range from traditional narratives to modern trickster tales to colonial and postcolonial histories. If we pay attention to the ground we cover, we can see these spaces as palimpsests, where different and even conflicting versions clash, interact, and merge.[13] Pauline reveals this multiplicity in her description of walking the death road with Fleur: "We glided west, following the fall of night in a constant dusk. We passed dark and vast seas of moving buffalo and not one torn field, but only earth, as it was before. . . . There were no fences, no poles, no lines, no tracks. The road we walked was the only sign of humans" (*Tracks* 159).

In her description of the death road and its apparent existence in a precolonial time, Pauline draws together traditional belief systems and non-Native systems. By marking both what *is* and what *is not* there, Pauline in effect peels back a layer of the palimpsest without wholly destroying it. The death road, like the other trails and paths in the novel, functions as an overlapping margin between worlds and between worldviews. The land of Erdrich's North Dakota novels is alive with trails and paths, with people moving along ancient migration tracks, traditional hunting trails, ceremonial spokes of the Medicine Wheel, trade routes, and modern roads and highways. Her characters' continual movement along, through, and around these spaces acknowledges and defies the impact of colonialism on the physical, spiritual, and communal lives of the Anishinaabeg.

Notes

1. In the late 1960s, Victor Turner adopted the term "liminal" to explore the state of "in betweenness" experienced in rites of passage and Christian pilgrimage. In "Liminality and Communitas," Turner writes that liminal individuals are "neither here nor there; they are betwixt and between the positions assigned and arrayed by law, custom, convention, and ceremonial" (95). Turner differentiates "liminality" from "marginality" by suggesting that while liminal individuals are *in transition* from one state to another, marginal individuals "have no cultural assurance of a final stable resolution of their ambiguity" ("Passages" 233).

2. In this paper, I use "liminal" and "marginal" to describe both the physical, spatial transitional sites of roads as well as the spiritual, psychic, and metaphorical experience of characters on those roads. Roads and trails and the characters' experiences on them are always in transition and motion; the question of "a final stable resolution of their ambiguity" is impossible to answer. Colonialism has irrevocably changed the world of the Anishinaabeg—what sort of "stable resolution" may evolve does not fit Turner's use of the terms to describe the limited experience of pilgrimage or rite of passage. Therefore, while these terms are useful in exploring the importance of roads and paths in Erdrich's novels, they must be altered slightly from Turner's original usage. Implicit in my use of "liminal"

is that arrival at a final destination is consistently deferred, while implicit in my use of "marginal" is that arrival at that final destination is always imaginable.

3. Franchot Ballinger warns scholars about the dangers of applying Western critical paradigms such as liminality to American Indian texts. She writes that such application "obscures the particulars and uniqueness" of American Indian stories and narratives "in favor of fitting them into critical theory and a more generic, cross-cultural characterization" (24). While I agree with Ballinger's uneasiness with applying Western critical language to American Indian literatures, I contend that the answer is not simply an avoidance of these useful concepts and scaffoldings. Rather, in adapting critical metaphors, scholars of American Indian literatures have a responsibility to recognize the specific cultural and literary contexts of the texts under investigation, to apply theories mindfully, and to pay close attention to the places where the critical lenses work, as well as to where and how they break down.

4. "Anishinaabe" (pl. "Anishinaabeg") is a phonetic transcription from the oral tradition of the name the people use for themselves meaning "the original people." More specifically, "Anishinaabe" designates the Three Fires of the Ojibwe/Ojibway, the Potawatomi/Bodewadmi, and the Ottawa/Odawa. The Ojibwe were considered the eldest brother; the Odawa, the middle brother; and the Potawatomi, the youngest brother (Dickmann and Leefers 73). Ojibwe/Ojibway and Chippewa are different spellings for the same name, though the former versions are perhaps more accurate representations. Both Anishinaabe and Ojibwe/Ojibway appear in this paper as they are used by different authors. In my own writing, however, I use "Anishinaabe" to reflect the people's self-designation.

5. The Anishinaabeg currently live on reserves in Ontario and Manitoba and on reservations in Minnesota, Wisconsin, Michigan, and North Dakota, as well as in off-reservation towns and cities (Vizenor, *People* 32). John Nichols notes:

> Ojibwe and the other languages grouped together in the Algonquian language family resemble each other so closely in sound patterns, grammar, and vocabulary that at one time they must have been a single language. . . . At the time of the European invasion of North America, the languages of the Algonquian language family were spoken by Indians along the Atlantic coast from what is now North Carolina to Newfoundland, inland across Canada to the Great Plains, and in the region of the Great Lakes, perhaps ranging as far south as Alabama and Georgia. (qtd. in Vizenor, *People* 16)

6. The North Dakota novels that connect through location and character are *Love Medicine* (1984), *The Beet Queen* (1986), *Tracks* (1988), *The Bingo Palace* (1994), *Tales of Burning Love* (1997), *The Last Report on the Miracles at Little No Horse* (2001), *The Master Butchers Singing Club* (2003), *Four Souls* (2004), *The Painted Drum* (2005), and *The Plague of Doves* (2008).

7. Movement framing the narrative is one of many ways that Erdrich's novels can be connected to trickster stories. Louis Owens writes of *Love Medicine*, "Like the traditional trickster narrative, the story opens with the protagonist, June

Kashpaw, on the move" (195), and he notes that 'Trickster was going along' begins "almost all trickster narratives in Native American tradition" (228).

8. Summer Harrison writes of the extended version of this passage:

    Nanapush links stories with the material world and specifically with the political context of land use. He draws attention not only to how roads, cars, and buildings affect the earth but also to the historical narratives of progress that legitimize their impact. The deep printing of modern technology disrupts both the local woodlands and the communal identity of a "people who [once] left no tracks." (39)

9. Louis Owens contends that June's role of "permanent traveler" is evidence of her "infinit[e] dislocat[ion]" with no family/community/tribe to expect her return" (195). In my reading, however, it is her movement that connects her closely with her "family/tribe/community"; rather than a sign of alienation, her movement is a sign of her ultimate connection to people and place.

10. "Nadouissioux" is a French rendering of the Anishinaabe term *Na:towe:ssiw* or *Naadwesi*, which refers to the "Siouan peoples and particularly to Dakota speakers" (Koontz). "Nadouissioux" was truncated to "Sioux."

11. Maria DePriest notes, "Tracking the moments when land becomes property, [*Tracks*] moves implacably from 1912 to 1924, just at the time when the consequences of the Allotment Act of 1887 and its several amendments were the most devastating for the tribe" (251).

12. Anishinaabe elder Lillian Pitawanakwat states, "The teachings of the Medicine Wheel are vast. There are seven teachings within each direction on the Ojibwe wheel, and all these have sub-teachings to them, such as where all the medicines like sweetgrass came from, and what they mean." The Medicine Wheel is visually represented as a circle divided into four quadrants representing the four cardinal points and the four seasons, as well as sacred colors, animals, plants, and stories. Pitawanakwat further explains that also contained in the Medicine Wheel are the Seven Grandfather Teachings ("Honesty, Humility, Courage, Wisdom, Respect, Generosity, and Love") and the Seven Stages of Life ("The Good Life, The Fast Life, The Wandering Life, the stages of Truth, Planning, and Doing, and The Elder Life").

13. Nancy Peterson lays out some of the connections between the two: "Episodes in the story of Naanabozho parallel episodes in Nanapush's story. Both share the ability to come back to life after death or near death; both are noted for their keen ability to track people; both avenge wrongs committed on family members; both are powerful storytellers" (990). The connection is also marked by the location of trickster's home on the crossroads—Barbara Babcock notes that the crossroads is a location common to trickster figures in Native American stories (162)—and by trickster's ability to survive. Andrew Wiget argues that traditional trickster narratives "shift the burden of meaning from the cognitive sphere to the moral one. . . . Instead of asking, What is Truth in the matter—an unanswerable question . . . one must ask, What is right?" (92–93). The circling, contradictory trickster narratives expose the limitations of "official" historical accounts and

suggest that cultural survival rests not in the certainty of factual truth but on the shifting ground of interpretation, adaptation, and ethics. Nanapush's role in *Tracks* keeps the other characters off balance. In one moment, he is telling a story with the sole purpose of causing Pauline to lose control of her bladder, and in the next, he is enacting sacred ceremonies. Such a contrast is not a contradiction, but rather a clear sign of trickster's vibrant character, both creator and fool, wise elder and prankster.

14. Victoria Brehm argues that Nanapush's ceremony reflects his initiation to the sacred medicine society of the Anishinaabeg, Midéwiwin or Midé: "In the center of *Tracks* Nanapush begins a 'medicine' hunt, in which he guides Eli to a moose by lying down and holding his otter skin bag to his chest. Such a bag signifies that Nanapush has been initiated into the first degree of the Midéwiwin" (705 56n).

15. Thank you to Daniel Cooper Alarcón, whose articulation of palimpsests in *The Aztec Palimpsest* has provided me with a vocabulary for this and other projects.

Works Cited

"About the Project." *Tracing the Trail: The Pictured Rocks Segment of the Anishnaabeg Migration Route*. National Park Service and Alex K. Ruuska, Northern Michigan University, n.d. Web. 5 May 2011.

Alarcón, Daniel Cooper. *The Aztec Palimpsest: Mexico in the Modern Imagination.* Tucson: U of Arizona P, 1997.

Babcock, Barbara. "'A Tolerated Margin of Mess': The Trickster and His Tales Reconsidered." *Critical Essays on Native American Literature*. Ed. Andrew Wiget. Boston: Hall, 1985. 153–85.

Ballinger, Franchot. *Living Sideways: Tricksters in American Indian Oral Traditions.* Norman: U of Oklahoma P, 2004.

Bird, Gloria. "Searching for Evidence of Colonialism at Work: A Reading of Louise Erdrich's *Tracks*." *Wicazo Sa Review* 8.2 (1992): 40–47.

Brehm, Victoria. "The Metamorphoses of an Ojibwa Manido." *American Literature* 68.4 (1996): 677–706.

Clifford, James. *Routes: Travel and Translation in the Late Twentieth Century*. Cambridge: Harvard UP, 1997.

DePriest, Maria. "Once Upon a Time, Today: Hearing Fleur's Voice in *Tracks*." *Journal of Narrative Theory* 38.2 (2008): 249–68.

Dickmann, Donald I., and Larry A. Leefers. *The Forests of Michigan.* Ann Arbor: U of Michigan P, 2003.

Erdrich, Louise. *Four Souls.* New York: Harper, 2004.

_____. *Love Medicine.* New York: Harper, 1984.

_____. *Tracks.* New York: Harper, 1988.

Furlan, Laura M. "Remapping Indian Country in Louise Erdrich's *The Antelope Wife*." *Studies in American Indian Literatures* 19.4 (2007): 54–76.

Gross, Lawrence William. "The Trickster and World Maintenance: An Anishinaabe Reading of Louise Erdrich's *Tracks.*" *Studies in American Indian Literatures* 17.3 (2005): 48–66.

Harrison, Summer. "The Politics of Metafiction in Louise Erdrich's *Four Souls.*" *Studies in American Indian Literature* 23.1 (2011): 38–69.

Johnson, Kelli Lyon. "Writing Deeper Maps: Mapmaking, Local Indigenous Knowledges, and Literary Nationalism in Native Women's Writing." *Studies in American Indian Literatures* 19.4 (2007): 103–20.

Koontz, John E. "Etymology." *Siouan Languages.* U of Colorado, 2003. Web. 5 July 2011.

Owens, Louis. *Other Destinies: Understanding the American Indian Novel.* Norman: U of Oklahoma P, 1992.

Peterson, Nancy J. "History, Postmodernism, and Louise Erdrich's *Tracks.*" *PMLA* 109.5 (1994): 982–94.

Pitawanakwat, Lillian. "Ojibwe/ Powawatomi (Anishinabe) Teaching." *Four Directions Teachings.* 4d Interactive, 2006. Web. 9 June 2011.

Rainwater, Catherine. "Reading between Worlds: Narrativity in the Fiction of Louise Erdrich." *American Literature* 62.3 (1990): 405–33.

Sands, Kathleen M. "Louise Erdrich's *Love Medicine.*" *Studies in American Indian Literatures* 9.1 (1985): 12–24.

Stratton, Billy J., and Frances Washburn. "The Peoplehood Matrix: A New Theory for American Indian Literature." *Wicazo Sa Review* 23.1 (2008): 51–72.

Turner, Victor. "Liminality and Communitas." *The Ritual Process: Structure and Anti-Structure.* Chicago: Aldine, 1969. 94–130.

_____. "Passages, Margins, and Poverty: Religious Symbols of Communitas." *Dramas, Fields, and Metaphors: Symbolic Action in Human Society.* Ithaca: Cornell UP, 1974. 231–71.

Turner, Victor, and Edith Turner. *Image and Pilgrimage in Christian Culture: Anthropological Perspectives.* New York: Columbia UP, 1978.

Vizenor, Gerald. *Fugitive Poses: Native American Indian Scenes of Absence and Presence.* Lincoln: U of Nebraska P, 1998.

_____, ed. *Narrative Chance: Postmodern Discourse on Native American Indian Literatures.* Albuquerque: U of New Mexico P, 1989.

_____. *The People Named the Chippewa: Narrative Histories.* Minneapolis: U of Minnesota P, 1984.

Wiget, Andrew. "His Life in His Tail: The Native American Trickster and the Literature of Possibility." *Redefining American Literary History.* Ed. A. LaVonne Brown Ruoff and Jerry W. Ward Jr. New York: MLA, 1990. 83–96.

"Life will break you. . . . You have to love": Historical/Intergenerational Trauma and Healing in Louise Erdrich's *The Painted Drum*

Patrice Hollrah

Introduction

Ojibwe author Louise Erdrich writes in her novel *The Painted Drum* a nonlinear narrative of intergenerational family stories that moves from contemporary times to the past and back. Similar to the drum in the novel, the metaphor of "story" depicts life and death: "The story surfaces here, snarls there, as people live their disorder to its completion" (4). Historical trauma accounts for some of the "disorder" in the novel, its roots traced to colonization, boarding schools, and cultural genocide. Multiple narrators tell and retell stories of Ojibwe history and culture, and when the drum returns to the community, people celebrate traditional songs and ceremonies. Bernard Shaawano describes the healing power of story: "My father [Shaawano] talked once he got sober, talked like his own father [Old Grandfather Shaawano] had, endlessly, hoping to be redeemed by the story" (100–101) and "the father [Old Grandfather Shaawano] had to tell what he saw, again and again, in order to get rid of it" (110–11). Both the drum and storytelling have power to save and heal the contemporary reservation Ojibwes, as well as the detribalized urban characters. To discuss *The Painted Drum*, this essay begins with a critical literature survey and presents a brief synopsis of the novel for context. An explanation of historical/intergenerational trauma from a Native point of view and a description of off-reservation boarding schools inform the narrative of *The Painted Drum*.

Critical Literature Survey

Several critical essays on *The Painted Drum* focus on Ojibwe identity, narrative structure, and storytelling. In "Finding a Rhythm: How Tribalism Creates Identity in Erdrich's *The Painted Drum*," scholar

Matthew J. Rickard writes about the stories: "In order for [the] characters to gain an Ojibwe identity, they must be exposed to stories. They must draw together to generate a tribal experience, an experience the characters can share in common with one another and use as a starting point for a new identity" (32). Scholar Jean Wyatt also discusses identity in her essay "Storytelling, Melancholia, and Narrative Structure in Louise Erdrich's *The Painted Drum*," arguing that the novel's narrative structure "conveys the means of [Faye Travers's] change. . . . The mechanism of change is dramatized, not described" (13). Wyatt goes on to claim that the storytelling in parts 2 and 3 of the novel create "Faye's conversion to a different way of knowing" and that her "revival stems from her rebirth as a member of the Bear clan" (14, 27). In "Native Spaces of Continuation, Preservation, and Belonging: Louise Erdrich's Concepts of Home," scholar Jonathan Max Wilson concentrates on the "treatment of home and home's connection to identity for its major characters" (120). Rather than primarily consider the detribalized characters' Ojibwe identity, this essay explores how the drum and telling stories heal the historical/intergenerational trauma that the Ojibwes have endured.

The Painted Drum

The Painted Drum's narrative structure has four parts: "Revival Road," "North of Hoopdance," "The Little Girl Drum," and "Revival Road." The reader sees a circular pattern, the conclusion returning to the beginning of the novel, a configuration that complements mythic time and explains how the past, present, and future are one and the same. The drum connects the four parts despite the differences in settings, periods, characters, and narratives. Faye Travers narrates parts 1 and 4 in the early twenty-first century. Part 2 contains the story of the drum's origins in the early twentieth century, and part 3 relates the drum's role in the lives of contemporary reservation families. Faye, in her early fifties, lives with her mother, Elsie Travers, in New Hampshire, and they run an estate sale business, "dealing with the physical estate, the stuff, the junk, the possessions" with a specialty in Native American antiquities (28–29). Faye finds the drum at the estate of a family whose grandfather, Jewett Parker Tatro, was an Indian agent on an Ojibwe reservation in North Dakota.

Faye's not-so-loving father has passed away, and her younger sister, Netta, died in the family apple orchard when Faye was nine years old (92–94). Netta sacrifices herself for her sister, and Faye's guilt over her sister's death prevents her from developing close intimate relationships with other people, including her mother and her lover, Kurt Krahe. Faye thinks, "I have always been afraid of talking to my mother on this level, of breaking through the comforting web of our safe behavior. We have knitted it daily and well" (263); of Kurt, Faye admits, "I never talk about who I really am with him" (10). Nonetheless, the title of part 1, "Revival Road," foreshadows the restoration of the sacred drum to its rightful Ojibwe owners, thereby reawakening Ojibwe sacred songs and ceremonies, and the revival of Faye's spirit and those of other characters in the novel.

In part 2, "North of Hoopdance," Faye and her mother travel to the North Dakota Ojibwe reservation to return the drum. Bernard Shaawano recounts for the Travers family the history of the drum, family stories within stories of three Shaawano generations, relating events from the early to mid-twentieth century. Faye learns about her ancestors, great-grandfather Simon Jack and great-grandmother Ziigwan'aage, and their connections to Old Grandfather Shaawano and his wife, Anaquot.

Part 3 details the story of another Ojibwe family, Ira and her three children, who have moved back to the Ojibwe reservation from the city in the early twenty-first century. The drum saves the lives of the young children during a daring night walk through the freezing snow.

Part 4 returns to New Hampshire, where Faye and her mother reconcile long-held secrets about their lives and the death of Faye's younger sister, Netta. In "Religion and Ethics in Louise Erdrich's *The Painted Drum*," scholar Marta Lysik explores "issues of personal religion, spirituality, and ethics . . . through the prism of the concept of *kairos*" and "applies this concept to . . . denote a religious or spiritual break-through in the life of a modern individual" (1). Still, Faye insists at the end of the novel that she has not had a spiritual conversion: "For to suddenly say, *I believe*, *I am convinced*, even *saved*, and to throw myself into Native traditions as Kit Tatro wishes so sincerely to do, is not in my character" (269). Despite her denials, Faye has changed her thinking with regard to her dead sister, Netta, and now with a differ-ent attitude, spends time in the apple orchard where Netta died. In the beginning of the novel, Faye does not want the orchard brought back to life and says she likes it "ruined" (56). With the orchard now produc-ing fruit, she has a new appreciation: "I step toward my sister's tree and see right away that her branch has cracked off under the weight of apples. . . . I think that I might eat one" (272). Faye has made peace with her sister's death. Thus, the painted drum connects all the charac-ters in the past and present and helps them all in one way or another to heal from emotional, physical, and spiritual wounds.

Historical/Intergenerational Trauma and Boarding School

In part 2, "North of Hoopdance," Bernard Shaawano articulates the stories of his grandfather, father, and himself, and he explicates histori-cal/intergenerational trauma: "We still have sorrows that are passed to us from early generations, those to handle besides our own, and cruel-ties lodged where we cannot forget. We have the need to forget. I don't know if we stopped the fever of forgetting yet. We are always walking on oblivion's edge" (116). Telling the stories paves the way for indi-vidual, family, community, and nation healing.

Hunkpapa/Oglala Lakota scholar Maria Yellow Horse Brave Heart has developed historical trauma and historical unresolved grief theory and interventions among American Indians. Her research branches off from the literature on Jewish Holocaust survivors and incorporates the history unique to Native Americans. Brave Heart maintains that Native peoples' history fits the definition of genocide from the Convention on the Prevention and Punishment of the Crime of Genocide, adopted by Resolution 260 (III) A of the United Nations General Assembly on December 9, 1948 ("Intergenerational Trauma" 5). Article 2 of that resolution defines genocide to mean, among other things, "forcibly transferring children of the group to another group." Ojibwes have experienced all six points of the definition of genocide and, in particular, the history of residential boarding schools for Native children, where they were under the control of "another group."

In part 1 of the novel, John Jewett Tatro, a collector of Native artifacts, dies, and his niece, Sarah Tatro, calls Faye to handle his estate. His grandfather, Jewett Parker Tatro, had been "an Indian agent on the Ojibwe reservation where [Faye's] grandmother was born and where she lived until the age of ten, at which time she was taken east and enrolled at Carlisle Indian School, in Pennsylvania" (29–30). The passing reference to the Carlisle Indian Industrial School is loaded with historical trauma for Native Americans. Captain Richard Henry Pratt founded the school in 1879 for the express purpose of turning Indians into "civilized" people by teaching them how to imitate white people. Teachers taught the children to speak and write in English, converted them to Christianity, erased all signs of their Indian culture, and showed them how to do manual work like white people. Pratt was fond of saying, "In Indian civilization I am a Baptist, because I believe in immersing the Indians in our civilization and when we get them under holding them there until they are thoroughly soaked" (qtd. in Witmer 19). Pratt's version of baptism was to "kill the Indian; save the man" (qtd. in Landis). Mistakenly, Pratt thought he could "save" Indians by turning them into white people.

In the Carlisle Indian Industrial School website introduction, Barbara Landis writes, "It is our purpose to respectfully *honor* those students and their descendants who lived the experiment, *celebrate* with those who prospered from it, and *grieve* with those whose lives were diminished by it." Erdrich presents a picture of those whose lives are negatively impacted by the boarding-school experience. Faye describes her grandmother Niibin'aage's boarding school experience with a negative tone:

> There, she learned to sew intricately, to add and subtract, to do laundry, scrub a floor clean, read, write, and recite Bible passages, Shakespeare's sonnets, Keats's odes, and the Declaration of Independence and the Bill of Rights. Carlisle Institute was also where she fell in love, or came to know her husband, I should say. It is hard for me to imagine that the cold little woman I remember, the anti-Grandma, I used to call her, ever fell in love or felt much in the way of human emotion. (30)

When the US government removed American Indian children from their families and the larger tribal community to live at the off-reservation boarding schools, they lost the opportunity to learn how to love within the extended family and how to parent their own children. Carlisle operated like a military institution, with students all wearing the same uniforms and having their hair cut short (Witmer 24). Although Erdrich does not add any details of physical or sexual abuse in this account, both were frequent at the boarding schools: "Not uncommonly, staff members at these schools engaged in horrific instances of violence and violation perpetrated against their wards, including sadistic acts of torture" (Gone 752). Faye's nickname of "anti-Grandma" is not surprising, keeping in mind that she probably does not fit the stereotype of a warm, loving grandmother. The lack of loving parenting is probably Elsie's experience and passed on to Faye, an example of intergenerational trauma, first experienced at the boarding school and representative of the history of Ojibwes.

In part 3, there is another character, Seraphine String, a social worker, who has a painful boarding-school experience. Her brother-in-law, Morris String, calls her War Wounds, and states that Seraphine was in the army, "the one that was conducted on us where they took our children prisoner" (236). Boarding schools have been compared to prisons. In fact, the Cariboo Tribal Council concludes, "'Residential school students were overloaded with activities more appropriate to a correctional institution than a school . . . [and] could not be considered appropriate for learning, growth, and personal fulfillment'" (qtd. in Gone 752; ellipses in orig.). Bernard Shaawano recalls the story of how Seraphine came to have a white scar across her lips:

> Seraphine was raised in a traditional way by her grandparents and she spoke little English. But then her grandparents died and Seraphine was sent to boarding school. . . . It was forbidden to speak what the teachers called Indian; sometimes those words seemed to inflame a special wrath from the teachers and the matrons who took care of the children. One day, Seraphine forgot or rebelled and began to speak her own language and would not stop. The matron was showing girls how to mend cushioned chairs. In her hand there was a thick needle for sewing together upholstery. She turned and struck Seraphine. The needle ripped across the girl's face, and although the doctor who sewed the wound together was sensitive and careful, the scar of speaking her language remained across her lips all of her life. (250–51)

The story of Seraphine's disfiguring abuse encapsulates the atrocities that Native children suffered in the boarding schools. Forcing children to give up their language, the means by which people transmit culture and identity, traumatized them. If Bernard Shaawano lived at the boarding school, then most likely his grandfather and father did as well, creating more intergenerational trauma. Joseph Gone summarizes the lasting effects of forced assimilation: "In addition to violence, widespread loss of indigenous language, culture, and ceremony has combined with multigenerational disruptions in parenting practices to yield a harrowing legacy of distress and disability for contemporary Native peoples" (752). The return of the drum to the Ojibwe reservation restores songs and ceremonies that were lost, and the healing begins.

Brave Heart's definition of historical trauma, given on her website, includes the history unique to Native Americans:

Historical trauma is cumulative emotional and psychological wounding over the lifespan and across generations, emanating from massive group trauma. Native Americans have, for over 500 years, endured physical, emotional, social, and spiritual genocide from European and American colonialist policy. Contemporary Native American life has adapted, such that, many are healthy and economically self-sufficient. Yet a significant proportion of Native people are not faring as well.

Brave Heart's definition notes a time span of "over 500 years," and the trauma continues not only because of what happened in the past and has been carried from one generation to the next, but also because of the colonizing forces and oppression of Native peoples that persist.

Brave Heart's website lists six phases of historical unresolved grief resulting from historical trauma, including the damage from the boarding-school period: "destroyed family system, beatings, rape, prohibition of Native language and religion; Lasting Effect: ill-prepared for parenting, identity confusion." In her essay on historical trauma in Erdrich's novel *Tracks*, scholar Connie A. Jacobs notes, "The long-lasting effects of historical trauma on American Indian communities testify to the extent of the damage wrought by colonization" (40). Brave Heart records the damage that Native peoples suffer as "trauma response features," and among those features are "low self-esteem, victim identity, anger, self-destructive behavior, and substance abuse," which compel people to find ways to numb the pain. ("Intergenerational Trauma" 6–8).

Characters in *The Painted Drum* display several of the trauma response features, most notably depression, psychic numbing, self-destructive behaviors, substance abuse, and internalized oppression. For example, physical abuse and alcoholism as a way to numb the pain pass down through several Shaawano generations because of historical trauma and Old Grandfather Shaawano's individual trauma in the death of his daughter and abandonment by his wife. Understanding the historical trauma of a community is necessary to begin the healing process. Brave Heart presents "four major community intervention components" about historical trauma—confronting, understanding, releasing, and transcending—followed by three major hypotheses for the intervention model to begin healing historical grief: education, sharing, and collective mourning/healing ("Welcome"). She differentiates people as belonging to one of several hierarchical groups: victim, survivor, and transcendence, or those who go beyond the identity of survivor to the goal of healing ("Intergenerational Trauma" 5). *The Painted Drum* offers examples of individual characters that go through this intervention process, and eventually the community gathers for sacred drum ceremonies to heal and transcend past trauma.

The Painted Drum and Sovereignty

Faye discovers the drum when she begins to go through the artifacts in the Tatro house. Erdrich critiques the well-known fact about Indian agents and their tendency to "amass extensive collections of artifacts" (30), an example of whites exploiting Natives for their possessions. Although Faye is detribalized, she knows enough about her Ojibwe heritage to remark, "Were I a traditional Ojibwe, I would have a special place in the community because of my line of work. . . . Those persons who distribute the objects should not wear the color red—it is the one color the dead are thought to see clearly. . . . I avoid wearing red in my work, for somehow I find that idea compelling" (33). Faye also understands the different values between Natives and whites: "I almost never think of non-Indians as white. After all, my own skin is pale. But I experienced a sudden bolt of prejudice that surprised me. *Just like a white lady, so stingy with her tears she kept them*" (35). Faye recognizes that traditional Ojibwe values are often the complete opposite of Euro-American or Western contemporary values. Don Coyhis (Mohican), who created the Medicine Wheel and 12 Steps Circle alcohol recovery program for Native peoples, is the inspiration behind the Wellbriety healing movement in American Indian communities. In the essay "The Native American Healing Experience," he and Richard Simonelli have published a chart of values to illustrate the differences between traditional Native American and contemporary Euro-American values. For example, Native Americans value "generosity," and Euro-Americans value "saving" (1936). Not surprisingly, Faye identifies the white woman as "stingy" because she has saved all her handkerchiefs.

When Faye goes near the drum, three more sets of values become evident: "spiritual-mystical" versus "skeptical," "belief in the unseen" versus "belief in the seen/proven," and "right brain orientation" versus "left brain orientation" (Coyhis and Simonelli 1936). Faye hears the drum: "When I step near the drum, I swear it sounds. One deep, low, resonant note. . . . I hear it, I know I hear it, and yet Sarah Tatro does not" (39) and "I set my hand on the drum and then I feel, pulled through me like a nerve, a clear conviction. It is visceral. Not a thought but a gut instinct" (40). Faye takes the drum and puts it in her car. She justifies her actions, which by Euro-American standards equal stealing: "I wouldn't have done it unless it was on some level *right*" (41) and "My instinctive theft signifies a matter so essential that it might be called survival" (44). Faye's spontaneous decision to take the drum surprises her, but her action that she calls "survival" is plainly an act of respect for Ojibwe sovereignty.

When Faye informs her mother about the drum, Elsie is upset that Faye has taken it. After Elsie educates Faye about the significance of the drum, she soon begins to warm to the idea of finding the rightful owner and learning the story about how Tatro came to own the drum (42–43).

Storytelling

Part 2 of *The Painted Drum* takes Faye and Elsie to the reservation to return the drum. They meet Chook String and Bernard Shaawano, who tell them the stories about the drum's origins and the families involved.

Chook talks about the power of the drum to heal: "'We all got sorrows. . . . See, that's what the drum was good for. Letting those sorrows out, into the open, where those songs could bear them away'" (105). Chook echoes Brave Heart's intervention model of confronting, understanding, releasing, and transcending the sorrows caused by historical trauma.

Bernard Shaawano begins with the story of Old Grandfather Shaawano, his grandmother Anaquot, and their two children, a son and daughter. Anaquot falls in love with another man, Simon Jack, and has his daughter, Fleur. Simon Jack is married to another woman, Ziigwan'aage, and they have a baby boy, an older daughter named Niibin'aage (Faye's "anti-Grandmother"), and an older son. When the marriage becomes too strained, Old Grandfather Shaawano sends Anaquot, her new baby daughter, Fleur, and her older daughter to live with Simon Jack. The older daughter is eaten by wolves on the trip, and Old Grandfather Shaawano does not recover from his grief. Bernard recites the story of "how when the wolves closed in, Anaquot threw her daughter to them" (111). Old Grandfather Shaawano drinks too much in order to numb his pain.

In the second story, Bernard Shaawano reveals how he and his two siblings, Doris and Raymond, survive their childhood and their father's drinking and physical abuse. Finally, Bernard, at thirteen years of age, decides to fight back, and that is when his father has his senses literally knocked back into his head. He says, "Did you know I had a sister once?" (115). Acknowledgment of his dead sister is the first step in the healing process: to *confront* the trauma. He divulges to his son Bernard how his older sister died, and sharing his story helps him to *understand* the trauma. Then Bernard revises the story, saying that Anaquot did not throw her daughter to the wolves, but instead, the sister "lifted her shawl and flew" because "she was, of the old sort of Anishinaabeg who thinks of the good of the people first" (117). The revised version of the sister's sacrifice helps Shaawano to *understand*, *release*, and *transcend* the trauma, leading him to sobriety and healing.

In addition, Bernard Shaawano references the termination and re-location period in Native American history, a government-imposed program of the 1950s and 1960s that added to the historical trauma. This policy, E. Jethro Gaede states, "was enacted to facilitate the long-standing goals of assimilation and self-determination and to end government programs supporting tribes." Bernard Shaawano gives his account of the period and its traumatic effects on his family and community:

> There was a time when the government moved everybody off the farther reaches of the reservation, onto roads, into towns, into housing. It looked good at first and then it all went sour. Shortly after, it seemed like anyone who was someone was either dead, drunk, killed, near suicide, or just had dusted themself. None of the old sorts were left, it seemed, the old kind of people. It was during that time that my mother died and my father hurt us, as I have said. But now, gradually, that term of despair has lifted somewhat and yielded up its survivors. (116)

Gaede summarizes the failure of the program: "While some Indian families did adjust to their new urban settings, the net effect of relocation for many American Indians manifested as loss of access to traditional cultural supports, economic hardship, social disenfranchisement, overt discrimination, and unemployment. . . . Termination and relocation policy wrought social havoc for Indians generally, and explicit, negative consequences for terminated tribes." The Shaawano family and the Ojibwes suffer trauma response features caused by this period of termination and relocation.

The third story Bernard Shaawano shares is about Ira's father (in part 3), the "old man . . . who wanted to be with the wolves and know their thoughts" (119). This man wants to learn how to survive, and he spends three days on the ice waiting for the wolves to communicate their thoughts to him. On the fourth day, the wolf asks him, "Do you want to die?" (120). The old man answers with a question of his own about how the wolves can survive when outside forces work to eliminate them: "How is it that you go on living with such sorrow? How do you go on without turning around and destroying yourselves, as so many of us Anishinaabeg have done under similar circumstances?" (120). The wolf answers, "We live because we live" (120). The old man returns to a traditional ceremony, the Sundance, to survive.

Coyhis and Simonelli recommend engaging Indian cultural practices for healing from addiction and historical trauma: "These include smudging with sage, cedar, and sweet grass, as well as speaking prayers in one's own tribal language or utilizing tribal drum groups, ceremonies, and songs as part of meetings and conventions" (1929). In 1883, the commissioner of Indian Affairs, Hiram Price, enacted the Indian Religious Crimes Code, which outlawed the practice of traditional spiritual ceremonies. Eventually, this code was reversed: "The Indian Civil Rights Act of 1968 (ICRA, 1968), and the American Indian Religious Freedom Act of 1978 (AIRFA, 1978) with its Native American Church Peyote amendment of 1994, made it possible for Native cultural ways to come out from behind closed doors" (Coyhis and Simonelli 1928–29). Ira's father, the old man, transcends historical trauma by a return to traditional ceremonial practice.

Anaquot's daughter, Fleur, gives Bernard Shaawano his fourth story, a tale about Anaquot's survival in Simon Jack's home, where his first wife, Ziigwan'aage, wants to kill her. Instead, the spirit of Anaquot's dead daughter keeps her safe and advises her how to avoid any poisonings. In time, Anaquot remembers what happened to her older daughter on the way to Simon Jack's home, and "her mind cracked open" (130). Anaquot acknowledges the traumatic death of her daughter, and in so doing, begins on the road to recovery. She and Ziigwan'aage become friends and conspire to do away with Simon Jack by sewing him a beaded dance outfit, an "elaborate set of clothes to be buried in" (144). The women also sew hoods and mitts from the fur of a wolf that Ziigwan'aage kills, and Anaquot learns that the dead wolf is the one that ate her daughter's heart (147). Reconciliation and forgiveness ensue with this new knowledge, and Anaquot can *release* the trauma of her older daughter's death and *transcend* it.

Bernard Shaawano returns to the story of Old Grandfather Shaawano and how he built the little girl a drum. Old Grandfather Shaawano suffers from guilt over sending his wife away, and his self-destructive behaviors turn to drinking and emotional abuse of his son (151–53). Old Grandfather Shaawano has a dream about his dead daughter, and she gives him directions for making a drum that will keep him alive: "She had given him a task that was meant to keep him here upon the earth" (155). The community contributes to Old Grandfather Shaawano's task, and soon he is building the drum that will help him and the community to heal. He even reconciles and forgives the wolves who killed his daughter: "The wolves had only acted according to their natures, after all" (169). Old Grandfather Shaawano *confronts*, *understands*, and *releases* the trauma of his daughter's death; he *transcends* it by building the drum.

The final story that Bernard Shaawano discloses in part 2 is about how Old Grandfather Shaawano completes the drum and how Simon Jack dances to his death: "He went the spirit world way around the drum" (184). After that dark event, Old Grandfather Shaawano put the drum away (184).

In part 3 of *The Painted Drum*, the reader meets Ira and her three children, Shawnee, Alice, and Apitchi. The drum saves Shawnee and her siblings from freezing to death in the dark of night by pounding and leading the children to safety at Bernard Shaawano's house. Shawnee is the only one who hears the drum when nobody is playing it, so her spiritual connection to the drum forecasts that someday she may be a keeper of it and the sacred songs. The youngest child, Apitchi, becomes ill from exposure to the icy cold, and Bernard Shaawano plans to hold a healing ceremony with the drum, an example of how it helps people physically heal in the community.

In part 4, Bernard Shaawano writes a letter to Faye and Elsie Travers to let them know how well the community is doing now that the drum has returned: "*With the drum back, there is a good feeling here. People have come together around it. I am surprised. That young girl Shawnee has moved back with her mother to a house built on the site of the old one. Our housing authority did come through there pretty good*" (268– 69). There are several parallels in the novel: daughters who die for their families (Netta Travers and Anaquot's daughter); mothers who have extramarital affairs (Elsie Travers and Anaquot); people who self-medicate with alcohol to numb their pain (Old Grandfather Shaawano, Shaawano, and Bernard Shaawano). All these characters ultimately find healing through their connections to the drum and the sharing of their stories.

Faye Travers arrives at a philosophy of life that advises love despite the heartaches and disappointments in life:

> Life will break you. Nobody can protect you from that, and living alone won't either, for solitude will also break you with its yearning. You have to love. You have to feel. It is the reason you are here on earth. You are here to risk your heart. You are here to be swallowed up. And when it happens that you are broken, or betrayed, or left, or hurt, or death brushes near, let yourself sit by an apple tree and listen to the apples falling all around you in heaps, wasting their sweetness. Tell yourself that you tasted as many as you could. (274)

Undoubtedly, telling the community/family stories illustrates their power to save, just as the characters in *The Painted Drum* learn by confronting their own personal histories, "endlessly, hoping to be redeemed by the story" (101). Forgiveness and reconciliation through storytelling and returning the drum to the rightful Ojibwe owners prove that Brave Heart's intervention model is successful; healing begins to take place, and the people become healthier, no longer victims but survivors.

Works Cited

Brave Heart, Maria Yellow Horse."From Intergenerational Trauma to Intergenerational Healing." *Wellbriety!* 6.6 (2005): 2–8.

_____. "Welcome to Takini's Historical Trauma." *Historical Trauma*. Maria Yellow Horse Brave Heart, n.d. Web. 31 Mar. 2011.

Cariboo Tribal Council. "Faith Misplaced: Lasting Effects of Abuse in a First Nation Community." *Canadian Journal of Native Education* 18.2 (1991): 161–97.

Coyhis, Don, and Richard Simonelli. "The Native American Healing Experience." *Substance Use & Misuse* 43.12–13 (2008): 1927–49.

Erdrich, Louise. *The Painted Drum*. New York: Harper, 2005.

Gaede, E. Jethro. "Termination and Relocation Programs." *Encyclopedia of Oklahoma History and Culture*. Oklahoma Historical Soc., n.d. Web. 18 Apr. 2012.

"General Assembly Resolution 260 (III) of 9 December 1948 (Prevention and Punishment of the Crime of Genocide." *Convention on the Prevention and Punishment of the Crime of Genocide*. United Nations, 2008. Web. 18 Apr. 2012.

Gone, Joseph P. "A Community-Based Treatment for Native American Historical Trauma: Prospects for Evidence-Based Practice." *Journal of Consulting and Clinical Psychology* 77.4 (2009):751–62.

Jacobs, Connie. " 'I Knew There Never Was Another Martyr Like Me': Pauline Puyat, Historical Trauma, and *Tracks*." *Louise Erdrich:* Tracks, The Last Report on the Miracles at Little No Horse, The Plague of Doves. Ed. Deborah Madsen. London: Continuum, 2011. 46–63.

Landis, Barbara. *Carlisle Indian Industrial School (1879–1918)*. Barbara Landis, 1996. Web. 18 Apr. 2012.

Lysik, Marta. "Religion and Ethics in Louise Erdrich's *The Painted Drum* and Alice Walker's *Now Is the Time to Open Your Heart*." *Ideology and Rhetoric: Constructing America*. Ed. Bożenna Chylińska. Newcastle: Cambridge Scholars, 2009. 135–44.

Rickard, Matthew J. "Finding a Rhythm: How Tribalism Creates Identity in Erdrich's *The Painted Drum*." Thesis. U of North Carolina, 2007.

Wilson, Jonathan Max. "Native Spaces of Continuation, Preservation, and Belonging: Louise Erdrich's Concepts of Home." Diss. U of Texas, 2008.

Witmer, Linda F. *The Indian Industrial School: Carlisle, Pennsylvania 1879–1918*. 1993. 3rd ed. Cumberland: Cumberland County Historical Soc., 2002.

Wyatt, Jean. "Storytelling, Melancholia, and Narrative Structure in Louise Erdrich's *The Painted Drum*." *MELUS* 36.1 (2011): 13–36.

From Wallace to Wishkob: Queer Relationships and Two-Spirit Characters in *The Beet Queen, Tales of Burning Love,* and *The Last Report on the Miracles at Little No Horse*_____

Lisa Tatonetti

In 1969, the year Kiowa/Cherokee author N. Scott Momaday's *House Made of Dawn* won the Pulitzer Prize for literature, I was three years old, riding barefoot on the handlebars of my older siblings' bikes around the neighborhood streets. Unsurprisingly, I was unaware that year marked what Kenneth Lincoln would later term the Native American Renaissance. It was not until I began an undergraduate degree in my late twenties that I discovered Momaday and, along with him, Leslie Marmon Silko, James Welch, and Louise Erdrich. I clearly remember the semester I took an honors class in American Indian women's literature. It was 1994, and among our course texts were Paula Gunn Allen's collection *Spider Woman's Granddaughters* (1989), Silko's *Ceremony* (1977), and Erdrich's *Love Medicine* (1983). That summer I read the rest of Erdrich's novels, which were then only four in number: *Love Medicine, The Beet Queen* (1986), *Tracks* (1988), and *The Bingo Palace* (1994). My passion for Erdrich's work during this time was closely paralleled by an interest in queer studies. In 1995, my first year of graduate work, I took a queer-theory course that introduced me to new ways of understanding desires, genders, and sexualities, as well as to the 1988 anthology *Living the Spirit*, which was then the only anthology of LGBTQ2 (lesbian, gay, bisexual, transsexual/transgender, queer, two-spirit) Native literature. I continued to expand my knowledge of both Native literatures and queer studies but found little beyond *Living the Spirit* that joined the two perspectives. While Latino and black literary studies seemed on fire with the possibilities of what would come to be called queer of color critiques, the intersections of indigeneity and queerness were only beginning to be explored in Native literary criticism.

Over fifteen years later, the face of Native literary criticism has changed, and as I have shown elsewhere, an important development in American Indian literary studies has been the emergence of an ever-increasing body of queer or two-spirit Native literatures and criticism.[1] Chronologically, the growth of the field has paralleled the rise of queer Native literatures: The inaugural issue of the Association for Studies in American Indian Literatures' regularly scheduled newsletter was published in 1977, just a few years after Mohawk author Maurice Kenny's overtly queer work in post-Stonewall publications such as *Gay Sunshine* and *Fag Rag* marked the publication of the first contemporary queer Native literature. Since the late 1980s, there has been a steady rise in the body of queer Native literature and a corresponding rise in criticism about such work since the late 1990s. Most recently, a number of significant publications situate the present day as a watershed moment in the study of queer Native literatures: a special issue of *GLQ: A Journal of Lesbian and Gay Studies* entitled "Sexuality, Nationality, Indigeneity" (16.1–2); a special issue of *Yellow Medicine Review* entitled "International Queer Indigenous Voices" (Fall 2010); a collection of critical work, *Queer Indigenous Studies: Critical Interventions in Theory, Politics, and Literature* (2011); and *Sovereign Erotics: A Collection of Two-Spirit Literature* (2011), the first new collection of queer Native literatures since *Living the Spirit.* If 1969 marked the Native American Renaissance, then perhaps the present day will be looked back upon as a queer renaissance in American Indian literary studies.

This history underlines the importance of Louise Erdrich's work: She has long been a trailblazer in terms of her depictions of alternate understandings of genders and sexualities. Her first inclusion of overtly queer characters occurs in *The Beet Queen* (1986), published four years *before* the term "two-spirit" was coined by indigenous people at the Third International Gathering of American Indian and First Nations Gays and Lesbians in Winnipeg (Jacobs, Thomas, and Lang 1–6; Driskill, Finley, Gilley, and Morgensen 10–18). As Driskill, Finley, Gilley, and Morgensen explain, "The community-based term

Two-Spirit . . . affirmed [Indigenous peoples'] belonging to cultural traditions by displacing anthropological terms—notably, *berdache*—thereby setting a new basis and method for Indigenous knowledge" (10). Erdrich's novels play an important role in such new understandings. Erdrich was the first among the five best-known Native American Renaissance authors—Momaday, Simon Ortiz, Silko, and Welch—to engage issues of queer sexuality, and as I will show, her depictions are by far the most nuanced and productive. While Silko and Welch offer problematic depictions of queers as murderers and monsters in novels such as *Almanac of the Dead* (1991) and *The Heartsong of Charging Elk* (2000), Erdrich represents lesbian, gay, bisexual, queer, and two-spirit identities as part of the everyday fabric of Native communities and, by the same token, represents the historical existence of gender variance as commonly accepted. This essay examines the images of queer identities in the first three of Erdrich's novels to spend significant time on such representations: *The Beet Queen, Tales of Burning Love* (1996), and *The Last Report on the Miracles at Little No Horse* (2001). While Erdrich presents queer characters in many of her texts, these novels can be juxtaposed to show how the depth and breadth of her characterizations develop across the body of her work: Her texts first highlight the fluidity of gender and the constructed nature of heterosexuality and later also invoke the importance of specifically indigenous, or two-spirit, understandings of the range and variety of genders and sexualities.

Erdrich's earliest foray into explicit representations of queerness comes in just her second novel, *The Beet Queen*. Notably, all of the central characters—Mary and Karl Adare, a brother and sister abandoned by their mother; Celestine James, an orphan who becomes Mary's lifelong best friend; Wallace Pfef, Karl's lover and surrogate father to Celestine's daughter; and Wallacette "Dot" Adare, the child of Karl and Celestine—stretch conventional gender norms in some way. Julie Barak argues that Mary, Celestine, and Dot can be read as "manly-hearted women," a term anthropologists historically coined for American Indian women who inhabited third gender roles by taking on the behaviors and occupations of men (55). J. James Iovannone contends that such characters should more accurately be read through a "transgendered" framework, as such a term "represent[s] gendered identities that exist beyond the binary categories of male and female, masculine and feminine, heterosexual and homosexual" (41). Tara Prince-Hughes, on the other hand, challenges work that relies too heavily on Western understandings of gender and sexuality. She maintains, "Despite recent theoretical fascination with identity instability, Erdrich demonstrates that for her characters, alternative genders are expressed as relatively stable identities marked by inclinations toward mediation, healing, community responsibility, and the work, dress, and behavior of the other sex" (8). While they differ over terminology and interpretation, these critics and others who have written on *The Beet Queen* agree that Erdrich regularly pushes the boundaries of gender and sexuality in her fiction, exceeding limited, normative definitions of each. Such recognition is reinforced when one realizes that, in terms of Native-authored novels, Erdrich's inclusion of queer characters as central figures in her fiction is preceded only by Paula Gunn Allen's 1983 novel *The Woman Who Owns the Shadows*.

Karl and Wallace, who share an on-again/off-again relationship, are two non-Native characters that function as the center of overt queer representations in *The Beet Queen*. Indeed, with the exclusion of Celestine, her half brother Russell Kashpaw, and brief references to their family, Erdrich's novel focuses primarily on the German American community in Argus, North Dakota. In the novel's 1932 opening, Karl is depicted as a character who straddles gender lines. He is "a tall fourteen" with a "sweetly curved mouth" and "skin fine and girlish" (1). The novel begins as he and his sister arrive in Argus, heading for the shelter of their aunt Fritzie's house after their mother's desertion. The two run different directions when a neighbor unleashes a dog upon Karl: Mary heads east, toward town and her aunt's butcher shop, while

Karl runs back to the boxcar that takes him away from Argus and his family for many years.

Karl's early meeting with Giles Saint Ambrose in the boxcar provides the first window into his desires. Giles, who mistakes Karl for a girl, offers the boy food and comfort. Giles's initial impression of Karl's femininity—"'You're a girl, aren't you?'" (23)—is underlined when his teasing causes Karl to burst into tears, to which Giles responds, "Quiet down. . . . You're going to have to practice. Boys don't do this" (24). This attempt to regulate how Karl performs gender highlights in a few short sentences both the malleability of gender and the social demands for the iteration of certain preferred gender performances. As Giles points out, expected gender behaviors—in this case, the old adage that men don't cry—rather than being inborn or biological expressions of gender, take "practice." Gender, Erdrich teaches her readers, is a set of learned behaviors. The theory of gender performance is interrogated most famously four years *after* the publication of *The Beet Queen* in Judith Butler's 1990 book *Gender Trouble*, where Butler argues that there is no "natural" tie between sex and gender. Butler explains, "There is no gender identity behind the expressions of gender. . . . Identity is performatively constituted by the very 'expressions' that are said to be its results" (25). In this case, the attempt to regulate Karl's gender performance is a resounding failure as, in the face of Giles' admonition, Karl cries himself to sleep.

Later that same day, Karl initiates sexual contact with Giles, but more telling than their sexual encounter is Karl's romantic daydream, which speaks volumes about the limits of his perception of queer identities. When he wakes from the exhausted sleep that follows his bout of tears, Karl "planned how he and Giles would travel in the boxcar, occasionally jumping off . . . stealing food, maybe finding an abandoned house to live in. He pictured them together, in danger from dogs or police, outrunning farmers and store clerks. He saw them roasting chickens and sleeping together, curled tight in a jolting boxcar, like they were now" (25). While Mary heads toward the relative safety and stability of family, Karl dreams differently in the liminal space of the boxcar. Notably though, Karl's imaginings all involve scenes of transgression and isolation. The homosocial bonding he envisions takes place outside of accepted societal boundaries, outside of a larger community, and in fact requires that he and Giles become outlaws who run from "police," "farmers," and "store clerks," figures that represent institutional authority, democratic agrarian ideals, and US capitalism. Karl's daydream suggests that to be together, he and Giles must exist outside of all that is valued in dominant US society. Additionally, it is significant that the enclosed boxcar itself mirrors the architecture of the closet, a spatial metaphor that has been interrogated by, among others, queer theorist Eve Kosofsky Sedgwick in *Epistemology of the Closet* (1990), a book often paired with *Gender Trouble* as a marker for the rise of contemporary queer theory. Sedgwick argues, "The relations of the closet—the relations of the known and the unknown, the explicit and the inexplicit around homo/heterosexual definition—have the potential for being peculiarly revealing" (3). As a metaphor for such relations, the boxcar, an unrooted space destined for continual motion, is always outside the bounds of whatever city or home it might pass, always outside the realm of community. Thus, like the content of his queer imaginings, the space in which Karl envisions his idealized relationship with Giles also serves as a symbol of disconnection and fragmentation.

Though their sexual encounter is ultimately short-lived, Karl sees his physical interaction with Giles as a landmark break with childhood: "He'd touched other boys before but just in fun, down the alleys behind the boardinghouse. This was different, and he was not sure he'd dare, but then his body filled with the rushing noise" (25). He reacts by twice telling Giles, "I love you" (25), a statement Giles dismisses with a brusque "Oh, Jesus, it wasn't anything. . . . It happens. Don't get all worked up over it, okay?" (25). For Karl, this rejection of his emotions tangles with memories of his mother's abandonment. Even while he parrots Giles's words to himself—"It happens. . . . It happens"—he feels "swallowed" by "the depth of his loss," which causes him to violently reject emotional attachment (26). Upon deciding never to "cry on the lap of anyone again," Karl jumps from the moving train, leaving behind his short-lived dreams of a romance and intimacy (26). Despite the fact that Karl later has multiple physical encounters with both men and women, he is depicted as nearly incapable of a fully formed relationship. Fittingly, he becomes a traveling salesman, who passes through towns and lovers indiscriminately. The queer possibilities Karl experiences in the boxcar are abandoned when he lands on stable ground.

Karl's association with Wallace, a queer connection that eventually leads to Karl's return to Argus, begins with another life-threatening jump. The two men meet at the Minneapolis Crop and Livestock Convention in 1952, twenty years after Karl abandons the boxcar. At the time of the convention, Karl's history includes "rendevou[s] with thin hard hoboes," but no lasting relationships as he "never let anything go far enough to cause [him] trouble" (55, 104). Karl and Wallace strike up a conversation and have dinner in Karl's hotel room, a place that mirrors the boxcar's enclosed and transient nature. They have sex quickly between the ordering and arrival of their meal. Wallace's subsequent admission that he has "never done this before" (105) causes Karl to scoff about the "little woman" he imagines Wallace keeps at home. Neither man, however, is attached, and in fact, though Karl claims numerous past liaisons with women, he overtly rejects "love and marriage" even as he silently recognizes "the truth" that he had "always found [a woman's] touch unbearable, a source of nameless panic" (106). Like Karl's headlong jump from Giles and the train, his encounter with Wallace, too, comes to an abrupt end through self-inflicted physical pain when Karl injures himself attempting to complete a somersault on the hotel bed. If earlier he fled a perceived rejection by leaping from the moving boxcar, here he attempts to distract himself from the possibilities of a queer connection that extends beyond the physical by jumping, high and wild, on the hotel bed. Karl explains:

When he looked at me with his clear sad eyes, I suddenly had the feeling that had always frightened me, the blackness, the ground I'd stood on giving way, the falling no place. Maybe it was true about him, the awkwardness, no experience, the awful possibility that he wanted to get to know me . . . just to do something, just to stop the feeling. . . . [I] leapt onto the bed. I had to stop myself from falling, so I jumped. (106)

In both cases, Karl's leap demonstrates his need to stem an emotional connection through physical action and injury. Thus, while *The Beet Queen* expands the parameters of its characters' sexualities, the novel also initially seems to represent queerness not only as an impossible dream, but also as a psychological and bodily threat.

As if offering readers the flip side of a coin, Erdrich shows a very different response to queer desire through her depiction of Wallace's perspective of his night with Karl. For Wallace, sex with Karl brings him not to "blackness" but instead to light and clarity through his definitive recognition of his own desires and identity. As he thinks back on their encounter, he realizes, "I never knew it, had probably hidden it away, but I found the attraction as easy as breathing. . . . There I was, member of the Kiwanis, eating prime rib and accepting choice bits of game hen from the fork of another man. Sheer madness. Yet I felt amazed, as if the clouds had blown away, as if the bare bones were finally visible. I was queer" (161). Karl's dark cloud, his "awful possibility," is for Wallace a revelation. Wallace's certainty about his queer identity is reinforced by an unexpected two-week visit from Karl. For that brief period, Wallace experiences his own version of domestic bliss: "It was enough for him to be there, wearing my clothes and towels, fixing toast for himself, at last making sense of my bed. I never knew what to ask from life, but now I did" (164). Through these two characters, Erdrich represents a spectrum of possible responses to queer desire, from romantic dreaming to violent denial to the everyday possibility of unexpected love.

Erdrich is known for her plot twists, and one of these occurs when Karl's abrupt departure from Wallace's home—where, he later explains, Wallace "drove [him] out of [his] mind with attention" (319)—brings Karl to Celestine. Their subsequent interactions shift the text's representations of both queerness and heterosexuality. While earlier descriptions of Karl link his femininity with his desire for men in a very traditional picture of Western homosexuality, his complex relationship with Celestine alters such a simplistic binary. Desire, Erdrich shows, is multiple and messy, by far exceeding dominant societal boundaries. Karl and Celestine's first encounter occurs when Karl stops at the family butcher shop that his sister Mary owns and that she and Celestine now run. Karl and Celestine almost immediately succumb to an awkward passion based on a parody of romance novels, moving from stilted conversation to a sexual encounter that in no way mirrors the Harlequin-inspired "tales of burning love" Celestine has read: "I lunge from his grip but he comes right with me. I lose my balance. He is fighting me for the upper hand, straining down with all his might, but I am more than equal to his weight-lifting arms and thrashing legs. I could throw him to the side, I know, but I grow curious" (128). Speaking of this encounter, Louise Flavin argues, "The comic deflation of the traditional lovers' scene affirms the absence of romanticized love" (20). Though there may not be romantic love between Celestine and Karl, there is an odd attraction, perhaps best characterized by Karl's inertia: Two weeks after they first have sex, Karl knocks on Celestine's door by chance in his role as a traveling salesman and does not leave. However, even as they are drawn together by a desire seemingly out of their control, the narrative continually points to their contradictions. For example, Celestine's female masculinity is set against Karl's femininity: Celestine compares his "polished fingernails" to her own hands, those "of a woman who has handled too many knives, deep-nicked and marked with lines, toughened from spice and brine" (133). Like their gender performances, their actions, too, are always in opposition—just when "love wears on"

Celestine, Karl proposes (135–36). Though Celestine declines and Karl moves out, they eventually marry in name only because of Celestine's pregnancy. Overall, in terms of Karl and Celestine's relationship, Iovannone's contention that "Erdrich's characters create . . . subversions through the enactment of various gendered performances that parody, undermine, and expose normative identity constructs" (43) could not be more apt. Through Celestine and Karl's relationship, Erdrich queers the discrete boundaries of desire by introducing bisexuality and also extends the conventional parameters of heterosexuality as Celestine's masculinity, Karl's femininity, and the collision of the two fall far outside the boundaries of most "tales of burning love."

In a final subversion, Erdrich offers an unexpectedly romantic conclusion to *The Beet Queen* through Karl's last transformation. In his youth and transient adulthood, Karl perceives queer affiliation as disconnection and fragmentation, as we have seen. At the close of the text, however, that affiliation is part and parcel of what returns him to community. The climax of the novel occurs when Wallace fixes a contest so that Dot, his namesake and Celestine and Karl's child, will win the Beet Queen competition. Karl sees "a newspaper photograph of the Beet Queen candidates. . . . Behind them, with a big square grin on his face and new wire-rimmed glasses, stood Wallace Pfef" (317). A subsequent reverie about his daughter, sister, and past lover evokes this epiphany: "I give nothing, take nothing, mean nothing, hold nothing. . . . And in that darkened, bleak, smothering moment, something came back to me. One thing. Not an object, not a plan, not even the nagging words to a song, but a sweetness" (318). That "sweetness" involves memories of Dot, Mary, and finally, Wallace, who Karl explains, "thought I was some sort of God he worshipped" and "drove me out of my mind with attention. . . . There was no question, ever, of staying. And yet I was coming back" (318–19). Karl arrives at the fair to find Wallace on the seat in the dunking booth, joking and laughing with townspeople. His earlier dismissal crumbles when a furious Dot, who has discovered Wallace's duplicity about the contest, mercilessly dunks Wallace. Karl sprints to the rescue: "He was out cold, I had to get there. I was running for my life" (323). Pulling Wallace from the water, Karl "drag[s] him close," and finally utters "the right words"—"Screw the management"—thereby recalling and humorously acknowledging the importance of their first night together twenty years earlier (323). Karl seems to have made a radical transformation in both thought and action by accepting his relationship with Wallace. As a result, the depictions of queerness in the novel can be seen to shift radically from the text's 1932 opening to its 1972 close.

The Beet Queen offers readers diverse and complex images of queerness. While the text begins with classic images of queerness as deviance and loss, long a trope in the literary canon, it concludes with an image of queerness as potential redemption. In the process, the text also engages ideas that will be key to the rise of queer theory in the early 1990s. Moreover, Erdrich repeatedly highlights the fluid nature of gender, desire, and sexuality, creating characters that exceed the boundaries of the conventional narratives about each. In doing so, her work destabilizes the foundation of the normative hetero/homosexual binary. A return to Butler demonstrates the importance of such an intervention:

> The heterosexualization of desire requires and institutes the production of discrete and asymmetrical oppositions between "feminine" and "masculine," where these are understood as expressive attributes of "male" and "female." The cultural matrix through which gender identity has become intelligible requires that certain kinds of "identities" cannot "exist"—that is, those in which gender does not follow from sex and those in which the practices of desire do not "follow" from either sex or gender. (17)

By focusing on just such disruptive gender representations, identities that should not exist according to dominant cultural beliefs, Erdrich challenges the very basis of such regulatory constructions and, in doing so, "provide[s] critical opportunities to expose the limits and regulatory aims of that domain of intelligibility" (Butler 17).

While neither of her two subsequent novels, *Tracks* or *The Bingo Palace*, explicitly centers queer desire as *The Beet Queen* does, all offer radical variations in gender identities through unconventional characters such as Fleur Pillager, Pauline Puyat/Sister Leopolda, Lipsha Morrissey, and Lulu Lamartine. These reconfigurations of gender norms have been the subject of a significant body of literary criticism. However, overt queer desire of the sort examined here does not reappear until *Tales of Burning Love*, which takes its name from the romance novels parodied in *The Beet Queen* and from 108-year-old Sister Leopolda's comment: "My prayer is a tale of burning love, child, but you aren't ready to hear it" (*Tales* 53).

Tales of Burning Love revolves around the five former wives of Jack Mauser: June Morrissey, Eleanor Schlick, Candice Pantamounty, Marlis Cook, and the Beet Queen herself, the adult Dot Adare. The novel moves back and forth in time from its opening scene in 1981 to its 1995 close. Part 1, "Jack of Sunflowers," begins with Jack's story of June Morrissey's death, which Erdrich readers will recognize from her first novel, *Love Medicine*. The section subsequently explores the present-day lives of Jack and Dot, who have just married after a brief courtship, and Eleanor, who flees a scandal by moving to Argus to research Sister Leopolda. The section concludes when Jack, who is drunk, broke, and single again, accidentally burns his house down. Part 2, "Blackjack Night," picks up at Jack's January 1995 funeral, where four of his former wives decide to find the fifth to settle a dispute over his remains. The section concludes with all five women trapped in a van during a raging blizzard. To remain awake and alive, Eleanor suggests, "Let's tell all. . . . Pretend this car is a confessional" (205). Dot agrees, adding, "Rule one. . . . No shutting up until dawn. Rule two. Tell a true story. Rule three. The story has to be about you. Something that you've never told another soul, a story that would scorch paper, heat up the air!" (206). Among the "scorching" stories told in part 3, "Tales of Burning Love," is that of Candice and Marlis's romantic relationship, which begins with a tug-of-war over Marlis and Jack's unborn baby.

One of the ways representations of queerness in *Tales* differ from *The Beet Queen* is in the novel's brief forays into outsiders' views of queer interactions. Ultimately, these limited forays into third-person perspectives reveal the covert ways heteronormativity reproduces itself. In *The Beet Queen*, the details of Karl and Wallace's relationship and Karl's other queer trysts remain hidden from public view in the shadowed spaces of train cars, back alleys, and hotel rooms, playing on the secrecy that is a classic trope in queer literature. By contrast, in *Tales*, as Michael Warner and Lauren Berlant might argue, "intimacy is itself publicly mediated" (553); the private is actually a public spectacle as the frequent outside perceptions of Candice and Marlis's love affair demonstrate. After deciding to flee his debts when he finds he has been declared dead, Jack stops to visit his son. Once he opens the bedroom door, "he knew it instantly, saw it, understood it . . . his two former wives slept together as lovers" (261). The realization stops Jack in his tracks, as he "stood in the doorway and could not set foot inside" (261). The power of this queer revelation, which brings that which society has deemed "private" into "public" view, has a visceral impact. Thus, from the first, queerness made visible disrupts the status quo.

The story that Candice and Marlis tell in the freezing van also first situates knowledge of their relationship in a perspective other than their own. Marlis is pregnant and broke when Candice, who is unable to have children, invites her on a trip to the Minnesota Northwoods in the hopes of persuading Marlis to relinquish the baby. Though they do not begin a physical relationship then, a woman in an adjacent hotel room perceives Candice and Marlis as lovers: "'You two whatevers, I get it now,' she said. 'I've heard about these things. . . . You inseminated her. I've read about this stuff,' she paused, looked darkly into the new drink she'd fixed. 'You've got to be from down in the Cities. That's where this stuff is happening. Up here we don't have the right equipment. Now you get out of here'" (346). Jack's response to his former wives' lesbian relationship keeps him out of the women's bedroom; similarly, this unnamed woman's response to such a possibility is to demand Candice and Marlis leave her room. Both reactions invoke separation and distance and reject queerness. The second scene additionally locates the possibility of nonheteronormative sex, reproduction, and family as inherently other. Berlant and Warner's discussion of how certain understandings of social relations construct heteronormativity is useful here. They point out, "The very category of heterosexuality . . . consolidates as *a sexuality* widely differing practices, norms, and institutions" (552). At the same time, "a complex cluster of sexual practices gets confused, in heterosexual culture, with the love plot of intimacy and familialism that signifies belonging to society in a deep and normal way. Community is imagined through scenes of intimacy, coupling, and kinship" (Berlant and Warner 554). As a result, very different types of interactions and "social relations becom[e] intelligible as heterosexuality, and this privatized sexual culture bestows on its sexual practices a tacit sense of rightness and normalcy. This sense of rightness—embedded in things and not just sex—is what we call heteronormativity" (Berlant and Warner 554). Erdrich, by offering these outside perspectives of queerness in *Tales*, makes the problematic and insistent construction of heteronormativity visible.

The chronology of the novel furthers this argument. The account of Candice and Marlis's lesbian relationship follows the narratives of Jack's heterosexual marriages. As the stories of Jack's relationships are told one after another, each is more twisted than the next. In the last, he is duct-taped to a bed, his leg hair removed with hot wax, his ears pierced with a silver brooch, and his feet superglued into red spiked heels (332–35). Yet this dysfunctional relationship is sanctioned not just by the romance novels, or "tales of burning love," that define romantic heterosexual coupling as the be-all, end-all of life, but also by the weight of national laws and institutions. Heterosexual marriage, like heterosexuality itself, is considered "right," "normal," whereas, with a handful of recent exceptions, "queer culture, by contrast, has almost no institutional matrix for its counterintimacies" (Berlant and Warner 562). By ending the stories of Jack's relationships with this ludicrous image and subsequently showing that outsiders view, not Jack's marriages, but *Candice and Marlis's* relationship as aberrant, Erdrich reveals the fractures in the supposedly stable foundation of heterosexuality. While *The Beet Queen* points to the performative nature of gender and the multiplicities of desire, *Tales* questions both the primacy and supposed normalcy of heterosexuality, thereby unmooring the "sense of rightness" that undergirds the continued circulation of a heteronormative ideology.

Erdrich's next book, *The Antelope Wife* (1998), offers a single scene that briefly introduces a two-spirit, or multiple gendered figure, to Erdrich's fiction, a role explored more fully in *The Last Report on the Miracles at Little No Horse*, a novel that centers issues of gender and sexuality. In one of Erdrich's most entertaining plot twists, *Last Report* reveals that Father Damien Modeste, a minor character in *Tracks*, was born Agnes DeWitt, a white, Chopin-playing former nun, who takes the robes and identity of the original Father Damien after he dies on his way to the text's fictionalized Ojibwe reservation. Agnes lives as a man and serves as the reservation priest from her 1912 arrival until her 1996 death. Along the way, she learns to perform masculinity, schooling herself as Giles schooled Karl. She makes an oft-cited list:

Some Rules to Assist in My Transformation
1. Make requests in the form of orders.
2. Give compliments in the form of concessions.
3. Ask questions in the form of statements.
4. Exercises to enhance the muscles of the neck?
5. Admire women's handiwork with copious amazement.
6. Stride, swing arms, stop abruptly, stroke chin.
7. Sharpen razor daily.
8. Advance no explanations.
9. Accept no explanations.
10. Hum an occasional resolute march. (74)

The novel's subsequent exploration of such gender b(l)ending has been the subject of much literary analysis. Maria Orban and Alan Velie read Agnes/Father Damien as trickster, "a shape-shifter of indeterminate sex and interchangeable gender who has the ability to create and re-create identity very much along the lines of Judith Butler's 'performative theory'" (28). Pamela J. Rader argues, "Erdrich's treatment of gender in *Last Report* reinstates a syncretic tradition wherein Ojibwe and Catholic beliefs fuse, marking Agnes's multilayered assimilation process" (221). Annette Van Dyke maintains that by "challenging the gender dichotomies of Euro-American culture, Erdrich also begins the reader's education as to what it is to be human" (67). Iovannone extends his transgender framework, contending, "While Agnes assumes the masculine role and position of a priest, she does not become a man in the Western binary sense of the word. She is positioned within the novel in a liminal space that transcends both masculine and feminine identity markers" (61). This sampling of the many fine analyses of *Last Report* mark the novel's importance in terms of Erdrich's depictions of the fluidity and transformative possibilities of gender performance.

As the number of articles on gender in *Last Report* suggest, Erdrich's portrayal of Agnes/Father Damien, with its mixing of gendered pronouns and interrogation of the boundaries and possibilities of shifting gender roles, extends the *depth* of the work she had already begun in terms of her depictions of gender performance. Thus, *Last Report* expands the examinations begun in *The Beet Queen*. One aspect of *Last Report*, however, also extends the *breadth* of Erdrich's queer representations: her inclusion of "an ikwe-inini, a woman-man called a winkte by the Bwaang [Lakota]" (153), and subsequently, her acknowledgement of two-spirit traditions among the Anishinaabeg. The "ikwe-inini" is significant on a number of levels in terms of mapping the range of Erdrich's queer characters. One marked shift is that queer sexuality is no longer solely the purview of white characters in her novels. Another is that Erdrich's historical representation of gender diversity provides an indigenous framework for readings of gender that are heretofore absent in her work. While critics such as Barak and Prince-Hughes have read Erdrich's earlier texts through the lens of two-spirit traditions, such work does not account for the fact that Erdrich's queer characters have, to this point, been white. Given the history of white appropriations of a romanticized two-spirit identity, reading non-Native characters as two-spirit is questionable. By contrast, in *Last Report*, both Agnes/Father Damien's adoption by the Anishinaabeg and Erdrich's inclusion of an explicitly two-spirit character open the possibility of two-spirit critiques.

Erdrich's flashback to an earlier moment in Anishinaabe history with the "ikwe-inini" is preceded by two scenes that show multiple-gender traditions are still known and accepted among the older Anishinaabeg in the text. When Agnes first arrives as Father Damien, she is brought to the mission by Kashpaw, who "sensed something unusual about the priest" whom he speculates is "a man like the famous Wishkob, the Sweet, who had seduced many other men and finally joined the family of a great war chief as a wife, where he had lived until old, well loved, as one of the women. Kashpaw himself had addressed Wishkob as grandmother" (64). Iovannone's discussion of this scene, though it invokes indigenous traditions, employs the term "transgender" and questions the limits of "two-spirit," which he suggests relies on gender binaries (42–43). In fact, the term "two-spirit" is specifically intended to cite the distinct histories of indigenous genders and sexualities.[2] Those histories *already* include the sort of nuanced understandings of gender and sexuality that Iovannone attributes to a transgender theoretical framework. Thus, while transgender theory can offer insight into Erdrich's texts, it cannot, or at least should not, supersede the specifically indigenous framework of a two-spirit critique in all readings of her work. Moreover, it is simply inaccurate when applied to multiply gendered Anishinaabe characters in historical scenes such as that under discussion. Replacing the problematic anthropological term "berdache" with "transgender" rather than "two-spirit" creates another historical elision. In a nuanced essay that parses the historical differences between transgender and two-spirit approaches, Deirdre Keenan maintains, "In the context of mainstream attitudes about transgender identities and Native American gender systems," *Last Report* "provides a theory and practice of gender identity formation" (2). That theory, in the case of Kashpaw and Nanapush, who represent the old-school Anishinaabeg, centers on an indigenous understanding in which multiple genders and sexualities are culturally appropriate, rather than radically transgressive. Thus, in the scene cited above, Kashpaw invokes a historical memory, not of transgender roles, but of accepted two-spirit traditions that precede and differ from transgender identities. Nanapush does as well when he tries to beat Father Damien at chess by asking, "What are you? . . . A man priest or a woman priest? . . . Are you a female Wishkob?" (230–31). After throwing Agnes/Father Damien off balance, Nanapush presses his advantage: "So you're not a woman-acting man, you're a man-acting woman. We don't get many of those lately. Between us, Margaret and me, we couldn't think of more than a couple" (232). Recognizing Nanapush's questions as chess strategy, Agnes "realized that this moment, so shattering to her, wasn't of like importance to Nanapush" (232). Each scene suggests that Anishinaabe attitudes toward sex and gender are wide ranging and complex and that positions existed for those whose gender performances exceeded the Western gender binaries that came to North America as part and parcel of settler colonialism.

The inclusion of a two-spirit history changes the conversation about queer identities in Erdrich's texts, and the recognition of that history, rather than Agnes/Father Damien's gender performance itself, is why *Last Report* occupies a particularly important place in Erdrich's many depictions of nonnormative genders and sexualities. Andrea Smith argues that we must recognize the context of settler colonialism to understand the importance of sexuality within both indigenous histories and indigenous peoples' present realities. Colonization took place "through sexual violence and through the imposition of European gender relationships on Native communities" (Smith 139). Daniel Heath Justice points to a well-known historical example of this pattern, explaining:

> Native and queer subjectivities have a long and quite vexed history of interconnectedness within the early modern context of colonialism and imperialism. In 1513 Vasco Nuñez de Balboa . . . led his soldiers against the village of Quarequa. . . . Balboa turned his attention to the "house of this kynge." . . . He found "the kynges brother and many other younge men in womens apparell, smoth & effeminately decked, which by the report of such as dwelte abowte hym, he abused wuth preposterous venus." Balboa ordered that the men, who numbered around forty, be fed alive to his hunger-maddened war-dogs. (Justice et al. 9)

Such violence occurs on the level of both action and ideology; thus, Balboa's savagery is sanctioned and driven by particular belief systems. Qwo-Li Driskill therefore maintains this settler colonial ideology "enforce[s] the idea that sexuality and non-dichotomous genders are a sin, recreating sexuality as illicit, shocking, shameful, and removed from any positive spiritual context" ("Stolen" 54). Karl's comparison of queers with outlaws and outsiders' shocked responses to Candice and Marlis's relationship stem from such beliefs. With this troubled history of erotic colonization in mind, one can see that Erdrich offers a radically different concept of sex/gender performances in *Last Report*. Her representation of Anishinaabe acceptance of two-spirit identities invokes indigenous understandings of sex and gender that both exceed and predate—by hundreds of years—those offered by theorists such as Butler, Sedgwick, Berlant, and Warner. Thus, while such theorists accurately describe the dynamics of Erdrich's earlier texts with their focus on how queerness circulates in the stories of white characters, *Last Report* shifts the conversation.

As I hope I have shown, analyzing the depictions of queer characters in *The Beet Queen*, *Tales of Burning Love*, and *The Last Report on the*

Miracles at Little No Horse highlights Erdrich's significant intervention in the field of American Indian literatures. The range of desires and
gender expressions represented in *The Beet Queen* was unprecedented
in Native fiction at that particular historical moment. Thus in the mid-
1980s, Erdrich was breaking ground in indigenous literary studies with
her wide-ranging and varied depictions of erotic attachments. *Tales of
Burning Love* subsequently extends the interrogation of heterosexuality that began in Erdrich's depiction of Karl and Celestine's affair. The
juxtaposition of Jack's dysfunctional marriages with Candice and Marlis's relationship calls into question the primacy and normalcy afforded
the former. Finally, *Last Report*, while extending Erdrich's previous
investigations of gender performance, shifts the focus to indigenous
understandings of genders and sexualities by introducing the historical existence of two-spirit people within the memory and history of
the Anishinaabeg in Erdrich's ongoing historical saga. The movement
from Wallace to Wishkob, then, speaks both to Erdrich's multifaceted
contributions to the field of Native literature and to the growth and importance of two-spirit texts and images within that field.

Notes

1. See my essay "The Emergence and Importance of Queer American Indian Literatures, or, 'Help and Stories' in Thirty Years of *SAIL*."
2. See Gilbert Herdt's "The Dilemmas of Desire: from 'Berdache' to 'Two-Spirit'"
   in *Two-Spirit People*, as well as Jacobs, Thomas, and Lang's introduction to that
   same volume. See also Driskill, Finley, Gilley, and Morgensen's introduction to
   Queer Indigenous Studies and Gilley's chapter "From Gay to Indian" in *Becoming Two-Spirit*.

Works Cited

Allen, Paula Gunn. *The Woman Who Owned the Shadows*. San Francisco: Spinsters,
   1983.
Barak, Julie. "Blurs, Blends, Berdaches: Gender Mixing in the Novels of Louise Erdrich." *Studies in American Indian Literatures* 8.3 (1996): 49–62.

Berlant, Lauren, and Michael Warner. "Sex in Public." *Critical Inquiry* 24.2 (1998): 547–66.

Butler, Judith. *Gender Trouble: Feminism and the Subversion of Identity*. New York: Routledge, 1990.

Driskill, Qwo-Li. "Stolen from Our Bodies: First Nations Two-Spirits/Queers and the Journey to a Sovereign Erotic." *Studies in American Indian Literatures* 16.2 (2004): 50–64.

Driskill, Qwo-Li, Chris Finley, Brian Joseph Gilley, and Scott Lauria Morgensen, eds. *Queer Indigenous Studies: Critical Interventions in Theory, Politics, and Literature*. Tucson: U of Arizona P, 2011.

Driskill, Qwo-Li, Daniel Heath Justice, Deborah Miranda, and Lisa Tatonetti, eds. *Sovereign Erotics: A Collection of Contemporary Two-Spirit Literature*. Tucson: U of Arizona P, 2011.

Erdrich, Louise. *The Antelope Wife*. New York: Harper, 1998.

_____. *The Beet Queen*. New York: Bantam, 1986.

_____. *The Bingo Palace*. New York: Harper, 1994.

_____. *The Last Report on the Miracles at Little No Horse*. New York: Harper, 2001.

_____. *The Master Butchers Singing Club*. New York: Harper, 2003.

_____. *Tales of Burning Love*. New York: Harper, 1996.

_____. *Tracks*. New York: Harper, 1988.

Flavin, Louise. "Gender Construction amid Family Dissolution in Louise Erdrich's *The Beet Queen*." *Studies in American Indian Literatures* 7.2 (1995): 17–24.

Gay American Indians, comp., and Will Roscoe, ed. *Living the Spirit: A Gay American Indian Anthology*. New York: St. Martin's, 1988.

Iovannone, J. James. "'Mix-Ups, Messes, Confinements, and Double-Dealings': Transgendered Performances in Three Novels by Louise Erdrich." *Studies in American Indian Literatures* 21.1 (2009): 38–68.

Jacobs, Sue-Ellen, Wesley Thomas, and Sabine Lang, eds. *Two-Spirit People: Native American Gender Identity, Sexuality, and Spirituality*. Urbana: U of Illinois P, 1997.

Justice, Daniel Heath, Mark Rifkin, and Bethany Schneider, eds. *Sexuality, Nationality, Indigeneity*. Spec. issue of *GLQ: A Journal of Gay and Lesbian Studies* 16.1–2 (2010): 1–339.

Keenan, Deirdre. "Unrestricted Territory: Gender, Two Spirits, and Louise Erdrich's *The Last Report on the Miracles at Little No Horse*." *American Indian Culture and Research Journal* 30.2 (2006): 1–15.

Orban, Maria, and Alan Velie. "Religion and Gender in *The Last Report on the Miracles at Little No Horse*." *European Review of Native American Studies* 17.2 (2003): 27–34.

Prince-Hughes, Tara. "Worlds In and Out of Balance: Alternative Genders and Gayness in the *Almanac of the Dead* and *The Beet Queen*." *Literature and Homosexuality* (2000): 1–21.

Rader, Pamela J. "Disrobing the Priest: Gender and Spiritual Conversions in Louise Erdrich's *The Last Report on the Miracles at Little No Horse*." *The Catholic*

Church and Unruly Women Writers, Critical Essays. Ed. Jeana DelRosso, Leigh Eicke, and Ana Kothe. New York: Macmillan, 2008. 221–35.

Sedgwick, Eve Kosofsky. *Epistemology of the Closet*. Los Angeles: U of California P, 1990.

Silko, Leslie Marmon. *Almanac of the Dead*. New York: Penguin, 1991.

Smith, Andrea. *Conquest: Sexual Violence and American Indian Genocide*. Cambridge: South End, 2005.

Tatonetti, Lisa. "The Emergence and Importance of Queer American Indian Literatures, or, 'Help and Stories' in Thirty Years of *SAIL*." *Studies in American Indian Literatures* 19.4 (2007): 143–70.

Van Dyke, Annette. "A Hope for Miracles: Shifting Perspectives in Louise Erdrich's *The Last Report on the Miracles at Little No Horse*." *Studies in the Literary Achievement of Louise Erdrich, Native American Writer: Fifteen Critical Essays*. Ed. Brajesh Sawhney. Lewiston: Mellen, 2008. 63–74.

Welch, James. *The Heartsong of Charging Elk*. New York: Doubleday, 2000.

There are No Burning Wagons, Beads, or Feathers in Louise Erdrich's *The Plague of Doves* _____

Debra K. S. Barker

The opening scene of arguably one of the most complex of Louise Erdrich's North Dakota novels, *The Plagues of Doves*, takes us back to the early twentieth century with the 1911 mass murder of a white family living outside fictional Pluto, North Dakota. Accused of the crime, four American Indians, including a thirteen-year-old boy, become scapegoats and are summarily lynched by the founding fathers of Pluto in an act of frontier justice. Only one of the accused victims survives, Seraph "Mooshum" Milk, whose granddaughter, Evelina Harp, will later tease out family and community secrets, as she explores the interrelationships between the descendants of both the lynching victims and the immigrant lynch mob. The central narrator, Evelina, narrates not only her grandfather's story but also her own coming-of-age, as she navigates the rough waters of identity formation. Part of Evelina's struggle entails grappling with her infatuations with descendants of two participants in the lynching, an Ojibwe victim and one of the vigilantes later regarded as a prosperous, upstanding citizen and a revered founder of this reservation border town. Later, in the throes of a nervous breakdown, haunted by the memory of the lynching story, Evelina realizes one ineluctable theme of both her life and of this novel: "History works itself out in the living" (243).

As I develop my discussion of *The Plague of Doves*, I argue that this is one of Erdrich's novels that performs a rich *tour de force* of subversion on many levels, subversion that unsettles the authority of non-Native readers tempted to ahistoricize American Indians in time within an imaginary "reservation" space unresponsive to time or the forces of history. Likewise, this novel challenges any tendency to romanticize the settlement of the American frontier and then ignore the consequences for the original denizens of that frontier. Clearly, the forces of history have shaped not only the material circumstances of the Ojibwes as a nation but also the consciousness of its individual members, even those surviving into the twentieth century. This essay will later devote attention to political issues around the colonial invasion and conquest of Pluto, North Dakota, tracing that legacy into the present time, ultimately resolving the conflicts presented in the acts of injustice and dispossession narrated in the earlier portions of the novel. Finally, I assert that *The Plague of Doves* challenges readers to interrogate their stereotypes of what ought to constitute American Indian literature and complicates their thinking about the lives of middle-class American Indians in the twenty-first century.

While some readers might expect an edgy, politically charged response to the racial violence narrated early in the novel, Erdrich elides readers' expectations with her focus on the destinies of the descendants of the victims and murderers, tracing their respective histories and interrelations. The novel's layered narrative strands include stories recounted by multiple narrators concerning the founding of the town of Pluto, as well as its slow demise at the hands of twentieth-century urban planning and economic progress. In a particularly fascinating embedded narrative titled "Satan: Hijacker of a Planet," Marn Wolde, a descendant of one of the early immigrant founders, recounts her difficult marriage to a charismatic religious cult leader whose ancestor was one of the lynching victims. Narrator Judge Antone Coutts, a mixed-blood descendant of one of the town's founding fathers, shares his memories of deathless love, confiding his long-term sexual liaison with the racist town doctor who refuses medical treatment to American Indians. Judge Coutts's other narrated section provides a chronicle of the original venture capitalists and homesteaders who sought their fortunes on the frigid plains of North Dakota. Finally, Evelina Harp reminisces the little childhood dramas shared with her brother as well as the comedy liberally provided by their irreverent grandfather, Mooshum, whom she describes as "happily disordered and profane" (22).

To date, literary critics have yet to explore *The Plague of Doves*, a 2009 Pulitzer Prize finalist, though the critical reception has remained overwhelmingly positive since its release. Anishinaabe scholar Margaret Noori situates the novel within the tradition of Erdrich's other polyphonic novels, layering plots and subplots, shifting seamlessly between generations and related narrative contexts. Noting Erdrich's prodigious stylistic influences, Noori points out, "Although many read her work as Native American, with each successive novel she challenges that boundary by writing more like Ernest Hemingway, William Faulkner, Albert Camus, or Arturo Pérez-Reverte than like N. Scott Momaday, Leslie Silko, James Welch, or Simon Ortiz" (12). Arguing for the sovereignty of Native artistic production, Noori asserts, "She has earned the right to write according to her own expectations" (12). Erdrich's expectations have continually ranged across the widening terrain of her lived and reading experiences. She is a postmodern Native author writing to audiences who can appreciate that although American Indians may appear to some non-Indians as surviving vestiges or living relics of a vanishing, mythic race, they are in fact complex American citizens who have hauled into this millennium some unique cultural baggage.

Erdrich is indeed entitled to the assertion of artistic sovereignty regarding not only her narrative style but also her choice of subject matter, including the representation of Native American family life in the mid-twentieth century. One of the many accomplishments of this novel lies in its challenge to readers to interrogate their assumptions about American Indians and class. Indeed, rarely have critics explored the subject of middle-class Indians, perhaps because, as Jack Forbes has pointed out, academics "sometimes seem to want modern-day chants and lots of symbolic beads and feathers. They want to read about the mystical, about rituals and ceremony. . . . They seem to be less interested in reading about genocide and politics or love and sex" (21).

In *The Plague of Doves*, Erdrich normalizes American Indians by situating her characters within domestic contexts already familiar to many readers of Erdrich's generation. For instance, she develops a series of Native characters, none of whom is looking stoic, wearing feathers, or bemoaning liminal identities. In fact, she repositions American Indians within a broader historical, racial, and socioeconomic context so non-Native readers new to Erdrich's fiction might elide knee-jerk stereotypical responses to a novel featuring American Indian characters: First, Indians—and middle-class Indians at that—really did and do exist, and they make an enormous contribution in the world, alongside their Euro-American neighbors. Second, Indians do not inhabit a space called "plight." For example, while Evelina notes that her mother's and aunt's clothing was purchased secondhand, she nevertheless occupies a socioeconomic stratum not unknown to the majority of middle-class Americans during the 1960s. She tells us early in the novel, "We are a tribe of office workers, bank tellers, book readers, and bureaucrats. The wildest of us (Whitey) is a short-order cook, and the most heroic of us (my father) teaches" (9).

Evelina's new uncle, mixed-blood judge Antone Coutts, reads the works of the Stoics, philosophers Marcus Aurelius and Epictetus, but he himself is not stoic in the least. Even as he refers to himself as "the clichéd mixed-blood" (114), the irony in his tone is clear: Judge Coutts holds both a law degree and enrollment in his tribe, quite mindful of the benefits his status has afforded him. Moreover, while Evelina grows up aware of the historical processes of colonization and dispossession, this dimension of her family background does in no way dominate her consciousness or contain her within a marginalized category. Indeed, as she grows up and goes to college, Evelina expresses multiple identities as a college student during the early 1970s, when drug experimentation and living in countercultural collective households were not at all uncommon.

In the twenty-first century, Erdrich's novel works to resolve the conflicts of internalized ideologies by cultural normalization of racial representations. Erdrich's representation of American Indians challenges readers by the very nature of their complexity, their humanity, thus normalizing American Indians as a racial category. The novel explores a twentieth-century childhood and coming-of-age through the eyes of Evelina, a curious, passionate girl who enjoys *The Three Stooges*, learns French and dreams of going to Paris, and experiments with her sexuality. If readers come to *The Plague of Doves* curious about the ethnographic dimensions of indigenous family life in the 1960s, they will be disappointed to discover that its background elements resonate with those of *To Kill a Mockingbird* or the 1960s television programs featuring benign and preoccupied "Ward and June" parental figures who move along the vague periphery, foregrounding their children's dramatic inner lives. Evelina suffers dramatic, romantic crushes on not only Corwin Peace but also her teacher, Sister Mary Anita Buckendorf. Her brother, Joseph, collects stamps and loves science. In every respect, the siblings' experiences reflect the influence of mainstream American pop culture. However, with the exception of John Rollin Ridge, Erdrich is the only Native writer to draw attention to the lynching of Indians, a subject that has remained largely ignored, except by historians of the American West.

Historical Background

In crafting *The Plague of Doves*, Erdrich anchors the novel's central plot in historical events, after having read a newspaper account of the lynching of three American Indians in her native North Dakota in the aftermath of the mass murder of a farm family. The 1897 *New York Times* article's headline reads "Mob Law in North Dakota: Three Indians Lynched for the Murder of Six Members of the Spicer Family." The caption goes on to announce, "The Courts Were Too Slow. The Alleged Ringleader of the Murders Had Obtained a New Trial After Having Been Sentenced to Death." The *Times* reports that the vigilante group was composed of forty masked men, all members of the fraternal Lodge of the Woodmen, who adjourned their meeting to carry out their self-appointed civic duty. As the *Times* narrates the events, "The lynching apparently had been planned carefully, and was carried out without a break in the programme." The accused men were lynched from a slaughterhouse windlass (a device used to suspend slaughtered cattle) in Williamsport, North Dakota, and left to hang as of the completion of the news article. We are told that a period of time elapsed before the arrival of the coroner, and no one had come to claim and bury the bodies ("Mob Law in North Dakota"). In his 2011 review of the novel, Jeff Baenen reports, "No one in the lynch mob ever was prosecuted, and two other suspects, who were jailed miles away in Bismarck, N.D., were released after the lynching" ("A Dark Event"). What was not reported or acknowledged in any of the historical accounts was examined evidence that the Native men indeed committed the crime of which they were accused.

A witness photographed the lynching, capturing for posterity this sensational local event. On its website, in anticipation of a 2005 auction, Cowan's Auctions featured a grainy black-and-white photograph titled "Photograph of North Dakota Triple Lynching," an image of the three victims, hanging from a windlass. After identifying the victims' names and summarizing the events leading up to the hanging, the annotation on the photograph concludes the memorialized narrative:

> Eventually all were caught, and jailed. Technicalities, a hung jury and the belief that all three would be set free prompted a November 13, 1897 "visit" to the Williamstown jail by 40 masked men. The jailer was quickly overpowered and the doomed trio was pulled from their cells. The mob attempted to hang the three first from a well curbing, then a log cabin, and finally succeeded using the beam of a beef windlass at the rear of the Williamsport Hotel. Although the identities of most of the vigilantes were known, none were ever prosecuted.

The catalog copy concludes, "Significantly, neither Winona—the town where the Spicers lived, or Williamstown—the place where the murderers were lynched—exists today." The photograph sold at auction for $3,105 under the category "Western Americana." A second photograph of the five accused, titled "Degraff Photograph of Indians Implicated in the Spicer Murder," sold for $352.50 at auction in 2009, a sale no doubt prompted by the opportune publication of Erdrich's novel. The catalog copy for it indicates the accused were Black Hawk, Phillip Ireland (Standing Bear), Paul Holy Track, George Defender, and Alex Coudot.

According to Ken Gonzales-Day's *Lynching in the West*, the number of American Indians lynched in the late nineteenth century rose exponentially in relation to the relentless encroachment of settler populations anxious to claim and establish land rights, citing California as a region where indigenous people were not only "driven from their lands" but "shot on sight" (83). Gonzales-Day points out, "The fact that due process was rarely extended to 'Indians' was complicated by their legal status. Because they were rarely brought to trial, one will never know the truth of the charges" (83).

Readers new to American Indian literature may be surprised to learn that at this time, the indigenous inhabitants of what is now known as the United States were not legally recognized as US citizens and were therefore denied the legal protection enjoyed by Euro-American immigrants. Legal recognition and enfranchisement would not be conferred until 1924 and then only under the pressure of European governments noting the battlefield valor of American Indians soldiers during the First World War. Peter Nabokov writes, "At long last, on June 2, 1924, the Indian Citizenship Act was passed—in large measure because Congress had become embarrassed over the obvious discrepancy between Indian status at home and Indian courage overseas" (382).

The status of American Indians has been determined, since contact with European settlers, by the ideologies of race and racism, which sunk its roots into the rocky soil of the early Puritan colonies. Indeed, the Puritans racialized early American society and its social systems around its need for slave labor and land. George Lipsitz explains, "The colonial and early national legal systems authorized attacks on Native Americans and encouraged the appropriation of their lands" (72). Categorized as nonpersons by virtue of their race, American Indians weathered a genocidal assault that reduced their total numbers

---

to 237,196 by the beginning of the twentieth century (Stiffarm and Lane 37). Invoking Herman Melville's expression "the metaphysics of Indian hating," to characterize a particular strand of racial animus in early America, Richard Drinnon historicizes the "deadly subtleties of white hostility that reduced native peoples to the level of the rest of the fauna and flora to be 'rooted out.' It reduced all the diverse Native American peoples to a single despised nonwhite group and, where they did survive, into a hereditary caste" (xxvi). Returning to the novel for a moment, I maintain that Dr. Cordelia Lochren's decision to refuse medical treatment to Indians suggests a long-held ideology that finds expression in ambivalence: She is drawn to, repelled by, and yet guilty about the presence of Native people in her community in a space that her ancestors seized and settled. While she has desired and retained Antone Coutts as her lover in a long, surreptitious love affair, she will not marry him nor will she be seen with him in public.

The Plague of Doves prompts readers to reflect on the origins and historical consequences of American racial ideologies and the purposes that racial animus served as the frontier was settled. Richard Drinnon maintains that the dehumanization of Indians in relation to white Christian social systems was a step in the process of colonial conquest that was "in a real sense the enabling experience of the rising American empire: Indian-hating identified the dark *others* that white settlers were not and must not under any circumstances become, and it helped them wrest a continent and more from the hands of these native caretaker of the lands" (xvii–xxviii; Drinnon's emphasis).

The dispossession of ancestral tribal land assumes the power of a psychic wound within Evelina's family. A tactless question posed by her aunt Neve Harp, a non-Indian and self-appointed Pluto historian, prompts Evelina's dawning recognition that she too will inherit the legacy of dispossession. Mooshum, incredulous at Neve's question, responds: "What you are asking . . . is how was it stolen? How has this great thievery become acceptable? How do we live right here beside you, knowing what we lost and how you took it?" (84). Neve's desire to hear an Ojibwe elder explain how the town of Pluto came to be situated within the original boundaries of the reservation strikes the reader as a display of callous ignorance borne of her own white privilege, as she has not considered the moral implications of how the land she enjoys has come at the expense of her homeless, landless Ojibwe neighbors. Like many Indian reservations that have fallen prey to land loss based on spurious treaty agreements and settler greed, the town closest to Evelina's home has been pried from her ancestral land base.

Ironically, there are almost no Indians living in Pluto, North Dakota. In an emotionally nuanced scene capturing her recognition of her elders' distress, Evelina begins to internalize the effect of the historical processes of American imperialism:

> Both men's faces became like Mama's—quiet, with an elaborate reserve, and something else that has stuck in my heart ever since. I saw that the loss of their land was lodged inside of them forever. This loss would enter me, too. Over time, I came to know that the sorrow was a thing that each of them covered up according to their character—my old uncle through his passionate discipline, my mother through strict kindness and cleanly order. As for my grandfather, he used the patient art of ridicule. (84)

Here, Erdrich captures an intimate domestic moment that the founding fathers of America certainly could not have imagined or projected into a twentieth-century Native American living-room scene. As she comes of age, Evelina's developing comprehension of these historical processes and their effects on the generations of her family emerges, introduced with no drama and certainly no polemics.

The ideology of white supremacy wrested more than ancestral land from Evelina's forefathers; it had dispossessed them of their own sense of personhood. At the opening of the novel, it is clear that by the early twentieth century, Native people have internalized colonial oppression. Young Mooshum and the other individuals who came upon the murdered Lochren family already feel helpless to evade what appear

---

to be certain inevitabilities attending their very presence in their own land. When Mooshum and the others stop to care for the surviving victims of the massacre, drawn by compassion to the wailing, dehydrated Lochren baby and the "bawling" of unmilked cows, one heard "scream[ing] like a woman in pain" (61), they know they will regret their act of human kindness. Asiginak, the great uncle of young Holy Track, rejects Cuthbert Peace's suggestion that they notify the sheriff of the existence of the surviving baby. Incredulous, he asks, "You're not drunk, so why do you say this? We are no-goods, we are Indians, even me. If you tell the white sheriff, we will die" (63). Young Mooshum adds, "They will hang us for sure" (63). Later, as they are taken to be hanged, Cuthbert pleads, "We found those people already dead. . . . We found them, but we did not kill them. We milked their cows for them and we fed the baby. I, Cuthbert, fed the baby! We are not your bad kind of Indians! Those are south of here!" (74–75). Clearly, they have internalized the ideology of white supremacy, along with the social and political inequity that attends being an American Indian in a world in which the settlers have normalized Euro-American racial practices and justified murder as a civic practice complementing legal justice. At this point in early twentieth-century America, Cuthbert is powerless to protest the degraded status of not only American Indians in the region but also of himself and his companions.

Another key act of subversion on Erdrich's part is her repositioning American Indians within a broader historical and racial context that initially defamilarizes conventional historical paradigms that have shaped the way Euro-American settlers have viewed Indians vis-à-vis the frontier and the conquest of the American West. With her recounted history of the founding of Pluto, Erdrich presents, through the narrative of Judge Antone Coutts, a critique that deromanticizes colonial exploration and conquest. Critic Seamus Deane, in refining his definition of colonialism, explains: "To disguise its essentially rapacious nature, colonialism has been represented in literary, historical, and political discourses as a species of adventure tale, dominated by an ethic of personal heroism that is embedded in a specific national-religious formation" (354). Erdrich's "adventure tale," embellished by details of blizzards, starvation, the temptations of cannibalism, and persistent lower gastrointestinal miseries, provides readers with a dark comedy rather than a saga of frontier heroics. Moreover, it presents a story dominated by an ethic of rapacity with Judge Coutts's reference to the Pluto "town-site expedition" as "a bunch of greedy fools" engaged in a "hideous trial" that nearly kills them. Speculating on the eventual construction of the railroad west of the eastern border of Dakota and dreaming of the "millions" they would make, the expedition party sought to "survey and establish claim by occupancy on several huge pieces of land that would most certainly become towns, perhaps cities, when the railroad reached that part of the world" (97).

In Erdrich's hands, Joseph Coutts's narrative foregrounds the real heroes of the tale, the Native guides, Henri and Lafayette Peace. The Peace brothers save the lives of the white land speculators and venture capitalists who have hired them and have unfortunately chosen the time to depart, "the dead of winter" (97), to secure a clever advantage over other expedition outfits setting out to claim the potential wealth of the plains. Having eaten their oxen, the food for the oxen, and then their shoes, the men come to rely on a drug remedy one of the men brought, "Batner's Powders" (105), which Erdrich later reveals to be opium.

In a 2010 interview with *The Paris Review*, Erdrich reveals that this fictional expedition was based on a documented one that found its conclusion in Wahpeton, North Dakota, her hometown. Erdrich explains, "I knew the exact route they took, and my description was based on reality. Daniel Johnston, who wrote the account, recorded that the party had bowel troubles and so took 'a remedy.' Then it only remained for me to look up what remedy there was at the time, and it was laudanum" ("Art of Fiction" 55). The Peace brothers, familiar with winter-weather camping, set up camp, entice and stalk bison, and deploy inherited survival skills to enable the party's survival. Meanwhile, their employers hallucinated, considered eating one of their deceased comrades, and coped with incessant diarrhea. An expedition survivor who would pass on to his grandson Antone this decidedly unromantic conquest narrative, Joseph Coutts pronounced himself "cured of town fever" and then "decided to become a lawyer" (113).

Erdrich's Cultural Appropriation

Native cultural studies scholars have already noted the degree to which American Indian imagery and cultural references have been appropriated by the dominant culture to promote everything from Leininkugels beer to Land o' Lakes butter. In an exercise of subversion and aesthetic sovereignty, Erdrich draws freely on potent American pop culture indexical signs. Asserting her aesthetic sovereignty and agency in shaping or frustrating expectations of Native American coming-of-age stories, Erdrich appropriates signifiers of baby boomer literary and pop culture, drawing on hybrid cultural materials to provide unexpected cultural textures and thereby informing the zeitgeist that shapes the consciousness of Evelina Harp, the central narrator.

The chapter Evelina narrates of the tragic lynching of 1911 presents a field of allusions that organizes layers of pathos and irony throughout the novel. The legacy of racial violence sorted out by its inheritors suggests the southern gothic of William Faulkner's and Harper Lee's imaginary communities. Faulkner's middle name was Cuthbert, and by appropriating that name for Cuthbert Peace, Erdrich implies broad cultural connections between race relations in the American South and those on the western frontier. By naming one of the lynching victims Cuthbert, Erdrich likewise lends an aesthetic and political poignancy to the lynching. Erdrich's novel, initiated at the shock of a historical event, in fact prompts one to wonder if Harper Lee might have constructed her own novel around an actual story of a thwarted lynch mob that sought an innocent scapegoat like Tom Robinson.

A common motif relates *To Kill a Mockingbird* and *The Plague of Doves*: A stranger provides odd little gifts to children. Thinking about the folded dollar bills Warren Wolde left for the orphaned child of the family he murdered and later tried to give to Evelina, readers may refer to the small gifts Boo Radley secreted in the tree for Scout and Jem. Furthermore, like Scout and Jem, young Evelina and Joseph are introduced to the reality of racialized violence, shocked out of their innocence by Mooshum, and initiated into their town's secret history of murder and racial hatred. As Evelina contemplates the implications of the lynching—that her own great-grandfather, John Wildstrand, was a leader and her beloved grandfather, Mooshum, an implied abettor in the discovery of the accused men—she realizes that the story had "its repercussions—the first being that I could not look at anyone in quite the same way anymore" (86). Later, as a patient in the state mental hospital, Evelina recalls one of Mooshum's old stories of her ancestors' will to survive not just hunger but the rapacity of colonial domination that sought to control the indocile, the land. Evelina recalls, "Mooshum told me how the old buffalo hunters looked beneath the robe of destruction that blanketed the earth. In the extremity of their hunger they saw the frail crust of white commerce lifting, saw the green grass underneath the burnt wheat, saw the buffalo thick as lice again, saw the great herds moving, flattening that rich grass beneath their hooves" (244). The imagery of recovery and of renewal of the natural world echoes descriptions of the power of the ghost dance, an indigenous religious movement of the late nineteenth century. Believers danced in prayer for a cataclysmic transformation of the world, praying for the disappearance of the white settlers, the renewal of the land, and the return of the bison.

"History Works Itself Out in the Living"

Living out the history of Pluto, the sole surviving member of the Lochren family massacre eulogizes the dying town. The "white commerce" that Mooshum refers to in his apocalyptic story has indeed been drawn back to reveal the frontier reclaiming the space once platted and mapped by the venture capitalists who could not have imagined one-stop shopping malls, interstate highways, or big-city entertainment.

Louise Erdrich's *The Plague of Doves*

Town streets have fallen into disrepair for lack of tax revenue; Dr. Cordelia Lochren envisions Pluto as "empty at last" and her house "reclaimed by earth" (310). She concludes the novel with this prediction: "The wind will blow. The devils rise. All who celebrate shall be ghosts. And there will be nothing but eternal dancing, dust on dust, everywhere you look" (313). Pluto will return to the rhythms of time, which beat for the ghost dance of posterity. Both she and Judge Coutts mourn the quiet apocalypse they are witnessing, understanding nevertheless that the spirit of the land will prevail.

The narrators' meditations lend an eschatological cast to the conclusion of the novel, suggesting that Pluto has collapsed under the weight of its own history. The displaced indigenous inhabitants of this region, the Ojibwes and the Dakotas, understood the power of the earth, seeing themselves as its stewards rather than its masters. As critic Anne Ursu points out, "Place has a sentience in Erdrich's prose; it murmurs memories and whispers fortunes" ("The Lay of the Land"). Judge Coutts, recalling his grandfather's perspective on the siren call for millions that almost cost him his life on the original Pluto site expedition, reflects on the futility of conquest:

> As I look at the town now, dwindling without grace, I think how strange that lives were lost in its formation. It is the same with all desperate enterprises that involve boundaries we place upon the earth. By drawing a line and defending it, we seem to think we have mastered something. What? The earth swallows and absorbs even those who manage to form a country, a reservation. (115)

The conclusion of *The Plague of Doves* challenges readers' expectations in unexpected ways, given the identity of the narrator who knots together the conclusions of the multiple storylines of the novel. Moreover, we are left with a sense that this is a rare Erdrich novel that meets an expectation of complete closure; we may see no future sequels. At the same time, readers are asked to ponder the persistent legacy of economic, social, and political oppression bequeathed through the generational politics supporting both the colonial presence of immigrant settlers in the Upper Midwest and the attending racial animus that was—and remains—a lived reality for Native people. Belying the eulogistic tone of the novel's conclusion, Erdrich offers an optimistic perspective on the survival of American Indians in the twenty-first century. The novel successfully naturalizes American Indians within a racial category previously deemed mythic, without denying the racism that remains the shared legacy of both the Native and non-Native descendents of the early denizens of places like Pluto, North Dakota.

Works Cited

Baenen, Jeff. "A Dark Event Inspires Erdrich's New Novel." *News from Indian Country*. News from Indian Country, 30 May 2008. Web. 20 Apr. 2012.

Cowan's Auctions. "Photograph of North Dakota Triple Lynching." Cowan's Auctions, 2005. Web. 25 Apr. 2012.

_____. "Degraff Photograph of Indians Implicated in the Spicer Murder." Cowan's Auctions, 2005. Web. 3 May 2009.

Deane, Seamus. "Imperialism/Nationalism." *Critical Terms for Literary Study*. Ed. Frank Lentricchia and Thomas McLaughlin. 2nd ed. Chicago: U of Chicago P, 1995.

Drinnon, Richard. *Facing West: The Metaphysics of Indian-Hating and Empire-Building*. Norman: U of Oklahoma P, 1980.

Erdrich, Louise. *The Plague of Doves*. New York: Harper, 2008.

_____. "Louise Erdrich, The Art of Fiction No. 208." Interview by Lisa Halliday. *The Paris Review* 195 (2010): 132–66.

Forbes, Jack. "Colonialism and Native American Literature: Analysis." *Wicazo Sa Review* 3.2 (1987): 17–23.

Gonzales-Day, Ken. *Lynching in the West, 1850–1935*. Durham: Duke UP, 2006.

Lipsitz, George. "The Possessive Investment in Whiteness." *White Privilege: Essential Readings on the Other Side of Racism*. Ed. Paula S. Rothenberg. 4th ed. New York: Worth, 2012. 71–94.

"Mob Law in North Dakota." *New York Times* 15 Nov. 1897. Web. 20 Apr. 2012.

Nabokov, Peter. "Glimmerings of Sovereignty, 1915–1924." *The Native Americans: An Illustrated History*. Ed. David Hurst Thomas, Betty Ballantine, and Ian Ballantine. Atlanta: Turner, 1993.

Noori, Margaret. "The Shiver of Possibility—*The Plague of Doves*." *Women's Review of Books* 25.5 (2008): 12–13.

Stiffarm, Lenore A., and Phil Lane. "The Demography of Native North America: A Question of American Indian Survival." *The State of Native America: Genocide, Colonization, and Resistance*. Ed. M. Annette Jaimes. Boston: South End, 1992. 23–53.

Ursu, Anne. "The Lay of the Land: Louise Erdrich." *City Pages*. City Pages, 9 Sept. 1998. Web. 20 Apr. 2012.

Western Michigan University New Bureau. "Researcher Collecting, Critiquing 'Lynching Narratives.'" Western Michigan University, Kalamazoo, 10 Aug. 2004. Web. 20 Apr. 2012.

Sister Lost, Sister Found: Redemption in *The Painted Drum* and *Shadow Tag*

Gwen N. Westerman

Toward the end of the novel *The Painted Drum*, the main character Faye Travers muses, "Life will break you. Nobody can protect you from that" (274). It seems that life is just as difficult for *Shadow Tag*'s Irene America, whose image has become an American icon in the paintings of her self-destructive artist husband. Louise Erdrich's fallible characters appear lost and defeated by situations beyond their control. The theme of loss and guilt is the undertow in both novels, which are dark and often violent in their portrayals of contemporary characters who find themselves struggling, out of balance, and defined or controlled by others.

Both Faye and Irene feel utterly alone and struggle to find a place of truth in a world where pain is held as concealed as Irene's Blue Notebook in the safe-deposit box, a box that requires two keys to open. In *The Painted Drum*, Faye hides behind her mother and from the mistakes of her past while she sifts through the debris of other people's lives. Childless, she ultimately becomes the carrier of the stories of other mothers' children. *Shadow Tag* reveals Irene disappearing behind a veil of alcohol as she tries to protect her own children from the shambles of an abusive home life. Seemingly hopeless situations for both characters could produce a sense of despair, but a close examination of Faye's and Irene's ultimate motivations and their connections to their sisters may generate a different response. Release and deliverance from their mistakes and guilt and connection to a cultural community bring an unexpected perspective to the narratives through the voices of the daughters who survive.

The Painted Drum takes place in the seemingly disparate locales of rural New Hampshire and a North Dakota reservation and links the characters from those two places through generations of interconnected family histories. Faye Travers, in her fifties, lives with her mother on

Revival Road, "just where the road begins to tangle" (4), and for nearly two decades, they have run an estate appraisal business that specializes in Native American antiquities. Faye narrates parts 1 and 4 of the novel and declares, "Death has set changes into motion all up and down Revival Road, and there is no telling when one event will stop bumping into the next" (65). When she is asked to assess the estate of the eccentric Tatro brothers, Faye finds amid the years of accumulation in their home not only valuable Native American artifacts, but also a rare drum—an Ojibwe ceremonial drum—that she hears sound, even though she did not touch it. Compelled by an instinct "so essential that might be called survival" (44), Faye takes the drum and eventually returns it to Bernard Shaawano, an Ojibwe man who lives on her grandmother's reservation and knows the drum's traditional songs. There, she learns why the drum was created and how its power changes the lives of everyone who has been connected to it. Those connections require Faye to reevaluate her own family history of lost sisters, secrets, and guilt.

Despite being a second-generation resident of the small New Hampshire town of Stokes and Stiles, Faye feels like an outsider in the community. She describes herself as "a former user of street drugs cured by hepatitis, a clothing store manager fired for lack of interest in clothes, a semi-educated art lover, writer of endless journals and tentative poetry, and, lastly, a partner in the estates business my mother started more than fifty years ago" (6). Faye's grandmother, born in North Dakota, was Ojibwe and taken to Carlisle Indian Industrial School in Pennsylvania when she was only ten years old. There, she met her future husband, a young man from Stokes, and settled in the East permanently after Faye's mother, Elsie, was born. "That is why," Faye explains, "we are not really Easterners" (30). Yet, Faye does not identify strongly with her Ojibwe heritage or her North Dakota roots:

Were I a traditional Ojibwe, I would have a special place in the community because of my line of work. . . . Those persons who distribute the objects should not wear the color red—it is the one color the dead are thought to see clearly. It attracts them. They wander toward it. I avoid wearing red in my work, for somehow I find that idea compelling. (33)

She is also compelled to remain on the boundaries of her town and her relationships, disconnected and somehow caught between the living and the dead.

Disconnection does not prevent Faye from being defined by those around her. A captive of the past, she admits, "All I have is other people's lives. What I do belongs to them and to my mother—her business, her legacy, her blood. Even the box of tears in my closet belongs to another woman, L.M.B." (44). She immerses herself in the daily existence of the successful business and guards her solitude, while harboring a dreadful secret: "I've tried over and over to wreck myself on another human, and always failed. I fail now. For it seems that my sorrow is deep in my bones and I'd have to break every single one to let it out" (47). The physical depth of her sorrow is a result of the traumatic death of her sister, Netta, in the family orchard when Faye was nine years old, an event that has shaped her into an alienated and lonely woman.

The source of Faye's grief is revealed slowly and subtly, in an understated way indicative of Erdrich's narrative style, at the end of part 1. Faye's beloved and impetuous younger sister represents everything Faye is not: "Netta had all of the sandy-haired sun in our joint personality. She burned hot. She was just my opposite. Where I was quiet, neat, untiring when it came to detail, Netta was bold and impatient; she could be careless and even cruel" (80–81). These lively images of her sister are bound with memories of playing in the orchard, climbing apple trees, and competing for their parents' attention. When six-year-old Netta falls from a tree and dies, Faye knows the death will be blamed on her, regardless of the true circumstances. She recounts, "I knew that my father wouldn't have to say anything to convince them all that I'd pushed her or shaken the branch or she'd taken a dare" (93). The betrayal of both parents makes this tragedy even worse— her mother's absence and neglect, her father's destructive and erratic behavior, and their inability to protect their children. It is there in the orchard that Faye turns inward emotionally and encloses her grief and guilt: "I knew that I had lost them both, or all three of them. I knew that now I was alone" (93).

What happened to Netta prevents Faye from fully engaging in her own life and leaves her emotionally paralyzed, as if she too had suffered irreparable damage in the fall from the tree. She recognizes her situation and admits that "over the years I've warped my life around her memory," an idealized memory of a "very good sister who loved me so much that she sacrificed herself for me without hesitation" (73–74). However, the presence of the drum has initiated a change in the way that Faye now responds to her sister's sacrifice: "I lost myself along with her back there, I know it. When I touch the drum and think of her, though, I feel much stronger. I feel she has come back to help me" (77).

The decision to return the drum to the Ojibwe reservation of her grandmother leads Faye to a community and a cultural connection of which she has been only faintly aware. Parts 2 and 3 of the novel are narrated in collective voice of Bernard Shaawano, who recounts the history of the drum within the frame of the Ojibwe community, past and present, for Faye and her mother, Elsie. Observant and patient, he knows more about the eastern visitors than they seem to know about themselves:

Those two don't know who they are, what it means that they are Pillagers. They don't know they came from Simon Jack and they don't know what he did to Anaquot, my grandmother, or to my aunt whose name is never spoken, or to himself. They don't know what the drum did to him, either, what the drum knows, or what it contains. They don't know why my father sold it in spite of the many persons it healed. They don't know the whole story, but I do know it. So I tell them. (107)

Throughout that "whole story" are the accounts of self-involved fathers, neglectful mothers, and heroic little girls who sacrificed themselves to save their siblings. This return to and engagement with an ancestral Ojibwe community and its stories helps Faye come to terms with her loss and begin to heal.

Faye picks up the narrative again in part 4, the shortest section of the novel. As the daughter who survives, strengthened by the drum, she returns to New Hampshire able to accept and enjoy the revived orchard, released from the past, and open to living again, as if she has "just returned from an unknown journey" (262). She understands that she has been a reflection of her mother: "We've really been one person, she and I. But we must go deeper now, and perhaps apart. We must see what each other is made of, what differing stories" (263). Those stories include what they know about Netta's death and the depth of their guilt. When Faye confronts her mother about her whereabouts that day, she realizes that Elsie's "guilt has been greater, deeper, and so black I've lived in its shadow" (264).

Released from this shadow of guilt, Faye begins to move forward, on her own terms, knowing it will take years to change their lives: "Yet change they will. Even now, nothing is the same as it was before I reached out of my untested rectitude and stole the drum" (269). She knows she could not save Netta that day, but she can now save herself from a life of mourning and loneliness. Returning to the children's cemetery where her sister is buried, she is filled "with a sharp happiness" from the scents of the earth and the warmth of the sun and the rhythm of ravens playing in the sky. She muses, "Aren't they [the ravens] the spirits of the people, the children, the girls who sacrificed themselves, buried here?" (276). A connection to a larger Ojibwe community and a new perspective on a traumatic past produce healing for Faye.

Set in a contemporary upscale neighborhood of Minneapolis, Minnesota, *Shadow Tag* reveals the decaying relationship of Irene America and her husband, Gil, a painter who has become known for his provocative portraits of his wife. Gil created images of her that she describes as "starkly sexual, stirringly tender," while others "were such cruel portrayals that her eyes smarted and her cheeks burned as if she'd been slapped" (31). She knows that he is devouring her identity in and out of the studio and tells him, "When you take away that person's privacy you can control that person" (34). Irene discovers that he has secretly been reading her diary, so she creates entries to manipulate him and begins to record her true thoughts in a second journal, which is locked in a safe-deposit box. Their three children are caught in an atmosphere of abuse, secrets, and insecurities that grows more violent as Irene takes steps to end the destructive marriage. Gil becomes even more possessive and controlling and attempts to win them all back with gifts, an effort that he calls "the heart's desire project" (64). He is motivated by remorse: "If you could have anything, he asked each one of them in turn, anything in the world, the sky is the limit, your imagination is the limit, what would it be?" (65). But even this desperate act cannot change the fact that Irene does not love him. In the span of a little more than six months, Irene's guilt and secrets are exposed and have tragic consequences.

Irene is the daughter of Calvin American Horse, an absentee father who claimed their ancestor was the famous Lakota chief American Horse, but "she didn't think so," and Winnie Jane Sourcier, an Ojibwe from the crane clan (39). A promising scholar, she is thirteen years younger than her renowned artist husband, whose unrecognized heritage is "a mishmash of Klamath and Cree and landless Montana Chippewa" (13) on his father's side and white on his mother's. After an eleven-year gap to care for her children, Irene wants to complete her dissertation on George Catlin, the nineteenth-century painter of "vanishing" American Indian subjects who often were posed against painted backdrops and just as often were suspicious of his representations of them. It seems that she is "losing her mind—over George Catlin's clumsy, repetitive, earnest depictions of people—all of whom would sicken and die soon after" (7). Irene is a devoted mother and struggles to keep things together for the children, fourteen-year-old Florian, eleven-year-old Riel, and six-year-old Stoney, who was born on September 11, 2001. To make matters worse, her husband's attempts to control her are escalating: "On days he didn't have the strength to woo her with surprise gifts, he used the children to get to her" (10).

In the classic artist-model tradition of Andrew Wyeth and Helga or Edward Hopper and Jo, Gil and Irene are viewed in the art world as having an "iconic marriage" (91). Those who have seen her portraits believe they know her, portraits "in which she appeared raped, dismembered, dying of smallpox in graphic medical detail" (30). She is repulsed by what she sees in the new catalog of Gil's work but returns to sit for him after she "had a drink, two drinks, and brought another with, so she could ease into the session with a pleasant buzz" (31). Gil controls her movements, her breathing, her representation to the world outside of his studio. Then she realizes the extent of his domination over her: "By remaining still, in one position or another . . . she had released a double into the world. It was impossible, now, to withdraw that reflection. Gil owned it. He had stepped on her shadow. . . . A soul could be captured through a shadow" (40). She had to get out.

Aware that Gil is reading her Red Diary to discover if she is deceiving him, Irene preserves her real thoughts in the Blue Notebook kept in the safe-deposit box. Nervous, it took ten or fifteen minutes before she could begin to write, and she records, "My heart was beating so fast. I couldn't tell if I was experiencing panic, grief, or, possibly, happiness" (4). It also here where she admits to herself that their marriage is over: "With every person whom I have left, there has always been a final moment where I have realized *I am gone*" (48). Her efforts to maintain some balance in her life, hold onto her own identity, and protect her family from Gil's abuse are being drowned by alcoholism to the point where Stoney draws pictures of her with a "stick with a little half-moon on the end of it," a wineglass. She is stunned, and Florian responds, "He thinks it's a part of you" (54). How can she save her children when it appears she cannot save herself?

In the midst of this dysfunctional environment, Riel is planning to preserve her family by learning the "old-time" Indian ways, the "knowledge passed through generations" (102), her mother tells her. Named for the Métis hero Louis Riel, she records her memories in a notebook and "could name any number of frightful scenarios because she had made a list of them, and how an Indian would survive" (117). Convinced she will be left behind in the event of a disaster, Riel reads up on survival skills and fills an emergency bag with a water bottle, wax-dipped matches, flashlight and extra batteries, granola bars, dry dog food, duct tape, money, and Krazy Glue. Regarding those last items, she notes, "Indians would not have needed Krazy Glue or money but, she reasoned, she was a contemporary Indian" (119–20). After the disaster struck, she would be safely camped on the island in the middle of the lake with their dogs, where she would wait for her family to return without her father. She believes that "although their mother cannot tell them, she was always, secretly, on their side" (121).

Feeling utterly alone, Irene benefits from Gil's "heart's desire project" in a way he could have never anticipated. Stoney's wish is for a cloud, so Gil hires Louise, a painter he knew from "way back." After Stoney's ceiling is painted with sky and clouds, Irene offers Louise a ride home, and they stop at a coffee shop. Their eyes and hair match; they are the same height. Louise asks Irene who her father is and then responds, "He's my dad, too" (71). Shocked and unable to absorb the information, Irene begs Louise not to tell Gil. In her Blue Notebook, she can barely contain her joy of finding a sister: "She is almost like another me, a twin" (73). Yet this "twin" is real, unlike the fierce "doubles"—the captives—in Gil's paintings created out of pain and rejection. Irene hopes that Louise would understand that she was not the heroic or degraded image portrayed in Gil's works and would not "be disappointed when she came to know that Irene was ordinary" (76).

As her home becomes filled with secrets, violence, and screaming matches, Irene moves to end the nightmare that is her marriage after

Gil slams Florian's head onto a table. She tells Gil he can let her and the children go, but he berates her again:

> I've kept track of your issues, Irene. Do you think a judge is going to give the children to a depressed, dysfunctional woman who drinks too much and can't support them? You can't work. You can't finish your degree. You're having trouble with this thing you're working on right now. You have how many pages? Six? I will have sole physical custody. They will be with me, Irene. He spoke emphatically, with a flat, chilling kindness. You know how I love them. (114)

Riel overhears everything and realizes that, in spite of all her preparations, she cannot save her family either.

With the children safe in Louise's care, Irene finally gives Gil the divorce papers. In his rage, he rapes Irene in their dining room and then retreats to his studio. Locked inside, he almost poisons himself with vodka left over from Irene's surprise party but does not die. In her Red Diary, Irene rages against him: "So live on, Gil. Endure. Because you cannot ever be replaced and to kill yourself means never having to say you're sorry" (240). In fact, he does kill himself on Memorial Day weekend by swimming into the icy waters of Lake Superior, and although she had promised Riel that she "can save anyone" (102), Irene drowns trying to rescue Gil.

The last section of the novel is titled "Riel," and it is here that the identity of the omniscient narrator is revealed. Riel tells the story, the project of her graduate writing program. Raised by Louise, she is connected to a larger community where she finds that "the old-time Indians are us, still going to sundances, ceremonies, talking in the old language and even using the old skills if we feel like it, not making a big deal" (250–51). Storytelling releases her from the trauma of her childhood, and in remembering the day her parents died, she recalls, "It was noon and there were no shadows under us, or anywhere around us" (255). Riel relives the powerful story Winnie Jane had told a young

Irene about "an evil windigo warrior whose strength was in his shadow but whom a little girl was able to kill exactly at noon" (40). She is free.

In *The Painted Drum* and *Shadow Tag*, Faye and Irene are caught in the images and reflections of the people who exert the most power in their lives, while suffering from the devastating effects of their own actions. In a Minnesota Public Radio broadcast, Louise Erdrich once explained that "one of the most challenging things to write is about a person who believes strongly that they are doing the right thing but they are causing destruction." Those beliefs drive Faye's and Irene's destructive habits of wrecking themselves against other humans or with alcohol. The men in their lives, Kurt and Gil, are also driven by what they think is right, but they cannot connect emotionally and attempt to control women in order to assuage their own insecurities.

However, in the midst of these seemingly hopeless situations, a reclaimed Ojibwe worldview saves the daughters who survive. With only a few Ojibwe words and a tenuous connection to their culture, they are brought back into a community that values stories. Reticent at first to identify herself with those values, by the end of the novel, Faye recognizes her connection to the drum and its people: "We will travel back home to be part of what Bernard calls feasting the drum, and we also will learn the songs that belong to it" (269). Bernard's stories have so deeply affected Faye that she now calls the North Dakota reservation "home." Riel's home is with Louise, where she reveals, "We had a traditional adoption and I got brothers, sisters, twenty cousins, and it was all of them who mainly raised me" (250). Her desire to know the "old-time" ways is fulfilled by her mother's sister.

Through storytelling, these daughters draw closer to their mothers. Faye and Elsie have listened to the stories of their Ojibwe ancestors as they faced abandonment, death, and loss, and have survived. Both women are changed by the experience in a way that allows them to connect not only to their community, but also to each other. Faye is released from the guilt of her sister's death and recognizes the resulting change with her mother: "She isn't forgiving me anymore. No, it is I who am forgiving her" (264). The change is similar for Riel. While she cannot share the intent conversations of her childhood with her mother, she has put the Red Diary, the Blue Notebook, and her memory charts together and been given omniscience. She says, "I am angriest at you, Mom, but there is this: you trusted me with the narrative" (253). For Riel and Faye, the new relationship they create with their mothers is based upon the stories they share with each other. New perspectives are offered. Perceived injustices and failures are diminished. While abandonment is a common theme in Erdrich's novels, she states that "the main thing a parent has to do is stay alive. It doesn't matter how rotten you are, or if you fail. A failed parent is better than a dead parent. A failed parent at least gives you something to rail against" ("The Art of Fiction").

It is the transformative power of story and cultural community that provides release from loss and guilt for characters in *The Painted Drum* and *Shadow Tag*. The sisters who are lost, the sisters who are found, and the daughters who survive blur the boundaries of time and identity as their stories are told and retold. In the end, it is the rhythm of Ojibwe storytelling and memory that compel Faye, Elsie, Irene, and Riel to understand their differences and to heal. After all, as Faye muses, "We must see what each of us is made of, what differing stories" (263).

Works Cited

Erdrich, Louise. "The Art of Fiction No. 208." Interview by Lisa Halliday. *The Paris Review* 195 (Winter 2010): n. pag. Web. 20 Apr. 2012.

_____. "Louise Erdrich across the Decades." Interview by Kerri Miller. *Midmorning*. Minnesota Public Radio, 21 Sept. 2009. Web. 13 Apr. 2012.

_____. *The Painted Drum*. New York: Harper, 2005.

_____. *Shadow Tag*. New York: Harper, 2010.

Picturing a Thousand Words: Story and Image in Louise Erdrich's "Fiction"_____

Joanne DiNova

Traditional medicines capable of affecting both the physical and spiritual realms have been understood among the Anishinaabeg[1] (Ojibwe) since time immemorial. However, these medicines have also been understood to hold the potential for destruction as well as for healing. Tom Peltier's roughly autobiographical *Bearwalk*, for example, recounts the events that plagued a young couple due to "bearwalking," a type of medicine documented in academic literature (Hallowell; Angel) but better understood in traditional Anishinaabe communities. Bearwalking was (and is) recognized as a particularly destructive form of medicine. According to the stories, a bearwalker might assume the form of a bear or some other, often benevolent-looking animal or human in order to gain an unwitting victim's trust. Once trust was established, the bearwalker could enter the person's life and wreak havoc. As such, the Anishinaabeg were traditionally slow to trust strangers because appearances could be so misleading (Angel 26). Outward appearances were considered almost irrelevant since they might cloak unpleasant realities beneath the surface.

The illusory nature of surface appearances is foregrounded in Anishinaabemowin, the Ojibwe language. For example, people identify themselves with the phrase "_____ *nindizhinikaaz*," meaning "My name is _____." The etymology of the phrase is revealing. *Nind-* is the first-person marker, while the verb *-kaaz* means "to hide behind" (Beardy 297–98). The translation for "Joanne *nindizhinikaaz*" then would be "My name is Joanne," but the literal meaning would be closer to "Joanne is what I hide behind." "Joanne," from an Anishinaabe perspective, is not who I am; it is simply the name I hide behind. Similarly, I might hide behind cosmetics and clothing, or, on another level, within skin and bones, but none of these is who I truly am. Surface identity markers, including my name, are simply the things behind and within which my true self hides. For this reason, from a traditional Anishinaabe perspective, a person's life-force, the actual person beneath all the guises, is what is sought out and trusted: According to A. Irving Hallowell, the Ojibwes believe that "outward appearance is only an incidental attribute of being" (34) and "what is uniform, constant . . . and vital is the soul" (qtd. in Black 100). Michael Angel further asserts that "the concept of soul or 'life force' is the central concept in Anishinaabe cosmology. . . . It plays a significant role in the Midewiwin" (26).

In her recent novel *Shadow Tag*, Anishinaabe author Louise Erdrich paints a disturbing portrait of a family that seems, on the surface, to model perfection but whose "soul or life force" reveals violently destructive patterns of familial relations. While an external observer would see a loving and happy family, within a few months of the novel's opening and after increasingly deceptive hostility, both parents take their own lives while their children watch helplessly. Prior to the suicides, Gil, the father, goes to great lengths to portray himself as a caring husband and wonderful provider. He is an established painter, whose art generates enough money to finance an exclusive home in an upscale neighborhood and an equally exclusive private-school education for his children. The discrepancy between the public image that Gil constructs and the horrible lived reality he imposes on his family, however, call to mind the traditional Anishinaabe skepticism concerning outward appearances as "only an incidental attribute of being." Since appearances, in this case, reveal so little about what is going on beneath the surface, Gil functions much like a bearwalker, hiding behind a constructed image of familial compassion while tormenting those whom he appears to nurture.

An early scene in the novel illustrates the incongruity between Gil's surface appearance and the actual life-force that prevails beneath the surface. Gil prepares a surprise dinner for his wife, Irene. He chooses a cheese soufflé because, he notes, Irene had mentioned the dish a few weeks earlier, and he has decided to surprise her with his attentiveness to her desires. He is precise and exacting in his preparations, chooses a soufflé recipe from his best cookbook, prepares the meal, and sets the table with meticulous attention to appearances: "Gil surveyed the organized table. Very satisfying. Green plates, yellow napkins. The cheese soufflé. Crusty baguette. A fresh salad of baby spinach, toasted walnuts, pears. A bottle of chilled white" (14). During dinner, he begins to engage his children in a discussion of their school day: "So, what did everyone do today?" Based on this information alone, an external observer would judge Gil to be an ideal husband and father. However, we quickly begin to see shades of his true self, the actual life-force beneath the carefully constructed image.

Gil exerts total control over the dinnertime discussion, demanding that six-year-old Stoney be the first to answer. As he waits for a response, Gil assesses his son, noticing the artistic similarities between the two of them, but he becomes increasingly envious of the material advantages his youngest child enjoys. Stoney has access to the finest art supplies, while Gil as a child had to make do with used, borrowed, and discarded materials. By the time Stoney answers his father's question, Gil is so resentful that he harshly criticizes his son's language: "We don't begin sentences with *like*. Could you rephrase that?" (15). Irene senses Gil's mounting hostility toward the child and moves to intervene, patting Gil's wrist and speaking in a solicitous manner: "Stoney painted a scene for a play, Gil. That's a cool thing for a six-year-old to do . . . [then] in a more ingratiating tone, Your soufflé is amazing. You're a great cook!" (15). Irene's actions, it should be noted, resemble those of the two family dogs that appear later in the novel, constantly monitoring Gil's moods and working to divert his outbursts. Both Irene and the dogs must be vigilant in their efforts to keep this seemingly ideal father from attacking his own family. Fourteen-year-old Florian, the oldest child, is beginning to acquire some of his father's personality traits, however. He mocks his mother's attempts to divert Gil's hostility: "Who would think an artist of such stature could also deal so brilliantly with the humble egg? said Florian. His face was faunlike, subtle with malice. Of them all, he looked most like Gil" (15). Later in the novel, Irene describes her son as "a starkly handsome version of Gil, keen as a blade" (199). It seems that Gil's cruelty, cloaked in seeming benevolence and similarly "subtle with malice," will be the inheritance of the next generation.

The similarities between Gil and his son are mirrored in the novel's discussion of fractals. Florian is a mathematical genius and has been fascinated by fractals from a very young age. Fractals are geometric shapes discussed most cogently by Benoît Mandelbrot, who noticed that if one were to observe the coastline of Britain from space and then at increasingly greater magnifications, down to the level of the grains of sand, the shape of the magnified coastline would always be similar to—and yet distinctly different from—the shape of the overall coastline. There is never a perfect duplicate but always a set of distinct similarities, or self-similarities, at each level of magnification: "A fractal set generally contains infinitely many points whose organization is so complicated that it is not possible to describe the set by specifying directly where each point in it lies. Instead, the set may be defined by 'the relations between the pieces.' . . . It appears always to be better to describe in terms of relationships" (Barnsley 4). Likewise, Florian is becoming disturbingly similar to, while also distinctly different from, his father. This statement on familial relationships—that they follow the almost deterministic but almost incomprehensible patterns of fractal geometry—is perhaps one of the more unsettling themes explored in this similarly complex novel: "She understood that Florian's fascination had a name. But she was also a little spooked. In everything around him, Florian had been seeking fractal self-similarity" (87). Nevertheless, during the brief time span covered in the novel, Florian is still decidedly a victim of his father's cruelty (and his mother's inadequate efforts to protect him).

Gil's fierce attempts to maintain an ideal image, even one so disturbingly divorced from reality, frequently leads him to abuse his children for public disturbances of the false image. For example, when Florian fails to submit a book report on time, Gil smashes his son's head against the dining-room table (107). The very fact and nature of the punishment highlights the incongruity of the image and further divorces the family's reality from the false public image. In addition, Gil begins to look at his eldest son with intimations of sexual abuse, suggesting that the abuse may be entering a new, even more destructive level:

> Gil looked at Florian, irritated, but then he was taken by surprise by his son's beauty. Florian wasn't wearing his glasses and his narrow brown eyes, picked out by short, perfect spikes of straight lashes, burned darkly against his pale skin. His hair came to a peak at the center of his hairline and shot forward in a tuft. The way Florian slumped his hips against the counter as he drank was unknowing, pre-sexual. He was going to be very handsome. As Florian was leaving the room, Gil called out, I love you. . . . His father had followed him and paused now in the doorway behind Florian. . . . Gil touched his son's shoulder as he passed him. He'd thought of painting Florian drinking the milk, standing against the counter, one hand on the wood, the black T-shirt, the jeans, bare feet. A boy drinking milk. Through that act both separated and linked to his mother. (132–33)

This description might be read simply as a touching display of parental affection, but given that Gil routinely paints nude portraits of his wife in disturbingly graphic and often pornographic detail, his nascent sensual and artistic interest in Florian is somewhat troubling. The important point to note for the present discussion, however, is that Gil's appearance, the image of himself that he presents to the world, masks a violently destructive life-force beneath the surface. The idyllic image of family life that Gil constructs is almost entirely a fiction, but the constructed image is widely misrecognized as actual by everyone except those within the family. In this way, the line between real and actual, between fact and fiction, are blurred by Gil's masterful construction of a fictitious family image. As the narrator notes, such illusory images have the potential not only to obscure but to negate the very existence of the actual: "So it was, the shadows stole their subjects and, for the rest of the world, became more real, until it seemed they were the only things left" (143).

Shadow Tag is a disturbing novel. The reader is left unsettled by the plot and characters, by the themes and underlying philosophy. We might dispel the uneasiness by simply remembering that it is just a story; however, in the Anishinaabe tradition, stories are never *just* stories. Hallowell speaks of a distinction between two types of traditional oral narrative: "anecdotes, or stories, referring to events in the lives of human beings" and "sacred stories" (26). In Hallowell's classification scheme, the former is by far the broader category, including stories of experiences ranging from the everyday to the almost legendary. Sacred stories are treated as such: sacred, with strict patterns governing the invocation of persons in the story (Hallowell 26–27). This latter category is not unlike prayer, in which words are sacred instruments with the potential to tap into the spirit realm and thereby affect the physical world. The story related in *Shadow Tag* would clearly seem to fall into Hallowell's more mundane category of "anecdotes or stories." However, from an indigenous perspective, the line between quotidian stories and the sacred is not so clear and distinct.

One of the most frequently mentioned characteristics of an indigenous worldview is interconnectedness: "The Aboriginal worldview, as often noted, is characterized by an emphasis on connectedness, the idea that all of existence is connected and that the connectivity encompasses, infuses, and constitutes everything. This connectedness is called *manitou, wakan tanka, usen,* etc., and, as Willie Ermine points out, it forms the basis for Aboriginal thought" (DiNova 6). The precepts of deep ecology, in which everything in the universe is connected and interdependent, are not unrelated to this worldview (Seed). It is important to note, however, that in the indigenous understanding, the interconnectedness encompasses even the conceptual realm: "Aboriginal people found a wholeness that permeated inwardness and that also extended into the outer space. Their fundamental insight was that all existence was connected and that the whole enmeshed the being in its inclusiveness" (Ermine 103). Since this orientation to everything (the worldview) is based on interconnectedness, there is a tendency to look for relatedness rather than distinction. In the conceptual realm, the realm of thought and language, this tendency leads one to emphasize the fluidity of relationships between concepts rather than the distinctions between them. In short, relating people, things, places, and ideas is more important than defining them into discrete categories—a means of accentuating separateness rather than relatedness. In other words, the orientation is not toward defining or isolating the sacred from the mundane in stories (or in anything else), but rather toward connecting or relating everything, including story forms. In the indigenous worldview, then, degrees of sacredness are evident in all stories, in all language. Furthermore, even from a mainstream perspective, it is possible to see elements of the sacred in stories. Art lovers, for instance, frequently speak of a magic that occurs in the presence of great art, including literature. Art is magic, and the more powerful the art, the more powerful its impact. That impact, however, like the Anishinaabe medicine discussed earlier, has the potential to be either positive or negative.

Shadow Tag has a pronounced impact on the reader, but its impact is somewhat troubling, in part because, as some reviewers have noted, the marriage in *Shadow Tag* bears a distinct resemblance to Louise Erdrich's real-world marriage to Michael Dorris. As such, the blurring of fact and fiction that occurs within the fictional world of the novel—that is, the difficulty distinguishing between Gil's public image and the disastrous reality of his relationships with his family—is mirrored, fractal-like, by the blurring of the story of Erdrich's actual marriage and the fictional marriage of the novel. As *New York Times* reviewer Leah Hager Cohen points out with respect to *Shadow Tag*, "It's a fool's errand to parse fact from fiction. Even given such glaring similarities [between the marriage in the novel and Erdrich's actual marriage], to acknowledge them in a review would seem prurient, loathsome—if Erdrich hadn't seeded her narrative with what feels like an imperative to do so." Likewise, to point out the similarities here would seem in poor taste, if, as Cohen notes, the reader were not being forced to make the connections with such obvious prompts as the introduction of a character named Louise.[2]

The similarities between the fictional marriage of the novel and Erdrich's actual marriage create a disturbing verisimilitude: The reader is awkwardly and uncomfortably aware of striking similarities but simultaneously wants to—is trained to—understand the novel as a work of fiction. As such, the lines between fiction and reality are jarringly blurred. It becomes difficult to avoid seeing *Shadow Tag* as a self-portrait, much like the self-portraits described in the novel:

> During that time, [Pierre Bonnard's] had painted a self-portrait that Gil found both unbearable and heroic. In this picture of himself alone, frail, old, staring into the bathroom mirror, Bonnard had used every color. His eyes were deep, all-seeing, steady. Every color he had used in his life was there in that self-portrait. It was a portrait of the artist's gathered spirit, the self wearily dissolving into weariless color and light. (217)

If we read the novel as a type of self-portrait, then Erdrich, like Bonnard, is harnessing all her narrative skill, "every color [she has] used in [her] life" to paint an "unbearable and heroic" portrait of "the self wearily dissolving into weariless color and light." However, to read the novel in this manner not only makes us uncomfortably aware of aspects of Erdrich's personal life, it also makes us uncomfortable in our own disturbing, if involuntary, voyeurism. We find ourselves unwittingly inspecting the details of someone else's private life. Fractal-like, we parallel the audiences for Gil's paintings, entertained and entranced by the intimate and grotesque details revealed by the artist.

If the novel is a self-portrait, however, Erdrich herself is also a Gil parallel. Like Gil, she has painted an image of her spouse that is at once beautiful (in its brilliant command of technique) and grotesque (in its meticulously unflattering portrayal of her subject): "He'd been working on a mythic level with the portraits—her portrayals immediately evoked problems of exploitation, the indigenous body, the devouring momentum of history. More than that—he'd progressed to a technical level that allowed him an almost limitless authority" (11). As with Gil's paintings, the portrayal of a spouse, particularly a spouse exposed in graphic detail and without consent, can be seen as both exploitative and an abuse of privacy:

> Irene lay on her back with her knees drawn up together, tilted neatly to one side. She fell asleep. Her empty wineglass toppled onto the lush dark green blanket as her fingers relaxed. Gil adjusted his lights and continued to paint. Eventually, he put down his brushes, walked over to his wife, and gently teased her knees open. She drew her thighs up, then sighed and they flopped nervelessly apart. Gil stepped back, adjusted his lights to shine starkly between her legs. Her face was thrown into shadow. (162)

The reader of the novel is appalled by Gil's violation of his wife in this manner. If, however, the novel is a self-portrait, then Gil's portrayal of his spouse is an uncompromising comment on Erdrich's portrayal of her spouse without consent.

The novel includes a discussion of artistic depictions of spouses:

> Hopper had painted Jo, Rembrandt had painted Saskia, then Hendrickje . . . de Kooning and Kitaj and John Currin painted their wives. It was a way of getting at the essential other, the unknown essence, and the painting was also an act of fascinated love. Although, it was true, in the depiction of Irene, he had not always been gentle, he thought that he had used her humiliation as something larger—as *the iconic suffering of a people*, one critic had said. (36)

If the novel is read as a self-portrait, then Erdrich, like Gil, is using her spouse's "humiliation as something larger." Quoting the previous passage invokes a brilliant inversion that implicates the "critic" (me) and points to the most obvious and realistic violation in this reading: our own intrusion, unwitting though it may be, into Louise Erdrich's private life. Fractal-like, we replicate Gil (albeit imperfectly) as we read the novel, examining the details of "Erdrich's" marriage, artistically if repugnantly rendered. Furthermore, we replicate Gil, who, at the moment of Stoney's birth, was mesmerized by the iconic destruction of September 11, 2001. Rather than participate in the miracle of his son's coming into being, he watches as countless lives are destroyed, over and over again in graphic detail on the television. Likewise, instead of simply being fascinated by the wonder of Erdrich's literary creations, her readers have displayed an unseemly interest in the collapse of two icons of American Indian literature, Michael Dorris and Louise Erdrich.

Numerous reports appeared in the media following the death of Michael Dorris, some unnecessarily long-winded, others aesthetically pleasing, and all, perhaps, wholly inappropriate:

> Now, Ms. Erdrich said, she wanted to talk about their lives and about the circumstances surrounding his death, to correct some misconceptions that "seem to be floating around in the media" and to help shift the emphasis from the "grotesque details" of Mr. Dorris's death and the "morbid fascination" with the most intimate details of their private troubles. (Lyman 14)

Members of the reading public, it seems, have shown a "morbid fascination" with the "grotesque details" of Erdrich's private family life. In writing this novel, Erdrich may be satisfying reader desires, just as Gil's paintings—grotesquely intimate portrayals of his spouse—satisfied the inappropriate desires of an artistic public. Erdrich highlights the "morbid fascination" we seem to have with catastrophe (whether the collapse of the Twin Towers or the collapse of a high-profile family) by forcing the reader to identify with Gil. By our invasion of the writer's personal space—reading her personal story, as it were—we mirror Gil. Like Gil, we find ourselves sifting through the narrative, eager to discover intimate details of a story best kept private, and also like Gil, we have no way of knowing whether we are getting the "real" story or some further fabrication.

The reader of *Shadow Tag* is introduced to multiple layers of story, a labyrinthine interlacing of versions and elements of "truth" that violates narrative trust as it calls into question the very act of representation. At the outset, two diaries are introduced with two different versions of the fictional reality. The "real" diary ("Blue Notebook")—the truth, as far as we know—is kept in a safe-deposit box in a bank. The other ("Red Diary")—fabricated, we assume—is hidden where Gil can find it. The latter is the original diary, but it ceases to be a repository of truth when Irene discovers that Gil has invaded her privacy by reading it. From that moment, Irene begins to manipulate her personal narrative, using it to establish a fictionalized version of her thoughts and actions, a false truth. Gil's trespass into the diary is an obvious violation of privacy and breach of trust, but Irene's construction of a false truth takes the deception in the marriage to an even deeper level and sets in motion an unraveling that culminates in their joint destruction.

While Gil is being manipulated by means of the Red Diary, the false truth, the reader nevertheless assumes that she has access to "the truth of the matter" because of the presence of an omniscient narrator and the Blue Notebook. However, when the reader is told (from Gil's perspective) that Irene sometimes presents fabricated stories as if they were factual accounts, the fictional ground on which the reader stands is destabilized. The narrator recounts a story, based on Irene's research, about George Catlin's painting[3] of the Mink (*Mi-néek-ee-súnk-te-ka, Mink, a Beautiful Girl*):

> The story Irene told Gil was of the time George Catlin was stopped on a riverboat by Mandan people, a tribe he'd just left. They had followed him in order to retrieve the portrait of a beautiful girl. They told him that the girl, whose name was The Mink, was dying. They believed that the picture Catlin had made of her was too much like her. Catlin had put so much of her into it that when he took his painting away from their village, it drew a

part of her life away with it. She had begun bleeding from the mouth. She was throwing up blood. . . .

But Catlin refused to give back the picture, said Irene. He said that he had also put himself into the picture by using his own spirit in the making of it. Should that picture go back, he would become ill himself.

The people offered to take the picture immediately and burn it. Such a thing that could diminish two persons really should not exist, they said, it was dangerous. Catlin said that he would burn it himself. The people went away not believing him, still in despair. By the time they returned home, The Mink was dead. Catlin exhibited her picture in Catlin's Indian Gallery in 1838, Albany, New York. (45)

Gil, aware that Irene's "factual" stories are sometimes fabricated, routinely checks her sources: "Often, he discovered she had enlarged upon an episode in order to make some point. She didn't want him, in fact, to go back to the original text and find she had mistold the story. . . . He believed that she was trying to communicate with him through metaphors" (44). Indeed, Gil discovers that Irene has again fabricated the story she presented as researched fact: "Gil thought that perhaps Irene was trying to tell him something by referencing and fal-sifying the story" (46). This admission of falsification, presenting lies as truth, has a profound effect on the reader. First, even in a work of fiction, a bond of trust is established between reader and narrator, an unspoken agreement that, where facts are related as facts, the truth will be told. The introduction of a protagonist who relates partial but un-specified fictions as if they were fact—as the protagonist is also doing with the Red Diary—raises the disturbing prospect that the reader is being misled as well. Our trust in the omniscient narrator is radically destabilized, and we begin to question whether anything we have been told about Catlin, anything we have been told in the novel, is true. Like Gil, we begin to doubt the veracity of Irene's stories in general, and like Gil, we are drawn to track down, in the real world, "the story Irene had [conveniently] referenced in the second volume of [George Catlin's]

Letters and Notes on the Manners, Customs, Conditions of the North American Indians. Letter 54" (45). There, we find what Gil has also uncovered: that Irene has mistold the story as reported by Gil.

Catlin writes that he returned the painting to the sick girl's family:

> I unrolled my bundle of portraits, and though I was unwilling to part with it (for she was a beautiful girl), yet I placed it in their hands, telling them that I wished her well. . . . They rode back at full speed with the portrait; but intelligence which I have since received from there, informs me that the girl died; and that I am for ever to be considered as the cause of her misfortunes. (*Letters and Notes* 206–7)

We also find that the story of the Mink in Catlin's letter is, as Gil notes, "a story within another, longer story—sort of a lead-up, or an aside" (46), and much of this letter and the next ("Letter—No. 55") concerns indigenous medicine and spiritual beliefs, particularly beliefs around the power of images. We learn that there were others, in addition to the Mink, who had had their images painted by Catlin and had subsequently died unexpectedly. Letter 55 includes the story, also related in *Shadow Tag*, of Little Bear (*Mah-to-tchee-ga*) who was painted in profile, half his face in shadow, after which the half of his face that was depicted in shadow is destroyed by gunshot (cf. 140–41). As the narrator in *Shadow Tag* notes, Catlin introduced a terrifying multidimensionality into pictorial representation in North America:

> The tribes Catlin visited were artistic and produced extraordinary objects, including pictorial art. . . . They were also one-dimensional and contained no shadows. In addition to so many other European inventions . . . Catlin brought shadows.
>
> Because of the shadows, his paintings had the direct force and power of the supernatural, the dream replica, the doppelgänger. . . . So it was, the shadows stole their subjects and, for the rest of the world, became more real, until it seemed they were the only things left. (142–43)

Catlin claims that the people he encountered were terrified of the power of his portraiture and saw it as a potent medicine, superior to their own: "I am a friend of the white men, but here is one whose *medicine* is too great—he is a great *medicine-man*! his *medicine* is too great!" (*Letters and Notes* 219). However, Catlin was a showman, who embellished his paintings with bombastic stories of his own reputation and adventures. Even in his own day, many doubted the accuracy of his information, as they did the quality of his art (Catlin et al. 48–61). In reading through the letters, we find that Catlin brought yet another European invention: shadow in verbal representation. As Gil notes in *Shadow Tag*, Irene's story about the Mink did not align with the account given in Catlin's *Letters and Notes*. There, Catlin claims to have immediately handed over the painting to the girl's distraught relatives. However, the painting is currently in the Smithsonian American Art Museum, a gift of Mrs. Joseph Harrison Jr., the widow of the man who purchased Catlin's entire collection in 1852 (Truettner 181). The painting was also apparently exhibited in the Indian Gallery in 1838, as Irene claims, since it is listed in the catalog for Catlin's traveling show: "*Mi-néek-ee-sunk-te-ka*, the Mink; a beautiful Mandan girl, in a mountain-sheep skin dress, ornamented with porcupine-quills, beads, and elks' teeth" (13).

Catlin's fabrication in the *Letters and Notes* strengthens the image he has constructed of himself as a powerful but beneficent preserver of the history of "a (perceived) dying race." He is, therefore, able to profit doubly from this symbolic exchange—appearing benevolent for having returned the painting to the Mink's family, while also profiting from the exhibition of yet another image in his vast Indian Gallery. However, the introduction of an obvious fabrication into an ostensibly factual account means that, like Gil in *Shadow Tag*, Catlin's constructed image is seriously and maliciously out of alignment with his real life-force. As such, nothing he tells us about indigenous people in North America can be trusted, since, like Gil, his seeming appearance cloaks a destructive life-force. We have no idea how much of Catlin's account is factual; we can therefore trust none of it. Nevertheless, Catlin's paintings and narrative accounts are widely accepted as historical records of indigenous people. Interested parties are less likely to ask indigenous people themselves about their culture and history and are more likely to consult Catlin's *Letters and Notes on Their Manners, Customs, and Conditions*: "So it was, the shadows stole their subjects and, for the rest of the world, became more real, until it seemed they were the only things left" (*Shadow Tag* 141).

Erdrich artistically incorporates Catlin's tendency toward fabricated facts into her own interlacing of fact and fiction. The result is a novel that flits beautifully, if dangerously, between fact and fiction as it highlights self-similarities between the two. Throughout, the reader finds herself caught in a game of shadow tag, chasing shades of fact through a labyrinth of fictional and factual worlds in a futile attempt to catch the truth. This blending of fact and fabrication, the construction of a portrait that bears a striking resemblance to reality, creates a fascinating novel, the complexity of which will only be unraveled with much further study. Like fractal art, the beauty and philosophical sophistication of this novel is as fascinating as it is enchanting. However, unleashing the shadow of fabrication into the novel also introduces arbitrariness of signification, the impact of which has yet to be fully realized. It is no accident that the Anishinaabe word for "tongue" (*midenan*) derives etymologically from the word for "heart" (*midehi*) (Beardy 328, 296). Both have the same root, as also evident in the term *Midewiwin*, an ancient Anishinaabe spirituality that has been translated loosely as "the way of the heart" or "the way of life in which one speaks from the heart." Words and images have an impact—whether they accurately reflect reality or not. For this reason, what has traditionally been valued in the Anishinaabe understanding is an accurate alignment of the heart (the life-force) with one's words and self-representation. Since the destructive potential of the bearwalker is only unleashed when she or he begins to deal in false representation, perhaps the narrator of *Shadow Tag* is correct: "Such a thing that could diminish two people really should not exist" (45).

Notes

1. *Anishinaabeg* (pl.) is the word for the Ojibwe people in their own language.
2. The name of this character was changed to May in the 2011 paperback reprint of the novel.
3. George Catlin (1796–1872) was a nineteenth-century American painter who specialized in the portrayal of indigenous peoples.

Works Cited

Angel, Michael. *Preserving the Sacred: Historical Perspectives on the Ojibwa Midewiwin*. Winnipeg: U of Manitoba P, 2002.

Barnsley, Michael F. *Fractals Everywhere*. San Diego: Elsevier, 1993.

Beardy, Tom. *Introductory Ojibwe: Parts One and Two in Severn Dialect*. Thunder Bay: Lakehead U, 1996.

Black, Mary B. "Ojibwa Taxonomy and Percept Ambiguity." *Ethos* 5.1 (1977): 90–118.

Black-Rogers, Mary B. "Algonquian Gender Revisited: Animate Nouns and Ojibwa 'Power'—An Impasse?" *Papers in Linguistics* 15. 1 (1982): 59–76.

Catlin, George. *A Descriptive Catalogue of Catlin's Indian Gallery*. New York: Piercy, 1838.

_____. *North American Indians: Being Letters and Notes on Their Manners, Customs, and Conditions*. Vol. 2. Edinburgh: Grant, 1926.

Catlin, George, et al. *George Catlin and His Indian Gallery*. Washington: Smithsonian Amer. Art Museum, 2002.

Cohen, Leah Hager. "Cruel Love." *New York Times Sunday Book Review* 7 Feb. 2010: 1.

DiNova, Joanne. *Spiraling Webs of Relation: Movements toward an Indigenist Criticism*. New York: Routledge, 2005.

Erdrich, Louise. *Shadow Tag*. New York: Harper, 2010.

Ermine, Willie. "Aboriginal Epistemology." *First Nations Education in Canada: The Circle Unfolds*. Ed. Marie Battiste and Jean Barman. Vancouver: U of British Columbia P, 1995. 101–12.

Hallowell, A. Irving. "Ojibwa Ontology, Behavior, and World View." *Readings in Indigenous Religions*. Ed. Graham Harvey. London: Continuum, 2002. 17–49.

Lyman, Rick. "Writer's Death Brings Plea for Respect, Not Sensation." *New York Times* 18 Apr. 1997:14.

Mandelbrot, Benoit. "How Long Is the Coast of Britain? Statistical Self-Similarity and Fractional Dimension." *The Fractal Geometry of Nature*. San Francisco: Freeman, 1983. 25–33.

Overholt, Thomas W., J. Baird Callicott, and William Jones. *Clothed-in-Fur, and Other Tales: An Introduction to an Ojibwa World View*. Washington: UP of America, 1982.

Sallot, Lynne, and Tom Peltier. *Bearwalk*. Don Mills: Musson, 1977.

Seed, John. *Thinking Like a Mountain: Towards a Council of All Beings*. Philadelphia: New Soc., 1988.

Truettner, William H. *The Natural Man Observed: A Study of Catlin's Indian Gallery*. Washington: Smithsonian Inst., 1979.

RESOURCES

Chronology of Louise Erdrich's Life _____

1954	Karen Louise Erdrich, the first of seven children, is born on June 7 in Little Falls, Minnesota, to Ralph and Rita Gourneau Erdrich.
1976	Erdrich receives her BA from Dartmouth College in the first coeducational class.
1979	Erdrich receives her MFA from Johns Hopkins University.
1981	Erdrich becomes the writer in residence at Dartmouth College. She marries Michael Dorris on October 10 and becomes mother to his three adopted children.
1982	"The World's Greatest Fisherman" wins the Nelson Algren Award for short story.
1983	"Indian Board School: Runaways" wins the Pushcart Prize for poetry. "Scales," a short story, wins the National Magazine Fiction Award.
1984	*Love Medicine*, Erdrich's first novel, wins the National Book Critics Circle Award. Her first volume of poetry, *Jacklight*, is published.
1985	Erdrich is awarded a Guggenheim Fellowship.
1986	*The Beet Queen*, Erdrich's second novel, is a National Book Critics Circle Award finalist.
1987	"Fleur" wins an O. Henry First Place Prize. It is later modified to become the first chapter of *Tracks*.
1988	*Tracks* is published.
1989	Erdrich's grandfather, Patrick Gourneau, former chair of the Turtle Mountain Chippewa Advisory Committee, dies. *Baptism of Desire*, Erdrich's second volume of poetry, is published.
1991	Erdrich and Michael Dorris coauthor the novel *The Crown of Columbus* and the travel book *Route 2*. Their oldest son, Reynold Abel, dies after being struck by a car.

1994	*The Bingo Palace* is published.
1995	Erdrich writes her first nonfiction book, *The Blue Jay's Dance*, which describes her experiences as a writing mother to her three biological daughters with Michael Dorris.
1996	Erdrich's novel *Tales of Burning Love* and picture book *Grandmother's Pigeon* are published. Erdrich and Michael Dorris separate.
1997	On April 10, Michael Dorris commits suicide in New Hampshire.
1998	*The Antelope Wife* is published.
1999	*The Birchbark House* is a finalist for the National Book Award for Young People's Literature.
2001	Erdrich opens Birchbark Books, an independent bookstore in Minneapolis, Minnesota. *The Last Report on the Miracles at Little No Horse* is a National Book Award finalist.
2002	*The Master Butchers Singing Club*, based on the experiences of her German grandparents, is published. Erdrich's second picture book, *The Range Eternal*, is published.
2003	Erdrich's third collection of poetry, *Original Fire: Selected and New Poems*, and travel book *Books and Islands in Ojibwe Country* are published.
2004	*Four Souls*, which focuses on the iconic character Fleur and her experiences off-reservation, is published.
2005	*The Painted Drum* is published. It extends the North Dakota story farther back in history and introduces nonreservation Ojibwe in New Hampshire. *The Game of Silence*, a sequel to *The Birchbark House*, is published.
2007	Erdrich declines an honorary doctorate from the University of North Dakota because of their mascot, the Fighting Sioux.

2008	In August, Erdrich marries Dan Emmel. She cofounds the Birchbark House Fund with her sister Heid E. Erdrich. *The Porcupine Year* completes the *Birchbark* trilogy.
2009	*The Plague of Doves* is a Pulitzer Prize finalist. Erdrich is awarded an honorary doctorate from Dartmouth College. She and Heid E. Erdrich cofound Wiigwaas Press, an Ojibwe-language press.
2010	*The Master Butchers Singing Club* is adapted by playwright Marsha Norman and staged at the Guthrie Theater in Minneapolis, Minneapolis. Erdrich is interviewed by Henry Louis Gates Jr. for *Faces of America*, a Public Broadcasting Service (PBS) program. She narrates *First Speakers: Restoring the Ojibwe Language* for Minnesota Public Television, which later wins an Upper Midwest Emmy Award. *Shadow Tag*, a novel about the failure of a marriage, is published.
2011	*Awesiinyensag Dibaajimowinan Ji-gikinoo'amaageng*, the first Ojibwe-language picture book, is published by Wiigwaas Press and chosen as Minnesota's Best Read for 2011 by the Center for the Book of the Library of Congress.

Works by Louise Erdrich

Long Fiction
Love Medicine: A Novel, 1984
The Beet Queen: A Novel, 1986
Tracks: A Novel, 1988
The Crown of Columbus, 1991 (with Michael Dorris)
The Bingo Palace, 1994
Tales of Burning Love, 1996
The Antelope Wife: A Novel, 1998
The Last Report on the Miracles at Little No Horse, 2001
The Master Butchers Singing Club, 2002
Four Souls: A Novel, 2004
The Painted Drum, 2005
The Plague of Doves, 2008
Shadow Tag, 2010
The Round House: A Novel, 2012

Short Fiction
The Best American Short Stories, 1993, 1993 (coedited with Katrina Kenison)
The Red Convertible: Selected and New Stories, 1978–2008, 2009

Poetry
Jacklight, 1984
Baptism of Desire: Poems, 1989
Original Fire: Selected and New Poems, 2003

Nonfiction
Imagination, 1982 (with Helen Cogancherry)
Route 2, 1991 (with Michael Dorris)
The Blue Jay's Dance: A Birth Year, 1995
Books and Islands in Ojibwe Country, 2003
Winter Reader, 2003–2004, 2003

Children's/Young Adult Literature

Grandmother's Pigeon, 1996
The Birchbark House, 1999
The Range Eternal, 2002
The Game of Silence, 2005
The Porcupine Year, 2008
Chickadee, 2012

Bibliography

Beidler, Peter G., and Gay Barton. *A Reader's Guide to the Novels of Louise Erdrich.* 1999. Rev. ed. Columbia: U of Missouri P, 2006.

Bowers, Sharon Manybeads. "Louise Erdrich as Nanapush." *Studies in Gender and Culture.* Ed. Regina Barreca. Philadelphia: Gordon, 1992. 135–41.

Chavkin, Allan Richard, ed. *The Chippewa Landscape of Louise Erdrich.* Tuscaloosa: U of Alabama P, 1999.

DiNova, Joanne, R. *Spiraling Webs of Relation: Movements toward an Indigenist Criticism.* New York: Routledge, 2005.

Hafen, P. Jane. "Let Me Take You Home in My One-eyed Ford: Popular Imagery in Contemporary Native American Fiction." *MultiCultural Review* 6.2 (1997): 38–45.

_____. *Reading Louise Erdrich's Love Medicine.* Boise: Boise State UP. 2003.

_____. "'Repositories for the Soul': Driving through the Fiction of Louise Erdrich." *Heritage of the Great Plains* 32.2 (1999): 53–64.

_____. "'We Anishinaabeg Are Keepers of the Names of the Earth': Louise Erdrich's Great Plains." *Great Plains Quarterly* 21.4 (2001): 321–32.

_____. "'We Speak of Everything': Indigenous Traditions in *The Last Report on the Miracles at Little No Horse.*" Madsen 82–97.

Hollrah, Patrice E. M. *"The Old Lady Trill, the Victory Yell": The Power of Women in Native American Literature.* New York: Routledge, 2004.

Jacobs, Connie A. *The Novels of Louise Erdrich: Stories of Her People.* New York: Lang, 2001.

Lansky, Ellen. "Spirits and Salvation in Louise Erdrich's *Love Medicine.*" *Dionysos* 5.3 (1994): 39–44.

Madsen, Deborah L., ed. *Louise Erdrich:* Tracks, The Last Report on the Miracles at Little No Horse, The Plague of Doves. New York: Continuum, 2011.

Maristuen-Rodakowski, Julie. "The Turtle Mountain Reservation in North Dakota: Its History as Depicted in Louise Erdrich's *Love Medicine* and *Beet Queen.*" *American Indian Culture and Research Journal* 12.3 (1988): 33–48.

McCafferty, Kate. "Generative Adversity: Shapeshifting Pauline/Leopolda in *Tracks* and *Love Medicine.*" *American Indian Quarterly* 21.4 (1997): 729–51.

McKenzie, James. "Lipsha's Good Road Home: The Revival of Chippewa Culture in *Love Medicine.*" *American Indian Culture and Research Journal* 10.3 (1986): 53–63.

McKinney, Karen Janet. "False Miracles and Failed Vision in Louise Erdrich's *Love Medicine.*" *Critique* 40.2 (1999): 152–60.

Peterson, Nancy J. "'Haunted America': Louise Erdrich and Native American History." *Against Amnesia: Contemporary Women Writers and the Crises of Historical Memory.* Philadelphia: U of Pennsylvania P, 2001. 18–50.

Pittman, Barbara L. "Cross-Cultural Reading and Generic Transformations: The Chronotope of the Road in Erdrich's *Love Medicine.*" *American Literature* 67.4 (1995): 777–92.

Purdy, John. "Building Bridges: Crossing the Waters to a *Love Medicine* (Louise Erdrich)." *Teaching American Ethnic Literatures: Nineteen Essays*. Ed. John R. Maitino and David R. Peck. Albuquerque: U of New Mexico P, 1996. 83–100.

Rowe, John Carlos. "Buried Alive: The Native American Political Unconscious in Louise Erdrich's Fiction." *Afterlives of Modernism: Liberalism, Transnationalism, and Political Critique*. Hanover: Dartmouth College P, 2011. 163–86.

Sanders, Karla. "A Healthy Balance: Religions, Identity, and Community in Louise Erdrich's *Love Medicine.*" *MELUS* 23.2 (1998): 129–55.

Sands, Kathleen M. "*Love Medicine*: Voices and Margins." Wong 35–42.

Sarris, Greg. "Reading Louise Erdrich: *Love Medicine* as Home Medicine." *Keeping Slug Woman Alive: A Holistic Approach to American Indian Texts*. Berkeley: U of California P, 1993. 115–45.

Sarris, Greg, Connie A. Jacobs, and James Richard Giles, eds. *Modern Language Association Approaches to Teaching Louise Erdrich*. New York: MLA, 2004.

Sawhney, Brajesh. *Studies in the Literary Achievement of Louise Erdrich, Native American Writer: Fifteen Critical Essays*. Lewiston: Mellen, 2008.

Schneider, Lissa. "*Love Medicine*: A Metaphor for Forgiveness." *Studies in American Indian Literatures* 4.1 (1992): 1–13.

Schultz, Lydia A. "Fragments and Ojibwe Stories: Narrative Strategies in Louise Erdrich's *Love Medicine.*" *College Literature* 18.3 (1991): 80–95.

Silberman, Robert. "Opening the Text: *Love Medicine* and the Return of the Native American Woman." Vizenor 101–20.

Slack, John S. "The Comic Savior: The Dominance of the Trickster in Louise Erdrich's *Love Medicine.*" *North Dakota Quarterly* 61.3 (1993): 118–29.

Smith, Jeanne Rosier. "Comic Liberators and Word-Healers: The Interwoven Trickster Narratives of Louise Erdrich." *Writing Tricksters: Mythic Gambols in American Ethnic Literature*. Berkeley: U of California P, 1997. 71–110.

_____. "Transpersonal Selfhood: The Boundaries of Identity in Louise Erdrich's *Love Medicine.*" *Studies in American Indian Literatures* 3.4 (1991): 13–26.

Stokes, Karah. "What About the Sweetheart?: The 'Different Shape' of Anishinabe Two Sister Stories in Louise Erdrich's *Love Medicine* and *Tales of Burning Love.*" *MELUS* 24.2 (1999): 89–105.

Stookey, Lorena Laura. *Louise Erdrich: A Critical Companion*. Westport: Greenwood, 1999.

Stripes, James D. "The Problem(s) of (Anishinaabe) History in the Fiction of Louise Erdrich: Voices and Contexts." *Wicazo Sa Review* 7.2 (1991): 26–33.

Towery, Margie. "Continuity and Connection: Characters in Louise Erdrich's Fiction." *American Indian Culture and Research Journal* 16.4 (1992): 99–122.

Van Dyke, Annette. "Questions of the Spirit: Bloodlines in Louise Erdrich's Chippewa Landscape." *Studies in American Indian Literatures* 4.1 (1992): 14–27.

Vizenor, Gerald Robert. *Narrative Chance: Postmodern Discourse on Native American Indian Literatures*. Albuquerque: U of New Mexico P, 1989.

Wong, Hertha Dawn Sweet, ed. *Louise Erdrich's* Love Medicine*: A Casebook*. New York: Oxford UP, 2000.

CRITICAL
INSIGHTS

About the Editor _____

P. Jane Hafen (Taos Pueblo) is a professor of English at the University of Nevada, Las Vegas. She serves as an advisory editor for the *Great Plains Quarterly*, on the Western Writers series editorial board, and on the editorial board for the Michigan State University Press American Indian series. She is on the board of the Charles Redd Center for Western Studies and is an associate fellow at the Center for Great Plains Studies. She is a Frances C. Allen Fellow, D'Arcy McNickle Center for the History of the American Indian, the Newberry Library. She was the founding director and is currently a clan mother of the Native American Literature Symposium. She was awarded a Black Mountain Institute Fellowship for Fall 2011. She edited *Dreams and Thunder: Stories, Poems, and "The Sun Dance Opera" by Zitkala-Ša* (2005) and coedited *A Great Plains Reader* (2003) with Diane D. Quantic. She is the author of *Reading Louise Erdrich's "Love Medicine"* (2003) and numerous articles and book chapters about American Indian literatures.

Contributors _____

P. Jane Hafen (Taos Pueblo) is a professor of English at the University of Nevada, Las Vegas. She is one of the clan mothers for the Native American Literature Symposium. She edited *Dreams and Thunder: Stories, Poems, and "The Sun Dance Opera" by Zitkala-Ša* (2005) and coedited *A Great Plains Reader* (2003) with Diane D. Quantic. She is the author of *Reading Louise Erdrich's "Love Medicine"* (2003) and numerous articles and book chapters about American Indian literatures.

A. LaVonne Brown Ruoff is professor emerita of English, University of Illinois at Chicago, and former interim director of the D'Arcy McNickle Center for American Indian History, Newberry Library (1999–2000). A former a member of the Modern Language Association's Executive Council (2001–05), she served twice on the Committee on the Literatures of People of Color (1980–83; 1998–2001; cochair 2000–01). In 2002, she received MLA's Award for Lifetime Scholarly Achievement. In 1998, Ruoff received a Lifetime Achievement Award from the American Book Awards/Before Columbus Foundation. In 1993, she was the first honoree of the MLA Division on American Indian Literatures and the Association for Study of American Indian Literatures. She directed four NEH Summer Seminars for College Teachers on American Indian literature and has received an NEH research grant and fellowship. Formerly general editor of the American Indian Lives series for the University of Nebraska Press (1985–2008), she is the author of *American Indian Literatures* (1990) and *Literatures of the American Indian* (1990) for middle school and high school readers. With Jerry W. Ward Jr., she edited *Redefining American Literary History* (1990). She has also published annotated editions of books by S. Alice Callahan (Muscogee-Creek), George Copway (Ojibwe), Charles Eastman (Dakota), and E. Pauline Johnson (Mohawk).

Margaret Huettl, whose family is from the Lac Courte Oreilles Ojibwe reservation, is a history doctoral candidate at the University of Nevada, Las Vegas. Her dissertation focuses on the transnational Ojibwe community in the Great Lakes region of the United States and Canada during the twentieth century.

Gregory A. Wright is an assistant professor of English at Snow College in Ephraim, Utah, where he teaches in both the English and philosophy departments and advises the Native American Student Association. He has previously published work on Sarah Winnemucca Hopkins. He has given a number of conference presentations at the Western Literature Association and the Native American Literature Symposium. His scholarship is largely devoted to issues of gender and violence in American literature.

Thomas Austenfeld is professor of American literature at the University of Fribourg, Switzerland. He was educated at the University of Münster, Germany, and at the University of Virginia, where he earned a PhD in English and American literature with a dissertation on Robert Lowell. His fifteen-year teaching career in the United States took him to Missouri, Utah, and Georgia before he returned to Europe. He is the author of *American Women Writers and the Nazis: Ethics and Politics in Boyle, Porter, Stafford, and Hellman* (2001), editor of *Kay Boyle for the Twenty-First Century* (2008) and *Critical Insights: Barbara Kingsolver* (2010), and coeditor of *Writing American Women* (2009) and *Terrorism and Narrative Practice* (2011). His articles discuss authors as diverse as Lord Byron, Wallace Stevens, Katherine Anne Porter, Peter Taylor, Thomas Wolfe, Josef Pieper, Derek Walcott, Louise Erdrich, Philip Roth, and Frank Norris. He contributed bibliographies to *Western American Literature* and bibliographic essays to the annual *American Literary Scholarship*. In more than fifty conference papers, he has discussed women writers, literature of the American West, and questions at the intersections of literature and philosophy. His recent work has centered on contemporary American poetry.

William Huggins is an independent scholar who has been published in *Studies in American Indian Literature*, wilderness blogs, and local media, and has participated in the Native American Literature Symposium. He graduated from the University of Nevada, Las Vegas, with an MA. His critical focus rests primarily on environmental literature. Beyond writing, he is active in wilderness and environmental justice issues on many fronts and has worked for a Nevada wilderness organization.

Margaret Noori / Giiwedinoodin (Anishinaabe heritage, waabzheshiinh doodem) received an MFA in creative writing and a PhD in English and linguistics from the University of Minnesota. She directs the Comprehensive Studies Program and teaches American Indian literature at the University of Michigan. Her work focuses on the recovery and maintenance of Anishinaabe language and literature. Her research interests include language proficiency and assessment and the study of indigenous literary aesthetics. She and her colleague Howard Kimewon have created an online space for language shared by academics and the Native community.

Dean Rader has published widely in the fields of poetry, American Indian studies, and popular culture. His debut collection of poems, *Works & Days*, won the 2010 T. S. Eliot Prize for Poetry and the 2010 Writers' League of Texas Book Award for poetry and was a finalist for the Bob Bush Memorial Award for First Book of Poetry. A poem from the book, "Twilight at Ocean Beach: 14," was named among the best poems of 2010 by Verse Daily, and others have been nominated for the Pushcart Prize. With poet Janice Gould, he coedited *Speak To Me Words: Essays on Contemporary American Indian Poetry* (2003), the first collection of essays devoted to Native American poetry. Along with Jonathan Silverman, he coauthored a best-selling textbook on writing and popular culture, *The World Is a Text* (2009), and has authored the scholarly book *Engaged Resistance: American Indian Art, Literature, and Film from Alcatraz to the NMAI* (2011). He also curated a special issue of *Sentence* that focused on recent

American Indian prose poetry. He is a professor of English at the University of San Francisco, where he won the 2010–11 Distinguished Research Award.

Jill Doerfler (White Earth Anishinaabe) is an assistant professor of American Indian studies at the University of Minnesota Duluth. She is interested in the diverse ways in which Anishinaabeg have resisted pseudoscientific measures of blood (race/blood quantum) as a means to define identity. Her article "An Anishinaabe Tribalography: Investigating and Interweaving Conceptions of Identity during the 1910s on the White Earth Reservation" was published in *American Indian Quarterly* in summer 2009. She coedited *Centering Anishinaabeg Studies: Understanding the World Through Stories* (publication forthcoming) with Niigaanwewidam James Sinclair and Heidi Kiiwetinepinesiik Stark. She was a member of the Constitutional Proposal Team of the White Earth Nation and cowrote *The Constitution of the White Earth Nation* (2009) with Gerald Vizenor and David Wilkins. Her provisionally titled manuscript *Blood v. Family: The Struggle over Identity and Tribal Citizenship among the White Earth Anishinaabeg* is forthcoming in the SUNY Press Native Traces series.

Sandra Cox completed her PhD in English at the University of Kansas in 2011 and is an assistant professor in the Department of Humanities at Shawnee State University. Recently, her article examining the craft and politics of two-spirit Menominee poet Chrystos was published in *Interdisciplinary Literary Studies*. She is working on her first monograph, which explores the ethical challenges of ethnographic criticism of contemporary fiction by American writers of color.

Amy T. Hamilton is an assistant professor of English at Northern Michigan University on Michigan's beautiful Upper Peninsula. Her teaching and research interests include American Indian, Chicano, early American, environmental, and Western American literatures. She is working on a monograph that explores walking in American literature from a cross-cultural perspective.

Patrice Hollrah is the director of the Writing Center at the University of Nevada, Las Vegas (UNLV), and teaches in the Department of English. She is the author of *"The Old Lady Trill, the Victory Yell": The Power of Women in Native American Literature* (2003) and various critical essays on American Indian literatures. She is a member of the editorial board of *Studies in American Indian Literatures*, serves as one of the clan mothers for the Native American Literature Symposium, and is a member of the UNLV American Indian Alliance.

Lisa Tatonetti is an associate professor of English and American ethnic studies at Kansas State University where she studies, teaches, and publishes on American Indian literatures with a focus in two-spirit studies. She is coeditor of *Sovereign Erotics: A Collection of Two-Spirit Literature* (2011), with Qwo-Li Driskill, Daniel Heath Justice, and Deborah Miranda, and is completing a book project entitled *Queering*

American Indian Literature: The Rise of Contemporary Two-Spirit Texts and Criticism.

Debra K. S. Barker, an enrolled member of the Rosebud Sioux Tribe (Sicangu Lakota Nation), serves as director of American Indian studies at the University of Wisconsin–Eau Claire and professor of English and American Indian studies. Her research interests include the work of modern American Indian writers (with a special interest in Lakota writers, past and present), the representation of American Indians in Euro-American culture, and the rhetoric of colonial discourses. Her publications include articles on the Indian boarding-school system, Lakota women's life writings, and the literary production of Louise Erdrich.

Gwen N. Westerman is director of the humanities program and professor in English at Minnesota State University, Mankato, and teaches courses in literature, technical communication, and humanities. Her essays and poems have appeared in *Western American Literature, Yellow Medicine Review, Water~Stone Review, A View from the Loft,* and *Natural Bridge*. An enrolled member of the Sisseton Wahpeton Sioux Tribe, she lives in southern Minnesota, as did her Dakota ancestors. She is coauthor with Bruce White of the forthcoming book *Mni Sota Makoce: Land of the Dakota, an Oral and Textual History of Dakota Land Tenure in the Upper Midwest from Creation through 1862.*

Joanne DiNova teaches in the School of Professional Communication at Ryerson University in Toronto. Her research interests include indigenous theory and literatures. She is currently part of a research project that is working to identify key differences between indigenous and colonizing languages by using traditional linguistics and poetics along with new media tools and analysis. The goal of the project is to reclaim indigenous languages while restoring indigeneity in language. She is a member of the Couchiching First Nation in Treaty Three territory. She is the author of *Spiraling Webs of Relation: Movements toward an Indigenist Criticism* (2005).

Index

Adare, Dot (*Beet Queen*), 157, 216
Adare, Dot (*Tales of Burning Love*), 218
Adare, Karl (*Beet Queen*), 160, 210–17
Adare, Mary (*Beet Queen*), 162–63
agency, views of, 143
Agnes, Saint, 82
AIM (American Indian Movement), 44
Alexie, Sherman. *See* "Unauthorized
     Autobiography of Me, The"
allotment
     assimilation through, 33, 178
     fictional depiction of, 34–38
     history of, 33–34
     land loss and, 33–37, 178
     worst period of, 188
Allotment Act of 1887, 33, 178–81
Almanac of the Dead (Silko), 209
America, Florian (*Shadow Tag*), 258–61
America, Gil (*Shadow Tag*), 249–53,
     257–61, 263–66, 267
America, Irene (*Shadow Tag*), 249–53,
     266
America, Riel (*Shadow Tag*), 252, 253
America, Stoney (*Shadow Tag*), 40, 258
American hero, Agnes/Father Damien
     as, 78
American Indian literature
     ecocriticism and, 86–87
     marginality in, 174
     nationalism vs. cosmopolitanism in,
          49–51
     queer literature in, 208
     Western critical approaches and, 13,
          187
American Indian Movement, 44
American national literature, 74–77
Anaquot (*Painted Drum*), 201, 203
Anishinaabe, origin of term, 106, 187

Anishinaabemowin
     cultural connection through, 115–18
     history of, 107, 187
     outward appearance and, 256
     reasons for Erdrich's use of, 105
     revitalization of, 12–13, 109–10
     saving power of, 148
Antelope Wife, The (Erdrich), 9, 23, 43
*Approaches to Teaching the Works
     of Louise Erdrich* (Sarris, Jacobs,
     Giles), 61–62
appropriation. *See* cultural appropriation
Argus, North Dakota, 155, 161, 210
assimilation
     allotment and, 33
     education and, 108, 147, 195
     internalized oppression and, 147
     resistance to, 147, 177
autobiography
     fiction and, 262–66
     persona poem as, 133–34
     race and, 124
     voyeurism of, 263

Baptism of Desire (Erdrich), 22, 81,
     121–22, 131–34
Barton, Gay. *See Reader's Guide to the
     Novels of Louise Erdrich, A* (Barton,
     Beidler)
bearwalking, 256
Beet Queen, The (Erdrich), 22, 154–70,
     209–17
Beidler, Peter G. *See Reader's Guide
     to the Novels of Louise Erdrich, A*
     (Barton, Beidler)
BIA (Bureau of Indian Affairs), 42
Bible, allusion to, 79, 142
Bingo Palace, The (Erdrich), 22
Birchbark Books, 11, 110

Birchbark House, The (Erdrich), 9, 24, 113

Blue Jay's Dance, The (Erdrich), 22

boarding schools
  fictional depiction of, 108–109, 147
  historical trauma of, 195–97

Books and Islands in Ojibwe Country (Erdrich), 11, 23, 112

Borges, Jorge Luis, similarity to, 10

branch, symbolism of, 164

Brave Heart, Maria Yellow Horse, 194, 198

Broken Cord, The (Dorris), 20

Bureau of Indian Affairs, 42

Burke Act of 1906, 33

Carlisle Indian Industrial School, 108, 147, 195–96

Cather, Willa
  comparison with, 99
  precursor to Erdrich, 79
  reinterpretation of, 76

Catholicism. *See* Roman Catholicism

Catlin, George, 250, 266–70, 271

chance
  love and, 142, 143–45
  reclamation through, 150
  theme of, 140

characterization
  gender critique through, 158–59
  queer identity and, 209
  stereotype vs. realism in, 139–40

Chavkin, Allan. *See Chippewa Landscape of Louise Erdrich, The* (Chavkin)

Childs, Craig. *See Finders Keepers* (Childs)

Chippewa. *See* Anishinaabe

Chippewa Landscape of Louise Erdrich, The (Chavkin), 60–61

city, 42–44

Civilization Fund Act of 1819, 108

Claire, Saint (*Baptism of Desire*), 132

class. *See* poverty; socioeconomics

colonization
  deromanticized, 238–40
  English language and, 107
  imposed gender and sexuality norms, 224–25
  internalized oppression, 237
  literary resistance to, 155
  trauma caused by, 198

community
  American fiction and, 74
  Erdrich's representation of, 185
  healing through, 254
  individualism and, 69
  queer identity and, 212

continuance theme, 141

Cook, Marlis (*Tales of Burning Love*), 218, 219–20

corruption, 36, 180

cosmopolitanism, American Indian literature and, 50

Coutts, Antone (*Plague of Doves*), 230, 232

Creator. *See* Gichi Manidoo

critical reception
  Erdrich's oeuvre, 47–65, 75
  The Beet Queen, 154, 169
  The Painted Drum, 191
  The Plague of Doves, 230

Crown of Columbus, The (Dorris, Erdrich), 8, 22, 89

cultural appropriation, 149, 240

Damien, Saint, 81

Dawes Act. *See* Allotment Act of 1887

"Dear John Wayne" (Erdrich), 127–29

death and rebirth, 141

death road, 159, 182, 185
DeWitt, Agnes (Last Report), 78–80, 221–22, 223
disconnection
    characters defined by, 91
    emotional rejection and, 212
    identity and, 247
Dismas, Saint, 81
dispossession. *See* land loss
domestic abuse, 250, 252–53
Dorris, Michael, 18, 20, 262, 265
drum
    ecological importance of, 96–97
    healing through, 201, 204–205

ecocriticism, 86–87
economic revenge, 38, 150
education, assimilation through, 108, 147, 195
eggs, symbolism of, 142
English language
    colonization and, 107, 117
    rejection of, 149
essentialism, postmodernism vs., 71
ethnocide, 147
European encounter
    Agnes/Father Damien as embodiment of, 80
    American history and fiction based on, 74
Everything That Rises Must Converge (O'Connor), 77
extermination
    allotment and, 37
    racial categorization and, 235
    ravens and, 90
    wolves and, 92
Eyke, Davan (*Painted Drum*), 92

fact and fiction, 266, 268–70
fairy tale, 158, 169

Faulkner, William, 3, 55, 73, 240
femininity. *See* gender
Finders Keepers (Childs), 95
first-person narration, 165–66
first-person plural narration, 125–28
Four Souls (Erdrich), 23, 175
fractals, 259
free indirect discourse, 159, 163–65, 168
frontier, deromanticized, 238–40
Frost, Robert, allusion to, 126

Game of Silence, The (Erdrich), 24, 113
gay identity. *See* queer identity; two-spirit identity
geese, symbolism of, 5, 145
gender
    fluidity of, 217
    performance of, 211, 221
    vocation vs., 82
    Western ideals, critique of, 158–59
gender diversity
    critical attention to, 156
    Western norms challenged by, 209
General Allotment Act of 1887. *See* Allotment Act of 1887
genocide
    definition of, 195
    racial categorization and, 235
ghost dance, 241
Gichi Manidoo, 113
Giles, James R.. *See Approaches to Teaching the Works of Louise Erdrich* (Sarris, Jacobs, Giles)
government policies. *See* individual laws and acts; allotment; termination and relocation
Grandmother's Pigeon (Erdrich), 24
Great Migration of the Anishinaabeg, 172
grief, 36, 93–94, 198, 247

Hafen, P. Jane. See *Reading Louise Erdrich's "Love Medicine"* (Hafen)

Harp, Evelina (*Plague of Doves*), 229, 230, 233, 241

Harp, Neve (*Plague of Doves*), 236

healing
historical grief, intervention models for, 199
Native tradition enabling, 168, 203, 254
natural connection enabling, 93
storytelling enabling, 253

Heartsong of Charging Elk, The (Welch), 209

heteronormativity, 220–21

historical trauma, 194, 198–99, 202

history
Erdrich's fictionalization of, 80, 130, 233
reclamation of, 44–45
recovery through, 30

home
reservation as, 32, 37
return to and departure from, 180
spatial understanding of, 173

homosexuality. *See* queer identity; two-spirit identity

identity
loss of, 158, 237
outward appearance and, 256
restoration of, 148, 149

Indian Citizenship Act, 235

Indian Religious Crimes Code, 203

individualism, community and, 69

interconnectedness
characters and plots, 55
ecology and, 87
history and, 30, 225
storytelling and, 261

intergenerational trauma, 194, 198–99, 201

internalized oppression, 237

"Jacklight" (Erdrich), 125–27

Jacklight (Erdrich), 21, 109, 120–21, 125–31

Jacobs, Connie A. *See Approaches to Teaching the Works of Louise Erdrich* (Sarris, Jacobs, Giles); *Novels of Louise Erdrich, The* (Jacobs)

James, Celestine (*Beet Queen*), 160–61, 215, 216

James, Dot. *See* Adare, Dot

Jesus, 142

Johnson, Albertine (*Love Medicine*), 180–81

jump, symbolism of, 213–14

Kashpaw, Eli (*Tracks*), 184

Kashpaw, Gordie (*Love Medicine*), 142

Kashpaw, King (*Love Medicine*), 139, 151

Kashpaw (Last Report), 223

Kashpaw, Margaret (*Tracks*), 180

Kashpaw, Marie Lazarre (*Love Medicine*), 142–46, 147–49

Kashpaw, Nector (*Love Medicine*), 5–6, 142–46, 147

Kashpaw, Nector (*Tracks*), 180

Kashpaw, Russell (*Beet Queen*), 158–59

Kozka, Sita (*Beet Queen*), 158, 159

Krahe, Kurt (*Painted Drum*), 92

Kröger, Mary (*Jacklight*), 21

Lamartine, Henry, Jr. (*Love Medicine*), 32, 149

Lamartine, Lulu Nanapush (*Love Medicine*). *See* Nanapush, Lulu (*Love Medicine*)

Lamartine, Lyman (*Love Medicine*), 149–50
land loss
  allotment and, 33–37
  movement and, 178
  psychic wound of, 236–37
language
  assimilation and, 108
  authenticity from, 118
  cosmology conveyed through, 113, 256
  culture transmitted through, 112, 197
  identity and, 115–16, 148
  sound and style of, 110–12
Last Report on the Miracles at Little No Horse, The (Erdrich), 9, 23, 78–83, 221–25
leap, symbolism of, 213–14
Lee, Harper, comparison to, 240
Leopolda, Sister (Love Medicine), 148
lesbian identity. *See* queer identity; two-spirit identity
liminality
  characters defined by, 91
  definitions of, 186–87
liminal space
  characters inhabiting, 60
  cultural syncretism in, 154
  queerness in, 211
  roads and paths as, 172, 174–81
Little No Horse Reservation
  culturally defined space of, 154
  ecocritical possibilities of, 87
  location of, 31
  microcosm of pan-Indian community, 155
Lochren, Cordelia (*Plague of Doves*), 236
Louise (*Shadow Tag*), 252
Louise Erdrich (Madsen), 63–65
Louise Erdrich (Stirrup), 57

Louise Erdrich (Stookey), 54
love
  chance and, 142, 143–45
  theological perspective on, 68, 83
"Love Medicine": A Casebook (Wong), 58–60
Love Medicine (Erdrich), 3–6, 21, 137–52, 174, 180–81
lynching, 233–35

Madsen, Deborah L. *See Louise Erdrich* (Madsen)
magic realism, 14
mapping, reservations erased in, 182
marginality, 60, 174
Mary, the mother of Jesus (*Baptism of Desire*), 132
masculinity. *See* gender
Master Butchers Signing Club, The (Erdrich), 10, 23
Master Butchers Signing Club, The (play), 10
Matchikwewis, 166–68
Mauser, Jack (*Tales of Burning Love*), 218–19, 220
Medicine Wheel
  allusion to, 176, 183
  teachings of, 138, 188
Métis. *See* mixed-bloods
Milk, Seraph Mooshum (*Plague of Doves*), 39, 229, 237, 241
Milk, Shamengwa (*Plague of Doves*), 39
Minneapolis, Minnesota, 42–44
minority literature, Americanness of, 70
mixed-bloods
  allotment and, 34
  Catholicism and, 40
  historical role of, 41–42
  Métis struggle for rights, 38
  nationalism vs. cosmopolitanism debate and, 50

Modeste, Father Damien (Last Report), 78–80, 221–22, 223
Momaday, N. Scott. *See* Native American Renaissance
Morrison, Toni, 72, 76, 77
Morrissey, June (*Love Medicine*), 141–42
Morrissey, Lipsha (*Love Medicine*), 5–6, 145–46, 150–51
movement, 172–89
My Ántonia (Cather), 99

NAGPRA (Native American Graves Protection and Repatriation Act), 94
naming
    Catholicism referenced in, 81
    continuance and resistance through, 40–41
    cultural past referenced through, 109
    human-wolf connection reinforced through, 98
    Western literary allusion in, 240
Nanabozho. *See* trickster
Nanapush, Gerry (*Love Medicine*), 43, 151
Nanapush (*Last Report*), 224
Nanapush, Lulu (*Love Medicine*), 143–45, 146–47
Nanapush, Lulu (*Tracks*), 177
Nanapush (*Tracks*), 6, 29, 178, 189
narration. *See* first-person; first-person plural; free indirect discourse; unreliable
narrative continuity, 4, 8, 21, 134, 173
narrative poetry, 123
nationalism, American Indian literature and, 49–51
Native American Graves Protection and Repatriation Act, 94
Native American literature. *See* American Indian literature

Native American Renaissance, 47, 207, 209
Native ceremony
    allusion to, 184, 189
    laws about, 203
    omission of, 96
    survival through, 98, 203
Native orality, Western literary conventions and, 129, 164
Niibin'aage (*Painted Drum*), 196, 201
nonlinear narration, mythic time and, 192
North Dakota cycle. *See* narrative continuity
North-West Rebellion, 39
Novels of Louise Erdrich, The (Jacobs), 56

O'Connor, Flannery, 69, 72, 76, 77
Ojibwe. *See* Anishinaabe
Ojibwemowin. *See* Anishinaabemowin
Omakayas (*Birchbark House*), 112, 113, 118
orchard, danger of, 93
Original Fire (Erdrich), 23, 122, 134–36
Ortiz, Simon. *See* interconnectedness: ecology and; Native American Renaissance; sovereignty: American Indian literature and
Oshkikwe, 166–68

Painted Drum, The (Erdrich), 24, 89–100, 191–205, 245–49, 254–55
palimpsest, 185–86
pan-Indianism, 155, 169
Pantamounty, Candice (*Tales of Burning Love*), 218, 219, 220
Paradise (Morrison), 68, 77
Peace, Cuthbert (*Plague of Doves*), 238, 240
Peace, Henri and Lafayette (*Plague of Doves*), 239

persona poetry, 123–24, 125–36
Pfef, Wallace (*Beet Queen*), 160–62, 213–14
Pillager, Fleur (*Painted Drum*), 201
Pillager, Fleur (*Tracks*), 179, 182, 183
Pillager, Simon Jack (*Painted Drum*), 201, 204
Plague of Doves, The (Erdrich), 7, 11, 24, 39–40, 229–43
Playing in the Dark (Morrison), 76
Pluto, North Dakota, 238, 241
poetic voice, definition of, 124
polyphony
    narrative evolution through, 185
    Native orality and, 53, 163
    Western ideology challenged through, 165
    white guilt mitigated by, 59
pop culture, appropriation of, 240
Porcupine Year, The (Erdrich), 24, 113
postmodernism, essentialism vs., 71
Potchikoo (*Jacklight*), 109, 121
poverty, 31, 34, 150
Pratt, Richard Henry, 108, 147, 195
privacy, violation of, 264, 265
Pulliam, Reverend (*Paradise*), 68, 83
Puyat, Pauline (*Tracks*), 6, 182

queer identity, 160–63, 208–26. *See also* two-spirit identity; two-spirit, origin of term

race studies, Erdrich's persona poems and, 130
racial categorization
    American identification based on, 70
    American Indians, normalization of, 231–33
    American social policy based on, 74
    history of, 235–36

white supremacy ideology, effects of, 237
racial violence. *See* extermination; genocide; lynching
Radley, Boo (*To Kill a Mockingbird*), 241
Range Eternal, The (Erdrich), 24
ravens, 90–91
Reader's Guide to the Novels of Louise Erdrich, A (Barton, Beidler), 55
Reading Louise Erdrich's "Love Medicine" (Hafen), 57
reclamation
    chance as, 150
    land restoration, 38, 241
    remapping as, 182–83
Red Convertible, The (Erdrich), 7
relocation and termination, 42, 202
repatriation, 94–96, 200
reservation
    characters' relationship to, 31, 32, 37–38
    mapping of, 182
revival, 89
"Rez Litany" (Erdrich), 135
Riel, Louis David, 38–39. *See* also mixed-bloods
right and wrong, 143, 146, 254
roads and paths, 172–89
Robinson, Tom (*To Kill a Mockingbird*), 240
Roman Catholicism
    melding and subversion of, 81–83
    Métis brand of, 40
    poetic exploration of, 131–33
romance novels, parody of, 215
Round House, The (Erdrich), 25

Saint Ambrose, Giles (*Beet Queen*), 211
Sarris, Greg. *See Approaches to Teaching the Works of Louise Erdrich* (Sarris, Jacobs, Giles)

Sawhney, Brajesh. *See Studies in the Literary Achievement of Louise Erdrich, Native American Writer* (Sawhney)

Schlick, Eleanor (*Tales of Burning Love*), 218

self-similarity, 259

sexual abuse, 260

Shaawano, Bernard (*Painted Drum*), 201, 248

Shaawano, Old Grandfather (*Painted Drum*), 96, 201, 204

Shaawano (*Painted Drum*), 201

Shadow Tag (Erdrich), 11, 24, 245, 249–55, 257–71

Shawnee (*Painted Drum*), 41, 98, 204

Silko, Leslie Marmon. *See Almanac of the Dead* (Silko); Native American Renaissance

Sioux, origin of name, 188

sisters, 166, 247–48, 252

socioeconomics, 231–32. *See also* poverty

soul, importance of, 257

sovereignty
American Indian literature and, 49–50
movement and, 173
repatriation and, 200

Spicer family murders, 233

stereotypes. *See* characterization; movement; vanishing Indian myth

Stirrup, David. *See Louise Erdrich* (Stirrup)

stone, 90, 114

Stone Child, 40

Stookey, Lorena L. *See Louise Erdrich* (Stookey)

storytelling
anecdotes vs. sacred stories, 261–62

healing through, 200–205
narrative evolution in, 4–5, 185–86
reconciliation through, 254
use of, 138

String, Seraphine (*Painted Drum*), 108, 196–97

Studies in the Literary Achievement of Louise Erdrich, Native American Writer (Sawhney), 62

suicide, 142, 152

survival
Native ceremony for, 98, 203
traditional knowledge for, 252

survival humor, trickster and, 5

survivor's guilt, 193, 248

Tales of Burning Love (Erdrich), 23, 218–21

Ten Cent Treaty, 31, 34

Tenskwatawa (prophet), 41

termination and relocation, 42, 202

To Kill a Mockingbird (Lee), 233, 240

Tracks (Erdrich), 22, 33, 34, 176–77, 178–80, 182–84

transgendered framework, 210, 222, 223

transgender identity. *See* queer identity; two-spirit identity

translation, lack of, 117

trauma, 194, 198–99, 201, 249

Travers, Faye (*Painted Drum*), 89, 245–49

Travers, Netta (*Painted Drum*), 193, 247

tribalography, 13–14

trickster
enactment of, 5, 6, 183, 188, 222
movement and, 187
survival humor and, 5

"True Story of Mustache Maude, The" (Erdrich), 7

truth and lies, 260, 266–68, 269–70

Turtle Mountain Reservation
  allotment and, 34
  location and history of, 31
  Métis relocation to, 42
Two Sister story cycles, 166–68, 170
two-spirit identity, 156, 221–24. *See
  also* queer identity
two-spirit, origin of term, 208

"Unauthorized Autobiography of Me,
  The" (Alexie), 124
unreliable narration, 6, 266–70
urban Indians
  Erdrich's experiences with, 19
  fictional depiction of, 42–44
urbanization, 42

values, differing, 199–200
Vanishing Indian myth
  mapping and, 182
  narrative resistance to, 29
  undermining of, 37, 138–39
Vizenor, Gerald. *See* Native American
  Renaissance; sovereignty: movement
  and
voyeurism, autobiographical fiction as,
  263

Waldvogel, Eva (*Master Butchers Signing Club*), 10
Waldvogel, Fidelis (*Master Butchers
  Signing Club*), 10
walking, 174–77

warriors, views of, 159, 169
Wayne, John ("Dear John Wayne"), 128
Welch, James. *See Heartsong of Charging Elk, The* (Welch); Native American Renaissance
Western literary conventions, Native
  orality and, 129, 164
whites and white culture
  Catholicism, 81–83
  gender and sexuality, critique of,
    157–59
  pop cultural appropriation of, 240
  subversion of, 129, 229
  white supremacy ideology, effects
    of, 237
Wiigwaas Press, 12, 110
wilderness, views of, 88
windigo, 44, 114, 129
Wolde, Marn (*Plague of Doves*), 230
Wolde, Warren (*Plague of Doves*), 240
wolf
  Ojibwe connection to, 97–99
  survival wisdom from, 202
wolf attack, misrepresentation of, 99–100
Wong, Hertha D. Sweet. *See* "Love
  Medicine" *A Casebook* (Wong)
"World's Greatest Fisherman, The"
  (Erdrich), 3, 47

young-adult literature, 9

Ziigwan'aage (*Painted Drum*), 201, 203
zwischenraum, 91